C0-GNC-039

COMPUTER APPLICATIONS IN READING

Second Edition

George E. Mason
University of Georgia

Jay S. Blanchard
Texas Tech University

Danny B. Daniel
Houston Independent School District

Published by the
International Reading Association, Inc.
800 Barksdale Road, Box 8139, Newark, Delaware 19714

INTERNATIONAL READING ASSOCIATION

OFFICERS
1982-1983

President Jack Cassidy, Millersville State College, Pennsylvania

Vice President Ira E. Aaron, University of Georgia, Athens

Vice President Elect Bernice E. Cullinan, New York University, New York City

Executive Director Ralph C. Staiger, International Reading Association, Newark, Delaware

DIRECTORS

Term Expiring Spring 1983
Elizabeth Hunter-Grundin, Schools Council, London, England
Dianne L. Monson, University of Minnesota, Minneapolis
Alden J. Moe, Louisiana State University, Baton Rouge

Term Expiring Spring 1984
Phylliss Adams, University of Denver, Colorado
John Downing, University of Victoria, British Columbia, Canada
Sara Scroggins, St. Louis Public Schools, Missouri

Term Expiring Spring 1985
Bobbye S. Goldstein, New York City Public Schools, New York
Doris Roettger, Heartland Education Agency, Ankeny, Iowa
Judith N. Thelen, Frostburg State College, Frostburg, Maryland

Copyright 1983 by the
International Reading Association, Inc.

Library of Congress Cataloging in Publication Data
Mason, George E.
Computer applications in reading

Includes bibliographies and index.
1. Reading—United States—Data processing—Case studies. I. Blanchard, Jay S. II. Daniel, Danny B. III. Title.
LB1050.37.M37 1983 428.4'028'54 83-4749
ISBN 0-87207-936-8

CONTENTS

ACKNOWLEDGEMENTS

In this, the Second Edition, the authors have again had help from a number of people. Some have mailed us manuscripts which we could not have found in the ERIC collection or in any library. Others have sent us copies of their publications as soon as reprints were available.

On this page we wish to thank again the people named in the Acknowledgments of the First Edition, and to extend thanks to these people not previously mentioned:

Faye Branca, IRA
John Edwards, Georgia College at Milledgeville
Peter Joyce, East York, Ontario
Peter Kincaid, U.S. Navy
Lloyd Kline, IRA
Gwen Peck, University of Georgia
Richard Venezky, University of Delaware

Just as we asked in the First Edition, we now ask again that our readers write to advise us of our errors, both of omission and commission.

GEM, JSB, and DBD

FOREWORD

When the first edition of this text was written in 1977-78, the electronic landscape was still dominated by maxi and minicomputers. Computer aided instruction was mainly drill and practice, a phrase that by its own redundancy reflects a generic blandness that was too often fully realized in practice. Microcomputers were flooding the market, but few reading lessons were available for them.

Since that time the prospects for computers in reading instruction have changed in both hue and value. Powerful microcomputers are now resident in many schools, some within school-based networks. Traditional textbook publishers, along with commercial software houses and some nonprofit organizations, have begun to produce reading lessons based on a variety of instructional paradigms. Instructional tools—word processors, spelling checkers, and management systems—have assumed a stage center position in the educational software market and in the software inventories of many schools.

For this rapidly changing environment, the second edition of this text provides not only an update to the material covered in the first edition but also a major new section on software, covering publications, authoring languages, evaluation, sources of computing services, and a variety of related topics. This emphasis on software is probably the most important contribution of the second edition. In a computing culture that appears inebriated with hardware capabilities, educators need, perhaps more than ever before, to retain a focus on the capabilities and quality of instructional software. Fortunately, resources for assisting in this task are rapidly expanding. User groups, software directories and exchanges, and evaluation standards (among other services) are available now, as the listings provided in this volume demonstrate. And the direction of change is clearly toward the availability of more extensive and more critical information.

Finally, for those interested in how rapidly the instructional computing world is changing, the authors have retained in the final chapter their projections for the future of computers in reading instruction as foreseen in 1977-1978, and appended their revised views as of Fall 1982. Perhaps by the time the third edition of *Computer Applications in Reading* is published we will know whether software developers and educators can acquire the imagination needed to utilize the amazing resources computers now offer.

Richard L. Venezky
University of Delaware

IRA PUBLICATIONS COMMITTEE 1982-1983 Joan Nelson-Herber, State University of New York at Binghamton, *Chairing* • Phylliss J. Adams, University of Denver • Roach Van Allen, University of Arizona • Janet R. Binkley, IRA • Faye R. Branca, IRA • Martha Collins Cheek, Louisiana State University • Susan Mandel Glazer, Rider College • MaryAnne Hall, Georgia State University • Dale D. Johnson, University of Wisconsin • Martha L. King, Ohio State University • Lloyd W. Kline, IRA • Elaine P. LeBlanc, Douglas County School, Atlanta • Irving P. McPhail, Johns Hopkins University • Nancy Naumann, North Haven, Connecticut, Board of Education • Caroline Neal, West Virginia College of Graduate Studies • P. David Pearson, University of Illinois • María Elena Rodríquez, Asociación Internacional de Lectura, Buenos Aires • Betty Roe, Tennessee Technological University • S. Jay Samuels, University of Minnesota • Ralph C. Staiger, IRA • John C. Stansell, Texas A & M University • Rosemary Winkeljohann, St. Ursula Villa Elementary School, Cincinnati.

The International Reading Association attempts, through its publications, to provide a forum for a wide spectrum of opinions on reading. This policy permits divergent viewpoints without assuming the endorsement of the Association.

Chapter 1

INTRODUCTION

The Development of Digital Computers

Large Central Processors

The first completely electronic computer, ENIAC, was developed at the University of Pennsylvania in 1945. It had 18,000 vacuum tubes. The heat generated by the tubes and the constant need for replacing worn out tubes made this and other early computers of little value to education or industry. However, the invention of the transistor in 1947 enabled computer engineers to reduce heat problems and to nearly eliminate tube replacement problems. Successes led to commercial production and sale of a variety of computers which have constantly increased in the complexity of function they perform.

The computers which have come to be used in education are digital computers. Their transistors are operated as switches that generally have only two states: on or off (conducting or nonconducting). The signals switched on or off are only two: high or low voltage. Since all the states in a digital circuit are one or the other of these dual values, the logic or arithmetic of a digital computer operates with a binary (base 2) number system. In a binary system, digits represent (from right to left) ones, twos, fours, and eights instead of ones, tens, hundreds, and thousands (i.e. to a computer 001 = 1, 010 = 2, 011 = 3, 100 = 4, and 1011 = 8 + 0 + 2 + 1 = 11). The binary system can be used not only for adding, subtracting, multiplying, and dividing but also for evaluating logic statements. The binary values of on/off, high/low voltage or 1/0 can be made to stand for true/false or yes/no. This system is what gives the computer its tremendous potential.

Even with this great potential, the transistorized digital computer did not come into wide use until the development of the integrated circuit at Fairchild Semiconductor in 1949. (Integrated circuits are printed or etched onto very small disks or squares of silica. Already, integrated circuits have replaced mechanical elements of the calculator and the watch.) As a result of the price reductions which followed the development of integrated circuits, computers became common in colleges, universities, large school systems, government institutions, and large corporations. Yet, since they were still very expensive and very complicated to own and operate, smaller organizations seldom could afford them. The large computer centers used powerful CPUs (Central Processing Units). In the early 1970s, the most commonly used were the CDC 6400 and 6600 (from Control Data Corporation), the IBM 360/40-50-67 and IBM 370 (from International Business Machines), the UNIVAC 1108 (from Sperry Univac), the GE 635-645 (from General Electric) and the Spectra 70 (from RCA).

The Development of Data Processing Languages

To make computers useful for the wide variety of large scale users, programs (sets of rules) had to be developed for converting typed-in commands or sequences of activities to the "machine language" of the computer (on/off, high/low voltage, or 1/0). These programs are called data processing languages, or "author languages." By 1969 at least 60 of these author languages had been developed.

These languages can be divided into four classes, according to their potential for instruction: 1) Description of successive frames or items, 2) provision (within a limited context) for conversation, 3) specification of a standard method of presenting content, and 4) detailing the conditions for program construction.

The first of these categories includes more than 20 languages. Those which the reading specialist is most likely to encounter are "Coursewriter II" and "TUTOR." These languages are "conversations." They do well at presenting written text, at correcting "open answers" (those not chosen from a multiple-option set), at recording the answers of various kinds and type, and at branching determined by answers or sets of answers.

In the second group are languages which have the characteristics of those in the first group, but which can simulate a conversation between the student and the program only within a limited context. Among those in this group are FIT, ELIZA, FOIL, MENTOR, MINORCA, GLURP, and PLANIT. (The last four of these could be listed in the first group.)

The third group includes CATO, XXX, TICCIT, and PICO (a French author language). In the languages of this group, a system of programing procedures is required. The user has no choice but to follow them. These languages are generally used for computer managed instruction. In this group are IMS (Information and Management System) of the Southwest Regional Education Laboratory and Systems Development Corporation; PLAN (Program for Learning in Accordance with Needs) of the American Institutes for Research and the Westinghouse Learning Corporation; and WIS/SIM (Wisconsin System for Information Management) of the University of Wisconsin's Center for Educational Research and Development and the National Computer Systems Company.

In the fourth group of author languages are those which specify the conditions or limits for program construction. Most of these were not intended to be used in instruction, but several were immediately so used (for teaching and learning). Of those intended to be used for instruction, the best known are LOGO and BASIC. Both are very easy to use and may be applied even by elementary school pupils, who can use them to program the computer to solve a variety of problems. BASIC (Beginner's All-purpose Symbolic Instruction Code), the first interactive language created for instructional purposes, was developed in 1966 at Dartmouth College.

As more and more computer centers were created in universities and other large organizations, a few of these became very popular and others disappeared. By 1973 the most popular languages were COURSEWRITER II, APL (A Programing Language—the IBM calculating language), and BASIC. Very popular, but less frequently used, were TUTOR and FORTRAN. By 1978 BASIC had come to be the major author language.

Newer Developments in Computers and Computer Use

When computers were first being used for instruction, each could operate only one terminal at a time. Project PLATO, at the University of Illinois, started in 1960 with an Illiac I which served only one terminal, and the PDP-1 with which the Stanford project started in 1963 served only six stations, none of which was more than 100 feet away. However, it was eventually connected to 600 teletype terminals in Mississippi, 800 in Kentucky, and 900 in California. By 1968, 6,000 New York City pupils were receiving computer assisted instruction processed by one RCA Spectra 70/45 located at 42 Street and Second Avenue. The sharing of one computer by a number of terminals was a very important development. The devices which allow such sharing of on-line time among computer users are called interfaces. With interfaces, the CDC 6400 at Illinois is one day expected to be able to handle 4,096 terminals on a time sharing basis.

Another important development was the formation of user groups. Some user groups such as TIES (a group of Minnesota High Schools), the Montreal Catholic School Commission, and the Northeast Ohio Computer Network actually share one computer. Others, such as EDUCOM, ARPA, CONDUIT, and CANUNET (Canadian), are groups of colleges which share computer based courses and other software. Furthermore, most computer manufacturers sponsor a user's group, which they have organized to facilitate sharing of computer courses, programs, and innovative uses by owners of the hardware (computing equipment) manufactured by that company.

Even as these groups were being formed, however, computer technology was taking another leap forward with the development of minicomputers ($10,000-$30,000). These are flexible and programable (but not portable) with direct access memory channels for storing information fed in by the user. Those most often used in teaching are the GE 255-235, the IBM 1130 and the HP 2000 (of Hewlett Packard), and the PDP-8 (of Digital Equipment Corporation). With these smaller computers, many high schools and vocational technical schools began to teach computer programing as an optional course in their mathematics sequence and to make available to their students both programs and courses developed in school, as well as predeveloped programs purchased from a commercial company or borrowed from another member of their user's group.

Schools and colleges operating the smaller computers frequently arrange interconnections with operators of large computers. The Georgia State Board of Regents Network is an example of such a network of computers. This network allows the smaller local computers to become terminals for the largest in the system when its capabilities are desired.

The capabilities of the smaller computers were not vastly different than those of the older large computers. In fact, many of the newer minicomputers have more power than the larger machines which were their predecessors. (The power of these computers is based on the number of bits [or digits] that it can process, with one circuit required for each bit. The number of bits also determines how many memory circuits can be accessed [i.e. a four-bit processor can access 15 locations, since there are only 15 binary numbers of four bits or less, while a 16-bit processor can access 65,536 memory bits]. The size of a computer memory is usually described in Ks or thousands of bits. A byte is eight or nine bits).

Even as individual schools began purchasing minicomputers, the four-bit microprocessor (MPU) was invented by personnel of the Intel Corporation in 1971. The microprocessor contains the most important circuits of a computer and is the size of a postage stamp. By 1973, more than 10,000 transistors could be integrated on a single silicon chip smaller than a postage stamp. In 1976, an 8-bit microprocessor was fabricated on a single chip which contained more than 20,000 transistors. As a result, microprocessor memory size is now specified in thousands (Ks) of bytes or characters rather than in bits.

The advent of microprocessors has been followed by the creation of a flood of very small portable computers, suitable not only for school use but also for home use. Most of these contain some random access memory (RAM) circuits for programing by the user, while nearly all have read—only memory (ROM) circuits preprogramed to hold the BASIC language and some computer games and/or mathematics drill and practice programs. To date, none have been preprogramed with stored reading instruction. However, they are bound to have an impact and what that impact may be will be discussed in the final chapter of this book.

The second chapter describes the colleges where reading programs were created—initially on the large expensive computers, later with interfaces and networks and, most recently, with minicomputers. The third chapter describes public school use of computers for reading instruction. The fourth details computerized readability assessment efforts, the fifth reports computer services in reading that are available to schools. The sixth annotates reports of research on teaching and learning reading with the aid of the computer. The seventh relates suggested uses of the computer in reading instruction, and the eighth predicts the future for computer based reading instruction.

Annotated References

1. Albrecht, B. *Teach yourself BASIC.* San Carlos, California: Technica Education Corporation, 1970.

   A two volume worktext for self-teaching of the BASIC author language. Includes practice exercises to do at the terminal.

2. Northwest Regional Education Laboratory. *REACT Relevant educational applications of computer technology*. San Carlos, California: Technica Education Corporation, 1971.

   Course I is composed of ten worktexts designed to give teachers and administrators a survey of the development of computers, kinds of computers, man-machine languages, author languages, instructions for using teletype terminals and two types of computers, and the use of computers for direct instruction and computer managed instruction.

Course II for teachers consists of six worktexts in which are listed and described the REACT programs developed at the Northwest Regional Education Laboratory. Included are programs in business education, English (poetry only), mathematics, science, and social studies. Course II for principals consists of eight booklets describing uses of the computer in record keeping and school management.

3. Noyce, R.N. Microelectronics. *Scientific American*, 1977, *237* (3), 63-69.

   Discusses the evaluation of microelectronic devices since the development of the transistor, pointing out that a $300 minicomputer of today has more calculating power than ENIAC, the first electronic computer.

4. PLANIT: *A computer assisted instruction language system.* Portland: Northwest Regional Educational Laboratory, n.d. (mimeo).

   Gives history of involvement of Michigan State University, Systems Development Corporation, and NWREL in developing PLANIT, which is briefly explained. Reference is made to a PLANIT user's group.

5. Zinn, K.L. *Computers in the instructional process: Report of an international school.* Ann Arbor: Center for Research on Learning and Teaching, University of Michigan, 1974.

   Describes and classifies a large number of author languages, relating their general utility.

Additional References

6. Association for Educational Data Systems. *Layman's guide to the use of computers.* Washington, D.C.: The Association, 1971.
7. Charp, S. *Computers in general education.* Harrisburg: Pennsylvania Department of Public Instruction, 1967.
8. Goodman, L.L. *Man and automation.* New York: Penguin Books, 1957.
9. Greenberger, M. (Ed.). *Computers and the world of the future.* Cambridge, Massachusetts: MIT Press, 1962.
10. Toong, H-M.D. Microprocessors. *Scientific American*, 1977, *237* (3), 146-147, 151-156, 158, 160-161.
11. Vacroux, A.G. Microcomputers. *Scientific American*, 1974, *232*, (5), 32-40.
12. *What is binary arithmetic?* Dayton, Ohio: National Cash Register, n.d.

The Programs Developed

As computer technology developed more complicated, faster, and yet cheaper equipment, programs for using computers for educational purposes were also being developed. The principal uses were computer assisted instruction (CAI) and computer managed instruction (CMI).

Computer assisted instruction is a term used to describe any instruction in which the material to be learned is presented by equipment under digital computer control and in which the students' responses are relayed to the computer for processing. The processing of responses generally includes storage of the responses in the computer's memory system, decision making as to reinforcement, and decision making as to the appropriate next presentation.

Typically, the presentation is a display on a cathode ray (television picture) tube or a plasma panel. Such displays can be printed text, graphed or charted material, and photographs or drawings in color or black and white. Less frequently the presentation is auditory, since groupings of recorded speech sounds are unlikely to produce words pronounced appropriately for the context of meaning intended.

The responses elicited are most frequently to be made with a keyset resembling a typewriter. The students type in the letters A, B, C, D, or E to indicate their choices for multiple choice questions or they type in Yes, No, True, False, or missing terms in incomplete statements. For young children only a few of the keys may be employed or a special key set using smiling faces or geometric designs may be used. As an alternative for young children, a light-sensitive cathode ray tube can be employed. Students using it point a light pencil at targets presented on the screen to indicate their responses. Even younger children can respond to the touch-sensitive panel which may be attached to Plato terminals. Plasma panels permit simultaneous display of machine controlled graphics and rear screen projected random access slides from microfiche.

Computer assisted instruction is generally programed instruction. Students are presented stimuli to which they respond at their own rate. Responses can be immediately confirmed by computer presented words or symbols, although in some cases a number of responses are expected before computer acknowledgement.

The programs of instruction available are of three types differing in complexity and in the amount of student-system interaction: *tutorial* programs which are self-contained courses of instruction with machine decisions and branching; simple linear *drill and practice* programs which are designed to supplement instruction initiated by a teacher; and *dialogue* programs which enable learners to converse with the computer in natural language wherein the student controls the information sequence. These programs are developed by educators or psychologists who direct the computer's activities using an author language.

Students can learn to use computer terminals with help from the teacher or another student. Usually very little help is required, even by elementary school children. Two or three ten-minute sessions are usually sufficient, even when audio disks and/or microfiche must be loaded. In some school systems, such as the Clarke County, Georgia, Schools, children belonging to the TAGS (Talented and Gifted) organization may elect to enroll in Saturday classes at a nearby college or university where they learn to solve problems by doing simple programing of the university computer in the BASIC language.

Computer managed instruction usually does not require that the student learn to operate the computer terminal. Instead, teachers give children criterion referenced tests to which the children respond by marking on machine-scorable answer sheets. These are mailed or shipped to the computer serving the school or college for batch-processing. Printouts are generated for the child, and class records are made up for the teacher. Some of these printouts may include individual prescriptions complete with materials and recommended pages for practice.

Progress in the development of both CAI and CMI programs is described in the annotated references in the final section of this chapter. Several additional references are listed at the end for reading specialists who desire to add depth to their knowledge in this area.

Annotated References

13. Association for Development of Computer Instructional Systems (ADCIS). *Minutes and proceedings of the semiannual meeting*. Ann Arbor, Michigan: August 1973.

    Abstracts are included of 23 reports given at the conference. Many deal with computer based instruction projects, including some in reading.

14. Baker, F.B. Computer based instructional management systems: A first look. *Review of Educational Research*, 1971, *41* (1), 41-70.

    Describes computer based instructional management systems existing in 1971. It is a complete review of early CMI programs and some CAI programs are mentioned. The author hypothesizes that computer based instructional management has greater possibilities than computer assisted instruction because of costs.

15. Baker, J.C. *The computer in the school* (Fastback number 58). Bloomington, Indiana: Phi Delta Kappan Educational Foundation, 1975.

A pamphlet giving an overview of computer assisted and computer managed instruction. It includes information on the following programs: PLATO, TICCIT, LOGO, and PLAN. Also included are the author's opinions on present and future capabilities of computers in education.

16. Barnes, D.O. & Schrieber, D.B. *Computer assisted instruction: A selected bibliography.* Washington, D.C.: Association for Educational Communications and Technology, 1972 (ED 063 769).

The most extensive and complete bibliography of computer uses in education and instruction. It contains 835 entries.

17. Beard, M. *Computer assisted instruction: The best of ERIC, 1973-May 1976.* Palo Alto, California: Stanford University. 1976 (ED 125 608).

An annotated bibliography containing articles about the entire spectrum of computer assisted and managed instruction. Included are such topics as PLATO, TICCIT, research, teacher training, author languages and costs.

18. Bukoski, W.J., & Korotkin, A.L. *Computer activities in secondary education: Final report.* Washington, D.C.: American Institute for Research in the Behavioral Sciences, September 1975.

This report is a follow up to a 1969 project entitled CASE. CASE surveyed secondary public schools to determine computer usage. The current project, sponsored by the National Science Foundation, surveyed 5,580 schools. The contents describe many new secondary computer based programs, with some in reading.

19. Bukoski, W.J., & Korotkin, A.L. Computer activities in secondary education. *Educational Technology*, 1976, *16* (1), 9-22.

This report deals with a survey initiated to determine the extent of computer usage (more than 13 per cent) in secondary public schools. Several secondary public school reading programs are reviewed and a large amount of information about computer availability in secondary schools is included.

20. Bundy, R. Computer assisted instruction—Where are we? *Phi Delta Kappan*, 1968, *49* (9), 424-429.

This article is an overview of the status of computer assisted instruction. The author provides a brief summary of results from research and several recommendations about areas in which further research is needed. He also reviews the research limitations of past projects and comments on the future of computer assisted instruction.

21. Clark, R.F. *The best of ERIC: Recent trends in computer assisted instruction.* Palo Alto, California: Stanford University, 1973. (ED 076 025).

This is an annotated bibliography which covers planning and utilization of CAI. Also included are reviews of computer assisted instruction programs at the elementary, secondary, junior college, community college, and university level.

22. Chevalier, G. *Classification of the uses of computers in education.* Service de l' Informatique Ministere de l' Education, Laboratoire de Pedagogie Informatique. Province de Quebec. Canada, 1972.

The author reviews the computer in four roles: as a laboratory tool, a teaching support system, teaching system / learning system, and as an educational research tool.

23. Dick, W.; Latsa, R.; & Rivers, L. Sources of information on computer assisted instruction. *Educational Technology*, 1970, *10* (3), 165-169.

The authors surveyed public schools, universities, and research and development centers in 1969 to determine the extent of computer assisted instruction. Several research and development center reading programs are mentioned as well as computer assisted reading instruction in public schools and universities.

24. Dirr, P.J. *Computers in education: A bibliography for the instructional technology course for teachers.* Buffalo, New York: State University College at Buffalo, 1974. (ED 105 677)

The bibliography lists 78 references from 1968 to 1974 on the uses of computers in education. Many articles mentioned deal with reading.

25. Doublier, R.M. *Interactive relationship with computers in teaching reading.* Paper presented at the annual conference of the International Reading Association, New Orleans, May 1974.

The paper reviews current man / machine communications and discusses a computer assisted reading educational system (CARES). The author also proposes CARES as a model for a reading laboratory.

26. Feldhusen, J.F., & Szabo, M. A review of developments in computer assisted instruction. *Educational Technology*, 1970, *10* (3), 90-97.

The authors alert the reader to potential sources of information available about computer assisted instruction.

27. Fletcher, J.D. *Computer applications in education and training: Status and trends.* San Diego, California: Navy Personnel Research and Development Center, 1975. (ED 108 681).

While this review concerns itself with computer based applications to training, some reading programs mentioned are: PLATO IV, Chicago Public Schools, TICCIT, Stanford University, Florida State University, Pennsylvania State University, and the University of California.

28. Fry, E. *Programed instruction and automation in beginning reading.* Paper presented at the annual conference of the International Reading Association, Seattle, May 1967.

A review of recent investigations into the effectiveness of programed instruction in reading. Included in one aspect of programed instruction is computer assisted instruction in reading.

29. Grayson, L.P., & Robbins, J.B. *U.S. Office of Education support of computer activities: 1965-1971.* (Report No. DE 12044-71). Washington, D.C.: U.S. Government Printing Office, 1972.

This report discusses 500 projects including reading projects and the $161 million spent on computer activities in education between 1965-1971. Unfortunately, follow up documents have never been produced. The report is summarized in the November 1971 issue of *Educational Technology*.

30. Halley, F.S. *Computer applications in teaching and learning.* Brockport, New York: State University of New York at Brockport, October 1973.

Gives examples of computer uses in teaching and learning with particular emphasis on testing.

31. Hickey, A.E. (Ed.) *Computer assisted instruction: A survey of the literature* (Vol. 3). Newburyport, Massachusetts: ENTELEK, 1968.

The survey contains an overview of computer assisted instruction from 1967-1968. Also included are programs in selected curricula (reading) and a listing of public and private computer assisted instruction programs as well as pertinent information about computer assisted instruction theory. An earlier second edition is also available covering 1966-1967.

32. Hickey, A.E. *Research guidelines for computer assisted instruction.* Newburyport, Massachusetts: A.E. Hickey Associates, 1974.

This is a survey prepared for the Defense Advanced Research Project Agency. It contains 59 recommendations for research and development in support of computer assisted instruction. Also covered are learning and instructional variables relevant to CAI and reading.

33. Hicks, B.L., & Hunka, S. *The teacher and the computer*. Philadelphia: W.B. Saunders, 1972.

Reviews the essential elements of computer based and computer assisted instruction programs. The authors also discuss, in depth, basic assumptions about CAI in the classroom.

34. Koch, W.J. *The use of computer instruction in secondary schools.* Washington, D.C.: National Association of Secondary School Principals, 1972. (Reprinted in *Education Digest*, 1973, *38*, 28-31.)

The booklet contains information about the following areas of computer assisted instruction: 1) hardware and software availability, 2) personnel needed, 3) reviews of ongoing CAI/CMI projects, and 4) a glossary of terms.

35. Majer, K. Computer assisted instruction and reading. *Viewpoints*, 1972, *48* (5), 77-97.

A comprehensive review of the development of CAI in reading. The author discusses the following questions: Can CAI be used effectively for reading? How do children respond to reading programs using CAI? What theoretical positions have been utilized with reading programs? What are the advantages of CAI programs? What are the new roles for teachers and the implications for teacher training with CAI? What about cost? What about the future of CAI in reading? A list of references is included.

36. Majer, K. Computer assisted instruction and reading: How, what, when, and where? *Educational Technology*, 1973, *13* (9), 23-26.

This article discusses where computer assisted instruction is being used, the advantages of computer assisted reading programs over other programs, student responses to computer assisted instruction, and the future of computer assisted instruction.

37. Mitzel, H.E. (Ed.) *An examination of the short range potential of computer managed instruction.* Proceedings of a Conference Sponsored by the National Institute of Education, Washington, D.C. (Chicago, November 1974.)

These proceedings are of particular interest to those educators concerned with computer managed instruction in reading. The abstracts include summaries of 27 operational computer managed instruction systems. A few are: PLAN, ISS (Instructional Support System), CISS (Computerized Instructional Support System), and CAM (Comprehensive Achievement Monitoring). Bibliographies included with most abstracts provide access to additional information.

38. Vinsonhaler, J.F., & Bass, R.K. A summary of ten major studies on CAI drill and practice. *Educational Technology*, 1972, *12* (7), 29-32.
The authors summarize the results of ten computer assisted programs of instruction. Reading related programs reviewed are: 1) Stanford—East Palo Alto, California; 2) INDICOM—Pontiac, Michigan; and 3) Harcourt Brace Jovanovich—New York City.

39. *Report on the instructional use of the computer* (3 vols.) Service de l' Informatique. Ministere de l' Education, Laboratoire de Pedagogie Informatique, Province de Quebec, Canada, 1973.
This report contains three volumes. The first, by Guy Chevalier and Bernard Gateau, is entitled "Types of Uses." It classifies and describes the types of instructional uses of the computer including public and private CAI/CMI programs. The second, by Francois Labrousse, discusses the costs of CAI/CMI programs. The third, by Lucien Dube, describes the extent to which computers were/are being used in education.

40. Wang, A.C. (Ed.). *Index to computer based learning* (1976 edition). Milwaukee: University of Wisconsin, Instructional Media Laboratory, 1976.
A complete guide to computer applications in education, especially CAI, it contains 1,837 separate entries. The index details voluntarily reported information about as many computer based projects as possible.

41. Yonder, W.W. *Computer literature bibliography: 1946 to 1963.* Washington, D.C.: National Bureau of Standards, Department of Commerce, Institute for Applied Technology, 1965.
Contains 6,100 references on computer literature from 1946 to 1963.

42. Yonder, W.W. *Computer literature bibliography: Volume 2, 1964-1967.* Washington, D.C.: National Bureau of Standards, Department of Commerce, Institute for Applied Technology, 1968.
Contains 5,200 references from 1964-1967.

Additional References

43. Dick, W. The development and current status of computer based instruction. *American Education Research Association*, 1965, *2* (1), 41-54.

44. Edwards, J., et al. How effective is CAI? A review of the research. Bibliography. *Educational Leadership*, 1974, *33* (2), 147-153.

45. Iverson, W. *The age of the computer and reading*. Paper presented at the Claremont College Reading Conference, Claremont, California, February 1967.

46. Swanson, A.K. The computer as a tool of instruction. An annotated

bibliography of selected 1972-1973 books and reports. AEDS *Journal*, 1974, *7* (1), 92-96.
47. Smith, N.B. *Reading for the seventies: An international challenge.* Paper presented at the International Reading Association World Congress on Reading, Sydney, Australia, August 1970.
48. Zinn, K., & McClintock, S. *A guide to the literature on interactive use of computers for instruction.* Stanford: ERIC Clearinghouse on Educational Media and Technology, Stanford University, 1970.

Chapter 2

COLLEGE AND UNIVERSITY CENTERS IN COMPUTER BASED READING PROGRAMS

It is important to note that in revising the 1979 edition of *Computer Applications in Reading*, few annotations or comments are being deleted. This was done to provide historical perspective for the reader. The rise of computer applications in reading is inexorably tied to college and university campuses. Chapter 2 chronicles the almost five decades of computer developments in reading at the nation's institutions of higher education. While the annotations and comments in this chapter should provide a catalog of college and university reading programs, some institutions may have been left out. The omissions are not intentional and probably exist only because their reading programs and projects have not come to our attention.

In the past, the vast majority of the programs for computer assisted reading instruction and many of the programs for computer managed instruction were developed on the campuses of colleges and universities with the aid of funding from the federal government and from private foundations. Many of the development projects were partnership arrangements in which computer manufacturers worked with the college and university personnel. In such partnerships, instructional program needs led to changes in computer construction and new developments in computer technology led to changes in educational programing.

These projects developed programs, many of which were field tested in public and private elementary and secondary schools. Such programs were modified to meet the demands of in-school operation and to continue operation with the minimal financing available for large scale, in-school, computer based education. Consequently, although the names of colleges and universities are used to organize the developmental efforts described in this chapter, the work was actually carried on by educators and programers from many backgrounds and fields of employment.

Stanford's Institute for Mathematical Studies in Social Sciences

The reading program at Stanford was developed by Atkinson and others over a period of years starting with a USOE grant awarded in 1964. The original program was intended to be a total curriculum which was independent of human teachers.

There were two major problems. No programed curriculum in reading was available for computerized delivery, and no integrated CAI system had been developed and marketed by any one manufacturer. Between 1964 and 1967 both problems were solved in a parallel effort by Stanford and IBM.

The resulting system, the IBM 1800/1500, consisted of a central computer with disk storage, two proctor stations, and an interphase to 16 terminals. Terminal equipment consisted of a high speed rearview filmstrip, typewriter keyboard, and an audiotape system delivering through earphones messages varying in length from a few seconds to fifteen minutes.

Using this system, Atkinson and his associates created a beginning reading program ("tutorial beginning reading program") in which students responded to video, audio, and rear screen projected displays by pointing the light pencil at the screen. The response was evaluated and a computer decision determined the next material to be presented. The interphase allowed the computer, with its ultrafast response capabilities, to serve 16 students in serial order so rapidly that it seemed to each that all were being individually served. (This is now standard practice in computer terminal allocation and is called time-sharing.)

The student terminals and the tutorial reading program were tried with first graders from November 1966 to June 1967. During October pupils met the adults who were to help them learn to use the terminals. The last week in October and the first two weeks in November were used to teach pupils to use the terminals. An adult proctor sat by them during their first five on-line sessions. At first students were allowed only a few minutes' work at the 16 terminals supervised by two student proctors and one machine proctor but, after six weeks, the time was increased to twenty minutes daily and by the end of the school year they were allowed half an hour daily. Evening hours were used for curriculum program debugging and early morning hours were for audio and course assembly work.

Prior to starting CAI instruction the children had been taught to respond to the written words YES and NO and to written forms of their own names. With this background they were able to walk into the terminal room, find the cathode ray tube showing their own names, put on their earphones, and start the program by touching the light pen to the display. Children soon learned to read "You have signed off," which was presented at the end of each day's lesson.

The curriculum presented six kinds of reading tasks to the students: letter discrimination and identification, initial vocabulary, word decoding, syntactic and intonation practice, syntactic and semantic practice, and informational processing tasks.

After deciding that the original program was successful, but exceedingly expensive, the Stanford personnel chose a new aim for their CAI Reading Program. The new objective was to create a low cost supplement to regular classroom instruction.

Consequently, the expensive CRT and slide projection equipment was eliminated. The terminals then consisted only of a Model 33 teletypewriter with an audio headset. While the keyboard was a limited one (uppercase letters only), the audio presentations were extensive. Six thousand messages were stored and any of them could be played at a terminal within thirty milliseconds of their demand by computer control. A list of all the words used in the reading program was filed in a disk memory file. Each word is described by four numbers giving its book and page number of first occurrence in Series B (for grade one), Series C (for grades two and three), or Series A (for supplementary and remedial work). Using this word file, the computer could easily draw words with the same endings (i.e. *-ick*), or of the same difficulty level.

The program to be presented by the computer was divided into six strands. When a student had demonstrated sufficient progress in a lower numbered strand, he automatically began receiving instruction in the next higher strand. The strands are described below:

Strand I	Reading Readiness—using the terminal, following directions.
Strand II	Letter Recognition—copying, recognition, recall of letters.
Strand III	Sight Word Vocabulary—learning seven graded lists.
Strand IV	Spelling Patterns—learning to discriminate, copy, and spell word families.

Strand V Phonics—construction of words from consonants, consonant clusters, and spelling patterns.

Strand VI Comprehension—categorizing words, filling in blanks in sentences.

Any one lesson might involve the presentation of learning material from several strands even though lesson length was set at only twelve minutes daily (unless otherwise specified by the teacher). Students completing all strands could be authomatically started in a CAI drill and practice language arts program designed for grades four to eight. Approximately every fifth lesson was for review.

Teachers desiring status reports on the progress of a class or individual could type their request on any of the teletypewriters. For each student, the computer would type the time accumulated, the unit that the student was working on in each of the strands, and his error rates. The same information was available for the class as a whole and for class averages.

An experimental comparison of the reading scores of students whose instruction was supplemented with twelve minutes per day of computerized reading instruction found the experimental students to have reading norm scores 1.2 years greater than those of their controls. The cost of this difference was estimated to be 40 cents per day or $70 per year. Even though the research on CAI in elementary reading has now been terminated, and children in schools around Stanford no longer sit at computer terminals, much of the knowledge gained has been of use in ongoing programs, such as those used at schools for the deaf and those marketed commercially.

Annotated References

49. Atkinson, R.C., & Hansen, D. Computer assisted instruction in initial reading: The Stanford Project. *Reading Research Quarterly*, 1966, *2* 5-25.
A description of the purposes of the CAI Reading Project, its organization, its potentials for research, the equipment to be used, and what commands were necessary to create one complete lesson. Also explained is the six strand reading curriculum.

50. Rodgers, T.S. *Linguistic Considerations in the design of the Stanford computer based curriculum in initial reading.* Stanford, California: Institute for Mathematical Studies in the Social Sciences, 1967.
Seven tenets of psycholinguists form the base for the curriculum in initial reading: 1) spelling and reading were to be taught independently; 2) reading was to be begun with decoding; 3) sight and sound were to be associated with letter patterns; 4) vocalic center groups were to be scaled in difficulty for presentation; 5) graphic patterns were to be presented as members of a rhyme and alliterative set in matrix

format; 6) word items were to be presented in various contexts emphasizing morphological syntactic and semantic functions; and 7) words were to be presented in contexts in which punctuation, grammar, and meaning conveyed the writer's intent.

51. Atkinson, R.C. *Instruction in initial reading under computer control.* Stanford, California: Institute for Mathematical Studies in the Social Studies, 1967.

Explains the presentation of reading instruction to beginners by computer. Sixteen children could be taught at one time. Extensive "debugging" of the program was one of the first requirements in implementing the computer controlled tape-filmstrip instructional program.

52. Wilson, H.A., & Atkinson, R.C. *Computer based instruction in initial reading: A progress report on the Stanford Project.* Stanford, California: Institute for Mathematical Studies in the Social Sciences, 1967.

Describes development and initial field testing of the first grade tutorial program in reading. Students responded to computer presented auditory and visual stimuli with light pens. Points out the tremendous number of coursewriter commands necessary to execute a typical 30-minute student lesson.

53. Spache, G.D. A reaction to computer assisted instruction in initial reading: The Stanford Project. *Reading Research Quarterly*, 1967, *3* (1), 101-110.

An evaluation of reference 49 listing six misconceptions said by Spache to be held by Atkinson and Hansen and pointing out that they ignored learner variables and employed questionable output variables in their research.

54. Atkinson, R.C., & Suppes. P. *Project for an automated primary grade reading and arithmetic curriculum for culturally deprived children: Progress Report Number 5.* Stanford, California: Institute for Mathematical Studies in the Social Sciences, 1967.

Describes how students began to "spread out" through the various levels of the program's reading exercises and problems.

55. Atkinson, R.C. *Computerized instruction and the learning process, Technical Report Number 122.* Stanford, California: Institute for Mathematical Studies in the Social Sciences, 1967.

Explains the use of the cathode ray tube and light pencil as well as relating problems in implementing the curriculum.

56. Sears, P.S., & Feldman, D.N. *Changes in young children's classroom behavior after a year of computer assisted instruction: An exploratory study.* Stanford, California: Institute for Mathematical Research in the Social Sciences, 1968.

Observations resulted in comparison of behavior ratings on CAI-taught and non-CAI-taught first graders. Social behavior scores of CAI group decreased, while those of the non-CAI group increased. It was posited that CAI may reduce the expected positive relations among academic behavior, IQ, and achievement.

57. Jerman, M. Promising developments in computer assisted instruction. *Educational Technology*, 1969, *9* (8), 10-18.

Explains how audio messages were digitized and stored for computer retrieval and use in the initial reading program.

58. Suppes, P. *Computer assisted instruction at Stanford.* Proceedings of an International Conference of Man and Computer, Bordeaux, 1970.

A history of the Stanford CAI project which provides an excellent description of the equipment used by the project and a year-by-year accounting of the schools involved with the project's various curricula. Finally, the author makes four kinds of projections about the future of CAI (see Chapter 5).

59. Suppes, P.; Jamison, D.; & Butler, C. Estimated costs of computer assisted instruction for compensatory education in urban areas. *Educational Technology*, 1970, *10* (4), 49-57.

Costs estimated as of 1970 (bears no relationship to today's rapidly shrinking costs).

60. Atkinson, R.C. *Ingredients for a theory of instruction. Technical Report Number 187.* Stanford, California: Institute for Mathematical Studies in the Social Sciences, 1972.

Lists criteria for a theory of instruction necessary for deriving optimal strategies of teaching reading. These are 1) a model of the learning process, 2) specification of admissible instructional objectives, and 3) specification of instructional objectives, and 4) a measurement scale permitting cost assessment and reinforcements for the achievement of instructional goals.

61. Fletcher, J.D., & Suppes, P. Computer assisted instruction in reading: Grades 4-6. *Educational Technology*, 1972 *12* (8), 45-49.

Describes implementation of Computer Curriculum Corporation reading curriculum with the Honeywell 1648 Computer and Model 33 teletypewriters with standard ASC 11 keyboards.

62. Atkinson, R.C., & Fletcher, J.D. Teaching children to read with a computer. *Reading Teacher*, 1972, *25* (4), 319-327.

Describes the "strand" structure of the drill and practice program designed to supplement reading instruction in grades one to three, providing a flow chart for the Word Strand and sample exercises and giving cost estimates.

63. Fletcher, J.D., & Atkinson, R.C. Evaluation of the Stanford CAI program in initial reading. *Journal of Educational Psychology*, 1972, *63*, 597-602.

A detailed analysis of scores of forty-four matched pairs of subjects. Results indicated that 1) five-and-one-half months of CAI instruction yielded significant gains in reading among first grade students; 2) boys were helped more by CAI than were girls; and 3) most significant results were in sentence and paragraph comprehension, areas hardly touched by the CAI program.

64. Atkinson, R.C.; Fletcher, J.D.; Lindsey, E.J.; Campbell, J.D.; & Barr, A. Computer assisted instruction in initial reading: Individualized instruction based on optimization procedures. *Educational Technology*, 1973, *13* (8), 27-37.

Describes the expanded eight strand drill and practice curriculum and how monitoring student performance leads the computer to prescribe more practice for slower learning students and to all students for learning tasks which the computer "recognizes" as more difficult through its constant monitoring. Also described is a method for computing amount of computer time required for reaching a given score on a reading achievement test.

65. Atkinson, R.C. Teaching children to read with a computer. *American Psychologist*, 1974, *29*, 169-178.

Describes three levels of optimization of instruction: 1) Decision making within an instructional strand—which items to present, which formats to present them in, and when to schedule review; 2) decision making about allocation of instructional time to the various strands, or subareas within reading; and 3) decision making about distribution of terminal use time among students.

66. Campbell, J.; Lindsey, J.; & Atkinson, R.C. *Predicting reading achievement form measures available during computer assisted instruction.* Technical Report Number 249. Stanford, California: Institute for Mathematical Studies in the Social Sciences, 1975.

When correlations were computed between rate of progress during CAI reading instruction and scores on standardized tests of initial reading skill, CAI measures were found to be better predictors than were reading readiness tests.

Additional References

67. Atkinson, R.C. Reading instruction under computer control. *American School Board Journal*, 1967, *155*, 16-17.

68. Atkinson, R.C. Learning aspects of computer assisted instruction. In R.W. Ferard (Ed.), *Computers and Education*. New York: McGraw-Hill, 1967.

69. Atkinson, R.C. The role of the computer in teaching initial reading. *Childhood Education*, 1968, *44*, 464-470.

70. Atkinson, R.C. Computer based instruction in initial reading. *Proceedings of the 1967 Invitational Conference on Testing Problems*. Princeton, New Jersey: Educational Testing Service, 1968.

71. Atkinson, R.C. Learning to read under computer control. *Programed Learning and Educational Technology: British Journal of the Association for Programed Learning*, 1968, *5*, 25-37.

72. Atkinson, R.C., & Wilson, H.A. Computer assisted instruction. *Science*, 1968, 162, 73-77.

73. Fletcher, J.D., & Atkinson, R.C. *Computer based instruction in reading: Grades K-3.* Paper presented at the annual conference of the International Reading Association, Anaheim, May 1970.

74. Atkinson, R.C.; Fletcher, J.D.; Cheten, H.C.; & Stauffer, C.M. Instruction in initial reading under computer control: The Stanford Project. In Romano and S. Rossi (Eds.), *Computer in Education*. Vari, Italy: Adriatica Editrice, 1971.

75. Atkinson, R.C., & Paulson, J.A. An approach to the psychology of instruction. *Psychological Bulletin*, 1972, 1, 49-61.

76. Fletcher, J.D., & Suppes, P. *Computer assisted instruction in mathematics and language arts for the deaf.* Final report. Stanford, California:

Institute for Mathematical Studies in the Social Sciences, Stanford University, 1973.
77. Chant, V.G., & Atkinson, R.C. Optimal allocation of instructional efforts to interrelated learning strands. *Journal of Mathematical Psychology*, 1973, *10* (1), 1-25.
78. Fletcher, J.D. *Transfer from alternative presentations of spelling patterns in initial reading. Technical Report Number 216.* Stanford, California: Institute for Mathematical Studies in the Social Sciences, 1974.
79. Atkinson, R.C. *Adaptive instructional systems: Some attempts to optimize the learning process. Technical Report Number 240.* Stanford, California: Institute for Mathematical Studies in the Social Sciences, 1975.

Illinois' Computer Based Education Laboratory

In 1960, research under the direction of Donald Bitzer, of the Coordinated Science Laboratory of the University of Illinois, developed a computerized teaching system named Programed Logic for Automatic Teaching Operation (PLATO).

The first system was implemented with one high speed digital computer and one terminal. PLATO II was used from 1962 to 1974. PLATO III, making use of time-sharing, reached a peak of 71 terminals with twenty in use at one time. It was used from 1964 to mid-1973, and during its last two years PLATO IV was being installed. PLATO IV has remained in use from mid-1971 until the present.

During this time, many different languages have been employed. PLATO I made use of an ILLIAC I computer and PLATO II used the Control Data Corporation 1604 computer belonging to the Coordinated Science Laboratory. With both of these, machine language was used, but when the Computer Based Education Research Laboratory (CERL) was formed and PLATO III begun, several different programing languages were used before TUTOR III was created. TUTOR IV was implemented in 1971 and TUTOR has remained the language of the present PLATO IV program.

The student using PLATO IV must learn to use a computer terminal which has three vehicles for presenting information: 1) a plasma panel, 2) a microfiche slide projector, and 3) a random access disk record player. It can accept input from a keyset (similar to a typewriter keyboard) and from touching the screen, which is sensitive to interruption of 32 photoelectric circuits just in front of the leading surface of the panel. These divide the screen (16 x 16) into 256 half-inch squares. Breaking these circuits is a means of responding to the computer.

The visual display unit is the plasma panel which presents red lines on a screen much like the character and digit lines on a common hand or tabletop calculator. The PLATO IV plasma panel (screen) is contrived of two layers of glass, 8½ inches square. Between these is a thin layer of trapped gases (neon and others). Each pane of glass has 512 thin wires running through it. The two panes are rotated so that their wires are perpendicular. By firing combinations of these 1024 circuits, 262,144 points can be lighted. Lighting of these points is sufficiently fast to allow the computer to write its maximum of 2,048 characters at the rate of 180 per second. Unlike the cathode ray tube, the plasma panel "has a memory." It continues to display indefinitely, or until a change is directed by the computer or the student using the terminal.

The panel is also used as a rear screen for the projection of slides printed on microfiche cards. This requires the connection of a peripheral device (accessory) called the "random access image selector." This slide projector can be computer directed to show any of the slides on a microfiche which is four inches by seven inches. Access time is one-fifth of a second. Each microfiche has space for 256 images. When both rear screen projected images and plasma panel characters are to be shown, the portion of the panel directly behind the lighted plasma characters usually will be blacked out. The terminal must have a source of compressed air in order to use the projection device, since air pressure is used to move the microfiche from one display point to another.

When directions were given to touch plasma characters, pictures, and diagrams, programs were successful. However, the accuracy of the screen placement of rear screen projected microfiche was not sufficiently accurate for using the touch panel as a response device. There are some problems with the touch response system in other situations, since the toucher may break several circuits in carrying out the touching of a particular point on the screen, or since the toucher with small fingers may not break any circuit.

The audio presentations to the terminal user are made through stenographic headphones. The audio presentations are stored on fifteen-inch mylar magnetic disks, each of which contains about 23 minutes of sound broken up into as many as 4,000 messages. No one message may be less than one-third second or more than 45 seconds long. The time required for locating and starting an audio presentation is one-half second or less. As of 1977, little use of the audio peripheral device, known as the "random access device" had been made by any group other than personnel developing the reading curriculum, persons who would have been hard put to teach reading without it. (The average reading lesson is nearly three minutes long. Almost a minute of this time is audio presentation—with simultaneous video, of course.) One reason is that the device runs on compressed air.

To be taught by the PLATO IV system, the student finds an operating (on) terminal and presses the NEXT key (one of 63 on the keyset). On the plasma screen then appears "Welcome to PLATO." The student responds by typing (in capital letters, since there are no small letters) the name by which the computer recognizes him and again presses NEXT. As directed by the computer display, the student then types the name of his course and presses STOP while holding down the SHIFT key. Then he types his password and presses NEXT again. From then on, the student interacts with the computer until finished, at which time he again presses the STOP key while holding down the SHIFT key.

Although PLATO was initiated in 1960, the PLATO Early Reading Curriculum (PERC) was not begun until funded by NSF contract C-723 in June 1971. The aims formulated at that time were 1) to create a complete K-6 computer based curriculum in reading; 2) to build in the possible use of a variety of instructional modes, thus permitting teachers to maintain their own styles of teaching reading; 3) to take full advantage of the advanced devices available to the user of a PLATO IV terminal; and 4) to demonstrate the feasibility of the resulting curriculum in a variety of school settings.

The first lessons were tested in 1972, even before the random access audio device was available. During a six week summer pilot session it was found that young disadvantaged children not only could pay attention throughout their ten- to twenty-minute sessions, but also could (and did) ask for repeats at the end of their sessions. (It was also found that poorly constructed lessons bored children when presented by computer, just as they do when presented by human teachers.)

In 1972, the PERC group, led by Priscilla Obertino, Materials Coordinator, and Robert F. Yeager, senior author and programer, found that children related to the terminal in four ways: 1) active aggression, exploring how the machine will respond to hitting, shaking, and probing; 2) conventional (expected) responding; 3) passive, responding only when told to do so by the terminal or by a human teacher; and 4) inactive, exploring the terminal not at all. Observing student behavior was the major means of evaluating early lessons and improving responses from all four types of students.

The early lessons were designed to teach students to use the touch panel, to type stories with the keyset, to remember items presented and then removed from the screen, to match letters, to match words, to choose objects with names which are spelled with a T, to choose letters representing the certain speech sounds, to match words with pictures, to type words pictured, and to touch direction words such as UP and DOWN. In addition, a number of well known children's books were presented in such a way that touching any word in the story caused it to be pronounced by the audio device.

Between 1973 and 1977, the development of the reading program continued and the number of lessons was increased to 200. These lessons, comprising more than 1,500 exercises, were grouped into the following categories to meet approximately 400 objectives.

1. *Orientation*—Freddy Frog helps students learn to use the touch panel and keyset.
2. *Date activities*—learning days of the week, months, and how to read a calendar.
3. *Letter discrimination*—covering parts of a letter until a match can be chosen.
4. *Word detail*—matching words which at first are chosen from dissimilar distractors and later are chosen from similar appearing distractors.
5. *Memory skills*—choosing "new" pictures (not in a previous display) or, instead, the "old" ones.
6. *Letter names*—hearing, seeing, and choosing words beginning with a particular letter.
7. *Alphabet*—completing a sequence by choosing letters.
8. *Letter sounds*—sorting groups of words by sounds and responding to alliterative stories.
9. *Blending*—typing three-letter CVC trigrams starting with the consonant given.
10. *High frequency sight words*—a look-and-say presentation in isolation and in context followed by typing the word and choosing it from a set of distractors.
11. *Enrichment sight words*—picturable words taught as high frequency words, plus being pictured.
12. *Word meanings*—by touching appropriate printed words the child makes the display respond.
13. *Sentence building*—by touching words on the screen in order, the student creates sentences which are then displayed. If grammatical, the sentence is illustrated by the computer.
14. *Stories*—picture stories are displayed so that touching a square next to a line causes that line to be read aloud by the computer.

15. *Timed reading*—students are given the time required for reading a story and are asked multiple-choice questions about it.
16. *Stories written by students*—students type their own stories for storage by the computer and reading by other students and the teacher.
17. *Games*—memory, discrimination, and location activities with computer reinforcement.

These activities are prescribed for each student by his own human teacher, who spends about an hour each week typing prescriptions for the class. Using an index of currently available activities, the teacher makes up a lesson called a "prescriber." Listed in the prescriber are *main* activities (primary instruction for a student), *start-the-day* activities (done at the beginning of each session), and *extra* activities (to be done if the student completes all *main* activities). Using the prescriber, the teacher also can set lesson time and the number of activities to be completed in each lesson, or can call for autoprescribing, in which lessons failed are automatically listed for the next day.

Upon request by the teacher the PLATO IV system provides data on lessons completed (time spent, date, score earned, number of repeats) and on skills learned (known, ready to be tested, needing work, or no information as yet). The teacher may also create lessons and activities, may send personal notes (like electronic letters), and may "talk" with another teacher or with PLATO IV advisors. PLATO IV, using main core or floppy disks (off-line) can deliver 7,500 instructional hours in 150 subjects. Recently, using the PLATO IV terminal, lessons have been developed for GED comprehension activities in social science and science, pre-GED language and grammar usage skills, rate and comprehension activities for fourth to eighth graders (PACER). Illinois at present (1982) has terminals in schools, prisons, job centers and university sites.

Annotated References

80. Bitzer, D.L., & Braunfeld, P. A computer controlled teaching system (PLATO), in Brown and Thornton (Eds.) *New Media in Higher Education*, Washington, D.C.: National Education Association, 1963.

An early description of the PLATO system as it was at that time, with indications of its potential.

81. Bitzer, D.L.; Lyman, E.R.; & Easley, J.A., Jr. The uses of PLATO: A computer controlled teaching system. *Audiovisual Instruction*, 1966, *11* (1), 16-21.

A review of the uses of the PLATO system in various kinds of instruction. Includes a description of the hardware components.

82. Avner, C.A., & Tenczar, P. *The TUTOR MANUAL, CERL Report X-4.* Urbana, Illinois: Computer Based Education Laboratory, University of Illinois, 1971 (rev.).

Gives directions for using the TUTOR author language to create CAI for the PLATO system.

83. Elliott, P., & Videbeck, R. Reading comprehension materials for high school equivalency students on the PLATO IV computer based education system. *Educational Technology*, 1973, *13* (9), 20-22.

A discussion of the planning preceding the development of a program to train adults to pass the GED (high school equivalency) test. Presents task analysis, the instructional strategy, and features of PLATO IV which are available to the student having trouble. An on-line dictionary responds to pressing the HELP key by showing a vocabulary list. When the TERM key is pressed and an unknown word is typed, the terminal displays the word and its definition.

84. PLATO (booklet). Urbana, Illinois: Computer Based Education Research Laboratory, University of Illinois, 1974.

Describes PLATO system, features, and uses. Gives a time-line history of the project.

85. Obertino, P. The PLATO reading project: An overview. *Educational Technology*, 1974, *14* (2), 8-13.

Presents the aims of the PLATO Elementary Reading Curriculum (PERC) group and details their early program tryouts and findings about children's interaction with computer terminals.

86. Obertino, P. *PLATO Elementary Reading Curriculum, 1974.* Urbana, Illinois: Computer Based Education Laboratory, University of Illinois, 1974.

Contains the previous article and 19 pages of program samples.

87. Meller, D.V. *Using PLATO IV.* Urbana, Illinois: Computer Based Education Research Laboratory, University of Illinois, 1974 (rev.).

A well-written guide to the potential user of the PLATO IV system. Contains a description of the terminal and peripheral devices available; a description of the system; directions for getting on-line; directions to authors, instructors, and students; and maintenance procedures.

88. Lyman, E.R. *PLATO Highlights.* Urbana, Illinois: Computer Based Education Research Laboratory, University of Illinois, 1975 (rev.).

Contains a timeline of important events in the history of the PLATO systems and lists 262 publications dealing with PLATO through 1975.

89. Lyman, E.R. *PLATO Curricular Materials.* Urbana, Illinois: Computer Based Education Research Laboratory, University of Illinois, 1976.

A catalog of CAI programs available to the operator of a PLATO IV terminal. Each listing followed by the name of a contact person and his/her phone number.

90. Francis, L. *PLATO IV Terminal Peripheral Devices.* Urbana, Illinois: Computer Based Education Laboratory, University of Illinois, 1976.

A frank assessment of the usefulness, potential, and the weaknesses of the various peripheral devices which can be attached to the PLATO IV terminal. Especially valuable is the section by Yeager. "Using Audio with CAI Lessons: Experiences of the PLATO Elementary Reading Project" (49-54).

91. Obertino, P., et al. *Elementary reading on PLATO IV.* Urbana, Illinois: Computer Based Education Research Laboratory, University of Illinois, 1977.

The most recent description of the PLATO IV reading program. Provides an introduction of the project (PERC), a description of the PLATO IV hardware, a survey of the 17 kinds of activities, and a listing of teacher management options.

92. Michael, G., & Sliger, M. *LARS instructor's manual.* Urbana, Illinois: Computer Based Education Laboratory, University of Illinois, 1976.

LARS (Language Arts Routing System) is a set of modules designed to teach elementary verbal skills that require following a set of rules. Students are routed to 54 topics in four areas of beginning College English by their performance on diagnostic tests.

93. Yeager, R.F. *The reading machine.* (ED 142 990), 1977.

Describes lessons in beginning reading developed by the PLATO Elementary Reading Curriculum Project (PERC) that place emphasis on the process of learning rather than on content. The lessons are for first grade students. They emphasize sight word recognition, compound words, sentence making, and listening skills.

94. Breland, H.M. *Planning for the evaluation of the PLATO Computer Based Instructional System: Attitudinal and Performance Evaluation in Elementary Schools.* Paper presented at the annual meeting of the American Educational Research Association, Chicago, April 1974.

Presents plans for testing, observing, and assessing attitudes of students in PLATO reading and mathematics programs.

95. Siegel, M.A. *Computer based education in prison schools.* Paper presented at the annual meeting of the Society for the Advancement of Learning Technologies. Orlando, Florida, February 1978.

Describes PLATO Corrections Project in Illinois prisons. Included is a description of approximately 40 hours of CAI in reading comprehension and vocabulary development. The PCP Word Study program is based on Dale and O'Rourke's work, *The Living Word Vocabulary* (1977). The six strands of the comprehension program include: 1) Information finding (answering questions—*who, what, what kind of, which whose, whom, why, when, where*, and *how*); 2) Paraphrase (find sentences meaning the same as other sentences); 3) Following written directions (filling forms, etc.); 4) Synthesis (putting elements together); 5) Inference (draw conclusions without all information); 6) Logical relationships (understanding logical connectors such as *if then, and, or, only, some, all*, or *none*). Twenty-five teaching formats used.

96. Lyman, E.R. *PLATO highlights*, seventh edition. Urbana, Illinois: University of Illinois Computer Based Education Research Laboratory, 1981, (ED 211 070)

The PLATO highlights represent the definitive sources on the development of the PLATO system at Illinois and adds some perspective on national developments of PLATO. While the seventh edition covers 1961 to 1981, it specifically covers the period 1978 to 1981.

Additional References

97. Trippon, M. PLATO at work. *Phi Delta Kappan*, 1968, *49* (9), 439-441.
98. Lyman, E.R. *A descriptive list of PLATO programs, 1960-1970.* Urbana, Illinois: Computer Based Education Research Laboratory, University of Illinois, 1970 (rev.).
99. Jordan, P. *Language arts curriculum.* Urbana, Illinois: Computer Based Education Laboratory, University of Illinois, 1974.
100. Alpert, D., & Bitzer, D.L. Advances in computer based education. *Science*, 1970, *167*, 1582-1590.
101. Anastasio, E.J., & Alderman, D.L. *Evaluation of the educational effectiveness of PLATO and TICCIT.* Princeton, New Jersey: Educational Testing Service, 1973. (ED 088934)
102. Eastwood, L.F., & Ballard, R.J. The PLATO IV CAI system: Where is it now? Where can it go? *Journal of Educational Technology Systems, 1975, 3* (4), 267-284.
103. Yeager, R.F. *Using audio with CAI lessons: Experiences of the PLATO elementary reading project.* Paper presented at the Association for the Development of Computer Based Instructional Systems, Minneapolis, August 1976.
104. Smith, S.G., & Sherwood, B.A. Educational uses of the PLATO computer system. *Science*, 1976, *192*, 344-352.
105. Steinberg, E.R. *The evolutionary development of CAI courseware.* Paper presented at the annual meeting of the American Educational Research Association, Washington, D.C., April 1965.

Wisconsin Research and Development Center for Cognitive Learning

There are two types of computer applications to reading under development at the University of Wisconsin's Research and Development Center, The Wisconsin System for Instructional Management (WIS-SIM) and an on-line program for diagnosing reading difficulties with a PLATO IV terminal. The more extensive development has been of the former, since it designed to capitalize on the well-developed set of goals and objectives of the Wisconsin Design for Reading Skill Development (WDRSD) and has been under development for a longer period of time.

WIS-SIM was originally financed by NIE and a Title III ESEA grant to the McFarland Community Schools. The purpose of the R and D

Center in developing WIS-SIM was to further the cause of individualized education by identifying school system, school building, classroom, and individual pupil needs through more efficient ingestion, storage, and retrieval of student and program information. The areas chosen for developing computer managed instructional schemes include elementary reading, mathematics, and science.

In order to implement WIS-SIM in reading, one must implement the management system it is designed to support (WDRSD). The first step, then, is to test all individual students with the criterion referenced placement tests of the three strands (Word Attack, Comprehension, Study Skills) of the WDRSD. Once the tests had been administered (usually at the beginning of a school year), a data base for reporting is stored in the computer's memory. Of course, the second step is arranging computer services. Having a local computer available is best. Next best is having a terminal available for on-line communication with a distant computer, and the least satisfactory is a "batch" system requiring tests to be mailed or carried to the computer.

Since the objectives and goals of the WDRSD are hierarchically ordered, the computer can generate both a list of tasks mastered and a list of possible next assignments. Since pupil data carry the designation of school attended, classroom to which assigned, and school district or system, printout profiles can be requested to show school or class performance on tests of particular units (areas). Also available are suggested topics for instructional groups and suggested members of those groups (those who *have not* mastered the topic, but who *have* mastered the prerequisite topics or tasks), as well as recommended topics for assignment or teaching to individuals who were omitted from the suggested groups.

Pilot testing of WIS-SIM took place in 1975-1976 in seven schools from four Wisconsin school districts and one district in Minnesota with six elementary schools. Pilot tests help the designers improve the system by making minimal demands on teachers attempting to learn and implement the system in their classrooms.

The diagnostic program developed at the University of Wisconsin uses a PLATO IV terminal with telephone line connections to the computers of the Computer Based Education Research Laboratory of the University of Illinois. The initial step in conducting such a diagnosis involved comparing results of a group administration of the Stanford Diagnostic Reading Test, Level II, Form W, with results of a computer administered version of the same test. At first, results were not comparable. By changing the required response (touching a word in a box next to the answer selected from a multiple-choice display) so that when the word was touched once a box appeared around it and with a second touch being required before the computer registered the response, comparability was achieved.

Earlier computer based reading projects at the Research and Development Center for Cognitive Learning appear to have ceased. However, the University of Wisconsin at La Crosse has designed readability software (from earlier time-share work) that is now distributed by the Minnesota Educational Computing Consortium (MECC). The La Crosse campus also publishes two microcomputer newsletters: *Munchline* and *Punchline*. Regional service centers in Wisconsin have also developed a cooperative computer user service group similar in design to MECC, but called WICC (Wisconsin Instructional Computing Consortium). Additionally, the Green Bay regional service center (CESA #9) has developed their own reading software.

Annotated References

106. Belt, S.L., & West, S.F. *Implementing individually guided education (IGE) with the aid of a computer.* Madison, Wisconsin: Wisconsin Research and Development Center for Cognitive Learning, University of Wisconsin (mimeo, n.d.).

Contrasts CAI with CMI and points out how CMI reports are superior to the "file-folder" approach to individualizing. Provides samples of the kinds of printout reports provided by WIS-SIM.

107. Belt, S.L., & Skubal, J.M. *Individually guided education and the Wisconsin system for instructional management* (WIS-SIM). Paper presented at the annual meeting of the Association for Educational Data Systems, New York, May 1974.

A clear and detailed presentation of how a CMI system (WIS-SIM) can be implemented in a public school setting and some logistics problems accompanying such an implementation.

108. Venezky, R.; Bernard, L.; Chicone, S.; & Leslie, R. *On-line diagnosis of reading difficulties.* Technical Report Number 327. Madison, Wisconsin: Wisconsin Research and Development Center for Cognitive Learning, University of Wisconsin, 1975.

A description of early efforts to develop computer aided diagnostic reading tests.

109. Belt, S.L. *Some CMI design considerations to meet the requirements of individually guided education.* Paper presented at the annual meeting of the American Educational Research Association.

Explains the advantages of an optional CMI system, WIS-SIM over the self-contained classroom, listing sources of computer service to schools.

110. Spuck, D.; Junter, S.N.; Owen, S.P.; & Belt, S.L. *Computer management of individualized instruction.* Theoretical Paper Number 55. Madison, Wisconsin: Wisconsin Research and Development Center for Cognitive Learning, University of Wisconsin, 1975.

Explains learning theory underlying the development of the CMI program for implementation of the Wisconsin Design for Reading Skill Development.

111. *Wisconsin system for instructional management: Overview.* Madison, Wisconsin: Wisconsin Research and Development Center for Cognitive Learning, University of Wisconsin, 1975.

A brief explanation of WIS-SIM with sample printout profiles.

112. *Wisconsin system for instructional management: Instructor's manual.* Madison, Wisconsin: Wisconsin Research and Development Center for Cognitive Learning, University of Wisconsin, 1976.

A manual for use in conducting inservice training for teachers about to try using WIS-SIM.

113. *Wisconsin system for instructional management: Teacher's guide.* Madison, Wisconsin: Wisconsin Research and Development Center for Cognitive Learning, University of Wisconsin, 1976.

Instructions to teachers participating in WIS-SIM of WDRSD.

114. Belt, S.L. *CMI design considerations which enhance transportability to IGE schools.* Paper presented at the annual conference of the Association for Individually Guided Education, Denver, November 1975.

Since immediate computer response is not necessary for managing IGE, Wisconsin personnel are readying WIS-SIM for control by a variety of computers which may be available to schools around the country.

115. Lawrence, G.F. *Numerical procedures in the optimal grouping of students for instructional purposes.* Technical Report Number 399. Madison, Wisconsin: Wisconsin Research and Development Center for Cognitive Learning, University of Wisconsin, 1976.

A doctoral dissertation leading to the conclusion that the best method for computer assigned skill grouping for reading instruction first matched topics (skills) to groups, then matched group sizes against appropriate sizes for skill groups, then assigned students to maximize homogeneity, and only then applied other restrictions required for administrative purposes.

116. Douglas, B.G., & Belt, S.L. *System design manual for the Wisconsin system of instructional management (WIS-SIM) for the management of the Wisconsin design for reading skill development (WDRSD).* Madison, Wisconsin: University of Wisconsin Research and Development Center in Cognitive Learning, 1977.

Discusses computer managed instruction, individualized education, and the areas of WDRSD supported by WIS-SIM. The capabilities of the software for entering information into the data base, generating reports, and providing grouping information for instructional decision making are detailed. Documentation is provided on program listings and descriptions, and the interactive function codes.

117. Johnson, D.D.; Pittelman, S.D.; Schwenker, J.; & Perry, J. *On-line diagnosis of reading difficulties: IV.* Technical Report No. 464. Wisconsin Research and Development for Cognitive Learning (ED 162 277), 1978.
Describes three studies conducted to evaluate various paradigms for assessing vocabulary knowledge on-line: synonym in context, synonym out-of-context, cloze, oral recognition, and self-screening. Authors concluded no single format was superior for the assessment of vocabulary knowledge.
118. McIsaac, D.; Bilow, C.; Macrides, G.; & Romstad, D. *An overview of MICRO-CMI.* Theoretical paper number 88. Madison, Wisconsin: Wisconsin Research and Development Center for Individualized Schooling, 1980.
Describes use of large microcomputer for large scale CMI of reading programs (or other school subjects). Requires approximately 65 kilobytes of memory and dual-disk capacity of 2,500 kilobytes.

Additional References

119. Belt, S.L., & Spuck, D.W. *Design specification for the generalized Wisconsin system for instructional management.* Report Number WRDCCL-WP-Parts 1 and 2. Madison, Wisconsin: Wisconsin Research and Development Center for Cognitive Learning, University of Wisconsin, 1974.
120. Rosenkranz, C.I. *COMP (Computerized Operational Materials Prescription).* Madison, Wisconsin: Division for Handicapped Children, Wisconsin State Department of Public Instruction, 1974. (ED 094 539).
121. Spuck, D.W., & Owen, S.P. *Individualized instruction: Its structure and management.* Madison, Wisconsin: Wisconsin Research and Development Center for Cognitive Learning, University of Wisconsin (mimeo, n.d.).
122. Spuck, D.W., & West, S.F. *Computer managed instruction as an aid to decision making for individualized reading programs.* Paper presented at the annual conference of the International Reading Association, Anaheim, May 1976.
123. Rossmiller, R. *1977 Bibliography of Publications.* Madison, Wisconsin: Wisconsin Research and Development Center for Cognitive Learning, University of Wisconsin, 1977.
124. Venezky, R.L.; Chicone, S.; & Perry, J. *On-line diagnosis of reading difficulties-II.* Technical Report No. 386 (ED 141 791), 1976.
125. Venezky, R.L.; Perry, J.; Chicone, S.; & Pittelman, S. *Summary of studies for an on-line reading diagnosis system-III.* Technical Report No. 409 (ED 138 967), 1977.

Florida State University's Computer Applications Laboratory

The Computer Assisted Instruction Center at Florida State University has conducted several investigations and has completed several projects involving the teaching of reading. The original central processing computer at FSU was an IBM 1440 programed for time-sharing between several keyset 1050 terminals, some of which were equipped to control slide projectors and/or tape recorders. The programing language was COURSEWRITER.

The first reading program developed at FSU for presentation by computer was entitled "Reading for Illiterate Youths and Adults." This program was intended to promote functional literacy for adults reading fifth reader level and below. Twenty-four lessons of the second reader level program were created, slides were made, and the lessons entered into the computer. Third reader lessons with slides were ready for computerization and lessons were written for the fourth, fifth, and sixth reader levels. The lessons were written so that audiotapes were optional. Although the software was developed, the computerizing of this program could not be completed because the funding (federal) was discontinued at the end of the first year.

A second project of the Florida State CAI Center was the implementation of the DOVACK model in cooperation with an ESEA Title III project at the nearby Monticello, Florida, Elementary School. The DOVACK (Differentiated, Oral, Visual, Aural, Computerized, Kinesthetic) model is a version of the language experience approach. Each day each student dictated a story to a teacher or aide who recorded it and then redictated it and typed it on the terminal of the CDC 6400 computer serving the project. Overnight the computer printed out each new story. The next day each student reread computer printouts of stories dictated earlier. Every sixth school day the computer created a test which was a random sample of words dictated by the student since the last examination. Since videotape and field trips were also used in the DOVACK model, the role of the computer was primarily that of printer, record keeper, and test producer. Records available to the teachers included the list of words dictated by each student, his or her test performance, the total number of words dictated, and his or her rate of word acquisition. The cost per student was given as $770, above the school board's usual price per pupil of $658 per year.

A third project involved teaching sight vocabulary to EMR students using an IBM 1500 instructional system and an IBM 1800 central processing computer. Thirty tutorial lessons, each presenting nine words to be associated with pictures illustrating them, were developed in the COURSEWRITER II language and field tested with the IBM 1510 terminal (CRT with light pen) in Wakulla County, Florida. This was partially funded by an ESEA Title VI grant. At the end of the first year, the project switched from computer assisted instruction to computer managed instruction which required only periodic testing by the computer. During the third year, the project made no use of computers.

A fourth project, conducted in cooperation with the English department, involves the use of the CDC computer which the Florida State Center for Educational Development and Evaluation now uses as the central processor for its CMI and CAI projects. The purpose of this project is to test students for their competency and give them prescriptive feedback about skills in which they need improvement. Students needing to be tested (for basic English competency or for earning grades in one or more of their courses) come to the Assessment Resource Center. The student fills in a machine scorable form indicating his identity and the unit of instruction on which he wishes to be examined. A proctor examines the student's ID card and verifies his identity before going to the terminal and asking the central computer to process the request and determine the appropriateness of the requested test for this student. If all is satisfactory, the computer tells the proctor which test to give the student. The student completes the machine scorable test and hands it in to the proctor. The proctor inserts it in a document reader which relays student responses to the computer. The computer then prints out a prescriptive report to the student, while holding the complete record of this student's performance available for the instructor whenever the instructor requests it. The advantages of this program are that the use of machine scorable tests limits the amount of on-line computer time (and money) required and that instant feedback is provided to students.

At Florida State University several other units of instruction were developed. Among these was a tutorial reading program (in COURSEWRITER I) for preschoolers. In this program words were to be matched to words, pictures matched to pictures, and words matched to pictures. This required the computer to control a tape recorder and a slide projector. Another was a tutorial program (in COURSEWRITER II) for slow learning second graders. This required a cathode ray tube terminal and light pen. Students were presented stories followed by analytic questions, vocabulary exercises, and thought problems. Unfortunately, neither of these programs is now available. Currently, Florida State University has a computer managed college testing program and college level reading programs.

Annotated References

126. Puder, W.H., & Hand, S.E. *Frontiers in Adult Basic Education.* A Compilation of Selected Papers and Group Reports Presented at the Southeastern Regional Institute for Teacher Trainers in Adult Basic Education. Tallahassee, Florida: Florida State University, 1966.

Describes the initiation of the FSU CAI literacy project.

127. Hankin, E.K.; Smith, E.H.; Smith, T.; & Ritchie, M. *The development of prevocational education literacy courses for use with computer assisted instruction of disadvantaged youth and adults.* Technical Progress Report Number BR-6-1458-PRI. Tallahassee, Florida: Computer assisted Instruction Center, Florida State University, 1967.

A report of the first three months of development of CAI programs in reading and mathematics to prepare young adults for vocational training.

128. Hankin, E.K., et al. *The development of prevocational literacy courses for use with computer assisted instruction of disadvantaged youths and adults.* Final Report. Tallahassee, Florida: Computer Assisted Instruction Center, Florida State University, 1968.

A complete report of the project to develop CAI programs in reading and mathematics for functionally illiterate young adults.

129. Way, F.L. The DOVACK model. *Educom,* 1969, *4* (5), 6-7.

A description of a federally funded program designed to be differentiated, oral, visual, aural, computerized, and kinesthetic. Essentially a language experience approach using computer printouts of dictated stories as reading material and computer storage and retrieval of word lists to assess progress.

130. Wills, M. DOVACK's machines help children read. *American Education,* 1971, *7* (5), 3-8.

Another description of the DOVACK program.

131. Way, F.L. The language experience approach in teaching reading—computerized. *Computer Automation,* 1969, *19* (9), 28-30.

Reports positive results of DOVACK with a population of primarily underprivileged black children.

132. Way, F.L. *DOVACK: Method for teaching reading.* Project report for July 1, 1968-August 31, 1971. Monticello, Florida: Jefferson County Board of Public Instruction, 1971.

Reports the final evaluation of the project with both elementary and secondary students.

133. American Institutes for Research. *Model programs: Childhood education: A computer assisted language experience which allows children to create their own reading lessons.* Washington, D.C.: National Center for Educational Communication, 1971.

A 24-page report of the DOVACK program originally presented to the White House Conference on Children, December 1970.

134. Dick, W., & Gallagher, P. Systems concepts and computer managed instruction: An implementation and validation study. *Educational Technology, 12* (2), 33-39.

A detailed description of the development and cost of a CAI college course.

135. Luyben, P.D. *The effects of pictures on acquisition of a sight vocabulary in rural EMR children.* Paper presented at the annual meeting of the American Educational Research Association, New Orleans, February 1973.

Thirty lessons of nine words each employed computer presented pictures to be matched with words by shining a light pen on the screen of the CRT equipped terminal. It was concluded that pictures could help.

136. Elfner, E. *Reading curriculum development project.* Final Report. Crawfordville, Florida: Wakulla County Board of Public Instruction, 1974.

A complete evaluation report of the Title VI project including pretest and posttest data on 40 EMR students. Contains the interesting comment that students taking more time to respond to test items on the computer demonstrated greater gains.

137. Oosterhof, A.C. *The assessment resource center.* Technical Paper Number 1. Assessment Resource System. Tallahassee, Florida: Center for Educational Development and Evaluation, Florida State University, 1977.

A complete description of the working of the center, showing how computer managed testing can complement college instruction at a low cost.

Additional References

138. Hansen, D.N. *Information processing models for reading skill acquisition.* Technical Report. Tallahassee, Florida: Compuer Assisted Instruction Center, Florida State University, 1973.

139. Hansen, D.N. *Computer Applications Laboratory (Computer Assisted Instruction Center) annual progress report, 1 January 1972 through 31 December 1972.* Tallahassee, Florida: Computer Assisted Instruction Center, Florida State University, 1973.

Penn State's Computer Assisted Instruction Laboratory

At the Pennsylvania State University, the application of computers to reading instruction took the form of inservice education. A huge project—funded by the Bureau of the Handicapped, the Bureau of Educational Personnel Development (USOE), and the Penn State Foundation—was mounted to bring fundamentals of remediation to teachers of children who would become educationally retarded by age nine or ten. This project, named CARE I (Computer Assisted Remedial Education), was intended to be the prototype for several similar projects.

The central computer, an IBM 1130, was connected by telephone lines to terminals housed in trailer trucks so that they could be taken to remote sites around the state. Each terminal consisted of a cathode ray tube with light pencil, a keyboard, an audio device, and a self-contained image projector and screen. Students read a handbook prior to working at the drill and practice exercises presented at their terminal. The instructional language used to create the exercise was COURSEWRITER II.

A similar program was created to teach the principles of phonics instruction and i.t.a. to teachers and prospective teachers. Again, a handbook was created and the CAI was supplemental drill and practice for the course. In an evaluation study, students were branched to CAI according to the pretest performance. The computer presented illustrative lessons, a student self-evaluation, and multiple-choice practice exercises. It was concluded that the CAI course was valid for preservice education of teachers.

In addition to the teacher education courses offered through computer assisted instruction, the Computer Assisted Instruction Laboratory at Penn State also created a literacy program called LITE (funded by USOE). This program used the computer to improve students' literacy levels (up to eighth reader level) by providing job oriented reading materials and constant feedback on their improvement in reading. A summative evaluation found students made some gains in reading and great gains in their knowledge of occupations. Furthermore, student attitude was found to be positive. The program (now available) appears to be useful for junior high, high school, and vocational students.

The Computer Assisted Instruction Laboratory has also created a program for teaching fourth and fifth grade students to read word problems in mathematics. However, after a field test, the CAI group scores did not exceed those of the controls.

The CAI Laboratory closed June 30, 1977.

Annotated References

140. Hall, K.A. *Curricular and computer system compatability of CAI programs for multiuniversity use.* Paper presented at the EDUCOM Fall Conference, Princeton, New Jersey, October 1973.

Gives a brief description of the CAI programs at Penn State. Includes a description of Project CARE.

141. Cartwright, G.P., & Cartwright, C.A. *Handbook for CARE 1—Introduction to the education of exceptional children.* Laboratory Report

Number R36. State College, Pennsylvania: Computer Assisted Instruction Laboratory, Pennsylvania State University, 1970.

The first handbook written to provide the basic information for the CARE course.

142. Hall, K.A. Computer assisted instruction: Problems and performance. *Phi Delta Kappan,* 1971, *52* (10), 628-631.

Points out problems and successes in CAI implementation.

143. Cartwright, G.P., & Cartwright, C.A. *Computer assisted remedial education: Diagnostic teaching of preschool children.* Handbook for CARE 2. Report Number R54. State College, Pennsylvania: Computer Assisted Instruction Laboratory, Pennsylvania State University, 1973.

The extension of the CARE course to deal with exceptional preschool children.

144. Thompson, R.L. *Computer assisted phonic analysis: A validation study.* Laboratory Report Number R52. State College, Pennsylvania: Computer Assisted Instruction Laboratory, Pennsylvania State University, 1973.

An evaluation of the phonics program as taught with CAI to 36 undergraduates in teacher education.

145. Caldwell, R.M. *Literacy development using a programed text and computer assisted instruction.* Paper presented at the annual meeting of the American Educational Research Association, Chicago, April 1974.

CAI students spent more time on literacy lessons and were more positive toward instruction than those using a programed text.

146. Dupuis, M.M. *We CARE about inservice education.* Paper presented at the annual conference of the International Reading Assocation, New Orleans, May 1974.

An excellent description of the CARE program for reading teachers.

147. Golub, L.S.; Mull, P.; & Thompson, R.L. *Phonics/i.t.a. handbook for teachers.* Laboratory Report Number R63. State College, Pennsylvania: Computer Assisted Instruction Laboratory, Pennsylvania State University, 1974.

A two-part mimeographed text basic to the CAI course in phonics and i.t.a.

148. Golub, L.S. *A computer assisted literacy development program for career oriented youths and young adults, Ages 14-24.* Laboratory Report Number R59. State College, Pennsylvania: Computer Assisted Instruction Laboratory, Pennsylvania State University, 1974.

Describes LITE, a tutorial program for simultaneous reading instruction and vocational education for poor readers in junior high school or beyond. Also gives program products, including an adult diagnostic reading test.

149. Golub, L.S. A computer assisted literacy development program. *Journal of Reading,* 1974, *17* (4), 279-284.

Includes a flow chart showing how the LITE program was operated.

150. Hall, K.A. *CARE: Computer assisted remedial education.* Paper presented at the SECOS Conference, New Paltz, New York, May 1974.

Lists and describes four CARE courses for teachers.

Additional References

151. Demshock, G.N., & Riedesel, C.A. *Use of computer assisted instruction to teach spelling to sixth graders.* Laboratory Report Number R14. State College, Pennsylvania: Computer Assisted Instruction Laboratory, Pennsylvania State University, 1968.
152. Cartwright, G.P., & Mitzel, H.E. *Computer assisted remedial education: Early identification of handicapped children.* Laboratory Report Number R44. State College, Pennsylvania: Computer Assisted Instruction Laboratory, Pennsylvania State University, 1971.
153. Cartwright, G.P., & Cartwright, C.A. A computer assisted instruction course in the early identification of handicapped children. *Journal of Teacher Education,* 1973, *24* (2), 128-134.
154. Hall, K.A., & Mitzel, H.E. CARE: Computer assisted renewal education —An opportunity in Pennsylvania. *Audio Visual Instruction,* 1973, *18* (1), 35-38.
155. Borman, K.G. *Computer assisted instruction laboratory teaching and coursewriting language (TACL): User's guide.* Laboratory Report Number R64. State College, Pennsylvania: Computer Assisted Instruction Laboratory, Pennsylvania State University, 1974.
156. Golub, L.S., & Kidder, C. Syntactic density and the computer. *Elementary English,* 1974, *51,* 1128-1131.
157 Hall, K.; Cartwright, P.; & Mitzel, H. A triumph for CAI. *Phi Delta Kappan,* 1974, *55,* 70-72.

Brigham Young's Institute for Computer Uses in Education

In the early 1970s, Brigham Young University's Institute for Computer Uses in Education began to develop the courseware for TICCIT (Time-Shared Interactive Computer Controlled Information Television) to be developed by the Mitre Corporation. The purpose was to take advantage of the informational and motivational strengths of color television by controlling its presentation with the computer and adding such CAI as might enhance the presentation. One major task accomplished was the development of a technology which could produce still frames on the TV screen for careful viewing and analysis.

The TICCIT terminal is supported by the TICCIT system which provides random access/retrieval of video cassette decks, the playing of which can be stopped, rewound, run fast forward (in specific time intervals), run forward (at the usual rate), run frame-by-frame, or held at pause. They can be played as part of an instructional sequence or as pure entertainment.

Eventually a special TICCIT computer keyboard was developed with several special keys. Some of these are listed and explained below.

RULE KEY: Gives an example or a particular case of the generalization or rule to be learned.

EXAMPLE KEY: Gives an example or a particular case of the generalization or rule to be learned.

EASY KEY: Gives an easier version of the rule or example.

HARD KEY: Gives a harder version of the rule or example.

HELP KEY: Gives the most simple or basic information about what the student is to learn.

PRACTICE KEY: Presents problems related to the rule or concept to be learned and provides feedback after the student's response.

MAP KEY: Displays list of options available to the student, suggests prerequisites, and orients student to state of his current progress.

OBJECTIVE KEY: Explains what is to be learned in the forthcoming lesson.

ADVISOR KEY: Advises student of his current progress and the merits of the particular path he has followed in attempting to master the objective.

By pressing any of these keys, the student caused the computer to present (on the screen) still color frames which performed the keyed functions. Each slide was labeled on the bottom for better orienting the student as to its purpose. The labels gave both the component upon which the student was working and the number of the frame (called page) of that component (i.e., PAGE 3 of 5, EASY, MAP, etc.).

The availability of these keys was accompanied by the requirement that program authors had to define the rules and concepts to be learned and then offer examples of varying degrees of difficulty and practice items to clarify and lead students to mastery of those concepts and rules.

Other visuals (drawings, cartoons, artwork) are entered into the computer's memory by a graphic digitizer which scans the visuals through three color filters (red, green, blue) three different times to allow storage of seven colors (red, green, yellow, blue, blue-green, white, and black) for transmission by the computer controlled TV screen. Audio for the system consists of the audio accompanying the videotape decks.

Computer record keeping allows teachers to determine which lessons students have completed and which ones they are working on. Progress within lessons and scores on lesson posttests are also available to teachers when requested of the TICCIT computer system. Log tapes of student on-line time provide item analyses of practice and test items. A "mailbox" feature allows a TICCIT user to send messages to any (or all) other TICCIT user(s). Receivers receive the messages only when they elect to "read their mail" at their own terminals.

The TICCIT Reading Program was developed at Brigham Young University at the same time as the General Education Critical Reading Program (GECRP—required of all freshmen). Both courses were begun in Winter 1975, and in Winter 1976 the latter course was taught to ten sections of students. Many of the students used the TICCIT Reading Program as a supplement to the once-a-week class discussions of GECRP. Those students using the TICCIT program who were helped most were those who started with the lowest scores. A one teacher pilot study indicated a 10 percent advantage on evaluation test scores for students using TICCIT and generally favorable student response to the computer program.

Financial problems and the small number (28) of available terminals led Brigham Young to discontinue some of the TICCIT Reading Program in 1976-1977. At present (1982) BYU is revising the TICCIT Critical Reading program after some extensive debugging work. The Critical Reading program is designed to support and complement a freshman college level English course. In addition, BYU is at work on an improved authoring language for TICCIT as well as ESL for the Apple II microcomputer.

Annotated References

158. Bunderson, C.V. *Team production of learner controlled courseware: A progress report.* Technical report number 1. Provo, Utah: Institute for Computer Uses in Education, 1973.

An initial description of team activity in producing courseware for the TICCIT system.

159. Bunderson, C.V. *The TICCII project: Design strategy for educational innovation.* Technical report number 4. Provo, Utah: Institute for Computer Uses in Education, 1973.

Includes description of procedures designed to enhance learning with the TICCIT system. Describes original funding by NSF Office of Computer Innovations beginning in 1971-1972.

160. Herlin, W.R.; Bance, G.; & Hansen, D.M. *Teaching college level reading in a computer assisted computer managed setting.* Paper presented at the annual conference of the International Reading Association, Anaheim, May 1976.

Presents and reviews TICCIT developed through an NSF grant to the MITRE Corporation. It also reviews progress and problems of a computer managed critical reading program devised to help meet the critical reading course required for all BYU freshmen through use of the TICCIT system.

161. Hansen, D.N. Personal correspondence, October 13, 1977.
Describes development of TICCIT Reading Program and the successes and failures to date in implementing it.

162. Merrill, M.D. *Premises, propositions, and research underlying the design of a learner controlled computer assisted instruction: A summary for the TICCIT system.* Working paper 44. Provo, Utah: Brigham Young University, Division of Instructional Services, June 1973.
Points out four aspects of TICCIT that make it a unique CAI vehicle.
1. It has a built-in learning strategy. The lesson author supplies the content but must follow the TICCIT presentation strategy.
2. The learner selects both his content and his strategy for learning that content.
3. The objective of the TICCIT system is to make the learner independent of the system—able to proceed without it.
4. Authors (teachers and instructors) prepare lessons in natural language. There are constraints on the displays they may use, but the constraints are very similar to those facing the teacher in non-CAI settings.

163. Goldberg, L.M., & Rubin, F.S. *An overview of the TICCIT + 10 computer system at the Model Secondary School for the Deaf.* Paper presented at the annual meeting of the Convention of American Instructors of the Deaf, Los Angeles, June 1977.
Describes TICCIT system operative at the Model Secondary School for the Deaf and briefly sketches research and development to be attempted in the future.

Additional References

164. Bunderson, C.V., & Faust, G.W. Programed and computer assisted instruction, in Gage, N.L. (Ed.), *National Social Studies Education Yearbook,* Part 1. Chicago: University of Chicago, 1976.

165. Merrill, M.D., & Boutwell, R.C. Instructional development: Methodology and research, in F.M. Kerlinger (Ed.), *Review of Research in Education.* Itasco, Illinois: F.E. Peacock, 1973.

166. O'Neal, F. *Learner control of instruction requirements and potentials.* Technical Report Number 3. Provo, Utah: Institute for Computer Uses in Education, Brigham Young University, 1973.

167. *An Overview of the TICCIT program.* Washington, D.C.: Mitre Corporation, 1976.

168. *Overview of TICCIT authoring.* San Diego: Courseware, 1976.

169. *Toward a market success of CAI: An overview of the TICCIT program.* McLean, Virginia: Mitre Corporation, 1972.

170. Watson, P.G. The utilization of the computer with deaf learners. *Educational Technology* (in press).

171. Volk, J.L.; Mason, W.F.; & Zraket, C.A. *An overview of the TICCIT program.* Washington, D.C.: Mitre Corporation, 1974.

Delaware's PLATO *Project*

The University of Delaware PLATO Project began in 1975-1976 with the purchase of CDC PLATO from the Control Data Corporation and a contract with the University of Illinois for access to the Illinois (CERL) PLATO system. By 1977, thirty-two PLATO terminals were installed on campus and by 1978, forty-eight were installed. All of them were equipped with touch panels (see section on University of Illinois); six terminals also had random access audio devices. With these six, John Pikulski and Peter Pelosi of the Reading Study Center began the development of CAI reading activities in four ways.

First, graduate students and faculty of the Reading Study Center familiarized themselves with PLATO reading lessons developed at the University of Illinois. Then the group began developing their own lessons, both for instruction of children and for teacher education in reading. In 1976-1977, approximately forty children (clients of the Reading Study Center) used PLATO for an average of six hours each. In 1977-1978, fewer children were expected to spend more time at the terminals.

One of the programs is "Read Along with PLATO," developed by Peter Pelosi and Jessica Weissman (chief programer for the Reading Study Center programs). The lesson starts by presenting the student with a list of twenty short stories from which to pick one to read. After the story is picked the terminal displays a page line by line and asks the student to read along as it reads to him. The child is guided to the proper line by an arrow that moves down the left side of the text.

There are three types of reading available. On the first reading of each page, the student listens while PLATO reads. On the second reading, the student reads along with PLATO. In both of these readings, the machine stops at the end of each line. The student touches one box (shown on the display panel) to start the oral reading of the next line, or another box to read again the line just completed. The third reading is computer assisted only if the student has difficulty. When he does, he can touch a box requesting that the computer read the line for him. If so desired, the teacher can direct the computer to offer only one (any one) of these three types of reading.

A second program is SWAT (Sight Word Attack Team), developed by Rosalie Bianco, Peter Pelosi, Jessica Weissman, and Bonnie Seiler. SWAT now includes a set of sight word teaching lessons, a test, and a test results program (giving results to the instructor). All lessons use a theme involving spies and passwords.

The sight words are first presented in groups of four so that the pupil can select one he wishes to learn. Then an amusing story, illustrated by animations, is printed on the screen. Pupils can read it for themselves or direct the computer to read it aloud to them. (In this program all instructions, explanations, and remedial messages are printed on the screen, but the student can call for any of them to be read aloud.) In this story, the target word appears once on each line.

Next, a "secret message" appears on the screen. The pupil chooses the target word from four foils, thus completing the message. After that, the pupil is presented a picture of a "DeKoder machine." By touching letters displayed on the machine, the pupil fills blanks in sentences with the target word. The final two activities in this lesson require the pupil to 1) choose the target word from a scrambled set of words and 2) identify the presence or absence of the password (a correctly spelled target word) in a sentence by touching a box labeled "yes" or a box labeled "no." The time required for this sequence is approximately ten minutes per word.

The SWAT promotion test was developed by Rosalie Bianco, Peter Pelosi, and Jessica Weissman. Three versions are available for the pupil to choose from. In the first, "letter linker," children hear a word pronounced and indicate their recognition by touching it on the display panel, where it has been displayed among several nonsense word foils. In the second version, "sentence sayer," the computer displays a sentence with a blank in it, along with the target word and several foils, which are other sight words from the program. The pupil is to touch the word which best fills the blank. The third version, "supreme decoder," is the same as the second, except the sentence is read aloud by the computer as it is displayed. A beep is substituted for the blank. Results are reported instantly to the student as a promotion or as failure to get the promotion (to the rank of letter linker, sentence sayer, or supreme decoder).

SWAT Promotion Test Results, developed by Rosalie Bianco, Peter Pelosi, and Jessica Weissman, is a program that gives the teacher a report (right at the terminal) of the pupil's correct responses to the test items and the time elapsed before each correct response.

The "Word Zoo," developed by T. Stevenson Hansell and Jessica Weissman, is a game format lesson in which students group words into boxes (called "cages") containing one class of words. To put a word *animal* in its *cage* the pupil first touches the word and then the box (cage) in which he wants it to appear. The word changes locations on the screen. One game calls for words to be classed into one of four groups—words with prefixes, words with suffixes, words with both prefixes and suffixes, and words with neither prefixes nor suffixes. Another game calls for classifying words according to the meaning of the prefix *re*, with which each word starts. When the student needs help, the computer will present a sentence containing the word which the pupil is unable to classify.

When the pupil decides that he has completed the caging of the word *zoo*, PLATO marks his misplaced words. If he makes new errors, the computer helps him until all the words are properly caged (classified).

Two programs have been developed for helping teachers and prospective teachers develop skills helpful in teaching reading. FASTER (Fast Accurate Symbol Transcription for Evaluating Reading), developed by John Pikulski and Deborah Braendle, includes four games. These teach the student to score and interpret a word recognition test, use error marks required for scoring an informal reading inventory (IRI), and interpet scored IRI passages and word tests.

The "Sight Word Method Trainer," developed by Peter Pelosi, Jessica Weissman, and Bonnie Seiler, requires the student to watch cartoon sequences displayed by the computer. Each sequence shows a teacher teaching a sight word with a particular method. The student is told to stop the cartoon when the teacher makes an error and tell what type of error has been made. If the student misses the error, PLATO stops the sequence and asks the student to identify the error which has been made. Delaware now has no new computer based reading projects underway and older programs have been dicontinued.

Annotated References

172. Hofstetter, F.T. *Second summative report of the Delaware PLATO project.* Newark, Delaware: University of Delaware PLATO Project, 1977.

Gives the history and development of the Delaware PLATO project, applications in 19 areas, and evaluation efforts. A section entitled "Education" describes the uses of PLATO made by College of Education personnel. Several reproductions of PLATO visual displays are included in the report.

173. Seiler, B., & Weissman, J. *Remedial reading on a computer called PLATO.* Paper presented at the annual convention of the Diamond State Reading Association, Dover, Delaware, November 1977.

Describes three units of instruction developed and tried.

174. Hofstetter, F.T. *Third summative report of the Delaware PLATO project*. Newark, Delaware: University of Delaware, 1978.
Includes brief descriptions and mock-ups of screen displays for *Factors in reading comprehension*, a program by Jack Murray and Judy Sandler and *Fast accurate symbol transcription for evaluation of elementary reading (FASTER)* by Pikulski and Braendle. Also includes *Pronoun agreement and paragraph editing: Word usage.*

Additional Reference

175. Seiler, B.A. Personal letter, October 18, 1977.

Pittsburgh's Learning Research and Development Center

Originally funded in 1965, the Learning Research and Development Center installed computers in its demonstration school (McAnulty School, Pittsburgh) in 1968. At that time the school was demonstrating Individually Prescribed Instruction (IPI), and the use of computers was envisioned as a way of further individualizing instruction by providing computer management of reading and computer assistance in mathematics and spelling.

Eventually the demonstration school was discontinued. However, the computers were directed toward the solving of other problems such as classification, and a CAI spelling program was developed.

Work on computer based reading projects developed in the 1960s has been discontinued. Nevertheless, funded by private contributions, the Learning Research and Development Center has shifted emphasis toward the development and refinement of game format reading programs. The programs cover phonics and comprehension on Apple and Terrac computers. The Learning Research and Development Center hopes to market the software commercially or through softswaps.

Annotated References

176. Ragsdale, R.G. The Learning Research and Development Center's Computer Assisted Laboratory. *Digital Equipment Company User's Society Proceedings*, 1966, *5*, 65-68.
Includes a description of Westinghouse designed CROWs (random access audio devices), usually thought necessary to CAI at lowest levels of reading, spelling, and mathematics.

177. Peake, Charles H.; Glaser, Robert; & Cooley, William W. *Program plan and budget request*. Pittsburgh: University of Pittsburgh Learning Research and Development Center, 1968.
Gives plans for CAI instruction in mathematics and spelling. Spelling includes these factors:

1. Study history file
   a) daily
   b) permanent (updated daily)
2. Answer processing (of all incorrect responses)
3. Variable word list
   The present list is fixed and all students proceed through it in linear fashion. However, plans underway for lists varied according to individual student error patterns.
4. Branching—a function of *both* immediate response *and* error-pattern data. The student's history file (see 1 above) will be interrogated to determine if immediate error is part of a long term pattern.

178. Beck, Isabel L., & Bolvin, John C. A model for nongradedness, the reading program for individually prescribed instruction. *Elementary English,* 1969, *46*, 130-135.

Predicted that a CMI reading program is to be in effect in the fall of 1968. It was to include: 1) Reports on which students were working on which objectives, and 2) daily progress summaries on each student.

179. Holland, J.G., & Doran, J. Teaching classification by computer. *Educational Technology*, 1972, *13* (12), 58-60.

Describes a 160-item classification CAI program using touch sensitive screen showing rear screen projected images. This served as the basis for the CAI spelling program.

180. Block, Karen K.; Tucker, S.A.; & Butler, P.A. *Spelling, learning, and retention under variation in focal unit of word presentations in a computer assisted spelling drill.* Pittsburgh: University of Pittsburgh Learning Research and Development Center, 1974.

Research leading to the improvement of the CAI spelling program is described. The authors conclude that focal unit and manner of presentation did not affect retention of spellings and that audio presentations had no effect. Focal unit did seem to affect initial learning.

Additional References

181. Cooley, W.W., & Glaser, R. *An information and management system for individually prescribed instruction.* Working Paper Number 44. Pittsburgh: University of Pittsburgh Learning Research and Development Center, 1968.

182. Bolvin, J.O. *Individually prescribed reading instruction—reading program.* Paper presented at the College Reading Association Conference, Knoxville, April 1968.

183. Judd, W.A. The development of an on-line laboratory for CAI and other behavioral research, 1964-1968. Technical report series. Pittsburgh: University of Pittsburgh Learning Research and Development Center, 1969.

184. Block, K.K., & Simon, D. *Computer assisted spelling.* Progress Report. Pittsburgh: University of Pittsburgh Learning Research and Development Center, 1972.

185. Bell, F.H. *Computer related laboratories: An interdisciplinary approach to learning.* Paper presented at the summer conference of the

Association for the Development of Computer Based Instructional Systems, Portland, Maine, August 1976.
186. Holland, J.G., & Soloman, C. *Komputer Konkocted Kurrickulum: A review of CAI spelling*. Pittsburgh: University of Pittsburgh Learning Research and Development Center, 1975.

New Hampshire's CARIS System

Partially funded by a grant from the University of New Hampshire Central University Research Fund, the CARIS (Computer Animated Reading Instruction System) program was designed to teach beginning reading to handicapped children using a low cost (under $15,000) computer animation system. The first phase of the prototypic system, which has been developed and pilot tested by Leo Geoffrion and Daniel Bergeron, presents a display of several printed nouns on a light sensitive CRT. The child learns to select one of the words by touching a light pen to that word.

When a word is touched, the noun list disappears from the screen, where it is replaced by a picture of the word selected. A list of verbs is shown on the left side of the screen at this time. By touching the verb (printed) the child causes the noun pictures to act out the intended meaning of the verb. (For example, DOG RUNS.) Following this action on the screen is the representation of the noun list. As the child becomes adept at recognizing the nouns and verbs, new ones replace old ones on the list.

The computer used for this program was a PDP 11/40 (an inexpensive computer utilizing floppy disk memory storage) with a DEC VT 11 graphics display (a newer version using a less expensive DEC LSI 11 is being developed in 1977-1978). No audio device was required. To tailor the system to the child, the program prescriber can vary 1) the number of words initially presented, 2) which words are included, 3) the rate at which new words are added, 4) the number of words displayed at once, and 5) the frequency of reordering of words in any list.

In the second phase, children select words to create a sentence. When all the necessary words have been selected in the proper order, the computer animation shows the meaning of the sentence.

A third phase is under development. In this phase of the program, the child will select a word, again using a light pen. The computer then will request that the child choose letters to spell the word. As development continues, more pilot testing and updated reports should be forthcoming.

The CARIS System is intended to fit into a larger program planned for aiding language development in deaf and language handicapped children. Projected activities will involve the learner in picture drawing, animation, and computer based games designed for teaching initial language and reading skills.

Annotated References

187. Bergeron, R.D., & Geoffrion, L.D. Computer animation as a tool for teaching reading to the physically handicapped, in M.R. Cannon (Ed.), *Proceedings of the Fifth New York Bioengineering Conference*, New York: Pergamon Press, 1977.
   Describes the development of the CARIS program, its basic commands, and its eventual goals.
188. Geoffrion, L.D., & Bergeron, R.D. *Initial reading through computer animation.* Paper presented at the annual meeting of the American Educational Research Association, New York, April 1977.
   Describes the CARIS system and its initial evaluation with four types of handicapped children. It includes two case studies and suggestions for improving the program.

Additional Reference

189. Geoffrion, Leo. Personal letter, October 18, 1977.

Norfolk State University

Annotated References

190. Williams, C.K. *A study to examine cognitive technology for implementation into a college reading program.* Paper presented at the 20th annual conference of AEDS, Orlando, May 1982.
   Describes examination of a reading department's needs and the potential of computer based instruction at meeting those needs.
191. Williams, C.K. The computer based academic development system. Norfolk, Virginia: Norfolk State University, 1982 (mimeo).
   Describes C-BADS program, an attempt to meet ten stated needs of the university using CMI and CAI. A Title II project, it is funded through 1985. It will provide learning centers and a computer based learning laboratory.

Purdue's Teacher Education Effort

At the time of this writing, educators at Purdue University were using a PDP 11/70 Microcomputer to create demonstration lessons in secondary reading. The author language being used was a revised version of PILOT. The lessons were stored on floppy disks (memory records) and on cassette tapes. The CAI consisted of tutorial and simulation lessons designed to cover about two-thirds of the content of the secondary courses to which they relate. The remainder of the context is expected to be presented in standard lecture-discussion classes.

Annotated References

192. Kamil, M. Personal Telephone Message, December 1977.
   Described equipment and author language used in developing Purdue's CAI secondary reading program for inservice education teachers.
193. Kamil, M.L., & Frederick, F. Using low cost microcomputers to train secondary teachers in reading. Paper presented at the 28th annual meeting of the National Reading Conference, St. Petersburg, Florida, December 1978.
   Describes microcomputers as low budget alternatives in training secondary teachers in reading.

Additional References

194. Elliott, T.M. *Computer based education at Purdue University.* Lafayette, Indiana: Computer Based Education Subcommitttee, Computing Center Advisory Committee, Purdue University, 1974.
195. Feldhusen, J.F. *CAI programs developed at Purdue University by faculty and graduate students.* Lafayette, Indiana: Educational Psychology Section, Purdue University, 1968 (mimeo).

University of Akron

Annotated References

196. Martha Holder Jennings Foundation. Results of computer assisted instruction at Bath Elementary School, Cleveland, Ohio, 1978. (ED 195 245)
   Using a mainframe from the University of Akron (via telephone lines), the Bath Elementary School used CAI in reading and mathematics with sixth grade classes from January 1978, to June of the same year. Of the seventeen students in the pilot program fourteen made gains of at least a month or more over what normally would be expected. Each student was scheduled for 15 minutes of CAI work and the program appeared to be tutorial. The software was developed by the Akron CAI Center.
197. *Computer based instruction: A new decade.* Proceedings of the Annual Conference of the Association for the Development of Computer Based Instructional Systems, April 1980. (ED 194 047)
   Two papers presented in the Proceedings seem of interest to reading educators: The University of Akron's Computer Based Education Network: A Report on Activities and Results of a Five Year Study,

describes Akron's involvement in computer based education (CBE), which includes reading and many public school reading projects are discussed (Woodridge School District; Sieberling, Akron Public Schools; Buchtel, Akron Public Schools; Revere Schools, Bath Township; Waterloo and Rootstown Schools, Portage County; Cuyahoga, Richland and Medina County School Districts). Another paper, "Microprocessor Applications in Reading Instruction, Diagnostic Testing, and Evaluation" discusses the impact of the microcomputer in reading.

St. Cloud State University

Annotated Reference

198. Rauch, M., & Samojeden, E. Computer assisted instruction: One aid for teachers of reading, 1981. (ED 204 702)
Discusses, in general terms, a college CAI reading program at St. Cloud State University in Minnesota. The authors describe the advantages and disadvantages of a CAI tutorial program for college students. The presentation includes several flow charts on how to design and implement a CAI college reading program.

Utah State University

Annotated References

199. Thorkildsen, R. A microcomputer controlled vido disc instructional program for mentally handicapped children. *Computers in Education*, 1980, sponsored by the University of Montana, Department of Computer Science, Reading Institute, Missoula, Montana.
The microcomputer videodisc (MCVD) system used an MCA videodisc player, Apple II microcomputer, SONY 12″ color TV monitor and a Carroll light interrupt touchpanel. PILOT language was used to prepare a CAI program in visual discrimination (sizes, shapes, colors) for mentally handicapped children.

200. Hofmeister, A. *Microcomputer applications for monitoring and management: Present and future.* Paper presented at the Annual International Convention, Council for Exceptional Children's 60th Anniversary, Houston, April 1982.
The multifaceted paper discusses: 1) problems of modern day microcomputer applications in education; 2) recent developments in CAI software, vocational education and information management systems; 3) videodisc and educational research; 4) a research project matching assessment with instruction; 5) the future of the videodisc; and 6) issues and potential and problem areas for microcomputers and videodiscs.

Additional References

201. Frenzel, L. Learning with micros. *Interface Age*, 1981, *7*(2), 26.
202. Wilhelms, F. The ABC/NEA school disc program. *Videodisc/Teletext*, 1981, *1*(1), 30-32.
203. Kemph, J. Videodisc comes to school. *Videodisc/Teletext*, 1981, *1*(2), 94-97.

Computer Applications in other Colleges and Universities

Colleges and universities have applied computer technology to reading instruction in a variety of ways. In 1966, San Bernardino Valley, California, College reported using the computer in diagnosis, in instruction, in evaluation, and in research as part of their college reading improvement program. Harvard personnel described the segments to be programed in Project ORACLE in 1970. About the same time (1969-1970), North Carolina State University was seeking to determine the applicability of computer use to adult basic education.

Nashville State Technical Institute used the computer in scoring a comprehension-based informal reading inventory, in writing prescriptions, and in monitoring student progress. In that same year (1971) a computer-aided remedial English program was tried at Bernard Baruch College of the City University of New York; CATTS (a tutoring and testing system) was being used at Pasadena, California, City College; and a similar program, CBI, was in use at the University of Buffalo. Also in 1971, Northwestern University tried out computer simulation as a means of training educators in diagnosis. The results were said to be promising.

Quiz based instruction, such as in the basis of CMI, was made easier by a computerized concept sampling procedure reported in 1972. That year, a University of Virginia researcher described his efforts to teach sixth grade remedial reading with a computer providing additional remediation after the child was shown not to have profited from his other instruction. And also in 1972, a CMI reading program was reported to be operative at Christopher Newport College, Newport News, Virginia.

Wang's *Index to Computer Based Learning* (ICBL) listed a number of computer based programs for reading instruction in 1973. According to ICBL, Red Deer College in Alberta was teaching spelling clues with CAI. Project READ, developed at Arizona State University, was in use with elementary and junior high students. A number of programs developed at Harvard University were available through the State University of New York at Stony Brook and a program, READING, designed for EMR children, was under development at Teachers College, Columbia University, where a test battery (SITE) for normal children completing grade one had also been developed. ICBL also listed two computerized early reading programs developed as part of a master's degree thesis at the University of Alberta, although these programs are no longer functional.

The CONDUIT program of the University of Texas was also reported in 1973, making that year a banner year for CAI/CMI reports from colleges. Unfortunately, only one was added in 1974. It introduced CMI as a model for teaching reading to college students.

In 1976, the development of project LERN was reported by representatives of the University of Arizona and TICCIT (Time-shared, Interactive, Computer Controlled Informational Television) was reported by staff members from Brigham Young University, who discussed a computerized college reading instruction program.

In 1977, a letter from the University of Edinburgh described the development of a new program to teach backward children to read, and Teachers College, Columbia University also reported a CAI reading program to be under development. A University of Minnesota letter reported a CAI program, SYLLO, designed to teach syllabication to nine-year-olds. A similar program to teach plurals was reported to be under development, and Human Resources Research reported a large number of exemplary college reading CAI and CMI programs (see reference number 298).

Annotated References

204. Adair, J.B. Computer assisted instruction in adult basic education. In J.A. Mangano (Ed.), *Strategies for adult basic education.* Newark, Delaware: International Reading Association, 1969.

CAI selling points are: 1) instructional programs may be prepared to meet the differing needs of the individual, 2) computer programs can carefully sequence materials, 3) CAI can provide immediate feedback, 4) continuous diagnosis is made easier, and 5) more students.

205. Adair, J.B. *The use of modern educational technology for instruction of undereducated adults.* Research report. Raleigh: Adult Learning Resources Project, North Carolina State University, 1969.

Contains reviews of a number of research reports on CAI. The goal was to generate research questions related to applying CAI in Adult Basic Education.

206. Serwer, B.L., & Stolurow, L.M. Computer assisted learning in the language arts. *Elementary English*, 1970, *47*, 641-650.

Describes plans for ORACLE, a computer aided language experience reading program, and relevant activities for children.

207. Watkins, L. Computers on campus: Three reports on what they're doing, what they can do. *College and University Business*, 1970, *48*, 71-73.

Reports that in 1969 thirteen of the fourteen smallest colleges surveyed had computer facilities available for faculty and student use, while all but two of the large institutions also made computer services available.

208. Muller, V. *A case for early reading*. Unpublished M.Ed. thesis. University of Alberta, 1971.

Describes 1970-1971 field test of AUPER, a preschool CAI sight word reading program using the IBM 1500 computer facilities of the University of Alberta. Three-, four-, and five-year-old children chose pictured objects on the CRT by pointing the light pencil at the screen. Instantly, a picture of that object was displayed on an image projector under the control of the computer. Under the picture was the printed word naming it. An audio message related the printed word to the picture. Then the word appeared on the CRT and the child was challenged to name it. Eventually the child chose from as many as four printed words displayed on the CRT, to match the picture shown by the image projector. Built-in branching provided remediation presentations. A field test showed the program to be successful in teaching its 40 words to two of the three children with whom it was tried.

209. Wares, M.B. *Use of the computer in individualized remediation at Nashville State Technical Institute*. Paper presented at the National Reading Conference, Tampa, Florida, December 1971.

Designed to provide remediation in mathematics, reading, and English, this program provides computer management for a reading instructional system featuring an IRI (scored only on comprehension), followed by computer scoring, prescription writing, and monitoring student progress.

210. Bossone, R.M., & Weiner, M. *Three modes of teaching remedial English: A comparative analysis: A pilot study*. New York: City University of New York, Bernard Baruch College, and Graduate School and University Center, 1973.

Compared computer based basic skills in English program to more traditional versions. Found no differences in achievement.

211. Lerner, J.W. *Computer simulation: A method for training educational diagnosticians*. Paper presented at the annual conference of the International Reading Association, Atlantic City, April 1971.

Through computer simulations, students at Northwestern University were able to diagnose reading disabilities of a nonexistent child who "attended" the clinic, was diagnosed and treated, and who responded differently to different treatments. Students tested, observed and wrote reports; the authors thought the technique had promise.

212. McMullen, D.W. *A concept sampling procedure for quiz oriented instruction*. Paper presented at the annual meeting of the American Educational Research Association, Chicago, February 1972.

The computer program sampled text from college materials in order to generate wordlists for content area vocabulary instruction. Students trying the program endorsed it.

213. Strang, H.R. An automated approach to remedial reading. *Psychology in the Schools*, 1972, *9*, 433-439.

A program of automated remedial reading instruction was made available to grade six students as soon as they failed any classroom reading tasks. Children making use of this program outperformed controls in word accuracy and task completion.

214. Randall, A.F. A computer managed reading laboratory program. *Reading World*, 1972, *11*, 286-295.

Describes development and implementation of a simple CMI reading efficiency program at Christopher Newport College. The cost of development was $100. Costs were estimated at $112 for one year of use for 150 students.

215. Wang, A. *Index to computer based learning*. Milwaukee: Educational Media Laboratory, University of Wisconsin, 1973.

All of the computer based learning programs reported in time for publication are listed and described in this index. Seven reading programs were reported to be available from L.M. Stolurow, State University of New York at Stony Brook. These are as follows.

RHYME: A dialogue program to test comprehending main ideas, finding purposes, drawing inferences, getting meaning from context, and recalling details.

DRILL I: A diagnostic reading cloze test presented by controlled slides.

VIPCON: A diagnostic instrument to detect visual preception problems.

PHONIC: A slide tape, computer controlled drill and practice program in word recognition for children in grades one to three who are having difficulty learning to read.

CONTEXT: Drill and practice questions keyed to the *Using the Context* series (grades one to six).

CONTEXT (Placement test): Prescribes which book to use from the *Using the Context* series.

One listed program, "Survey of Reading and Study Efficiency," was developed at Loyola University of Los Angeles. It was designed to involve the pupil with the computer through inquiry; dialogue; and prescriptions of texts, manuals, and audiovisual presentations. The purpose was to improve study skills of college students.

Two were listed as being developed at Teachers College, Columbia University.

READING: Drill and practice, gaming, and simulation used to teach initial reading to EMR students.

SITE: A test battery for determining end of grade one reading achievement.

Other references to reading programs in ICBL are not reported in this section because they were reported fully elsewhere.

216. Newman, I. *A systematic approach to the use of instructional objectives as an aid in teaching.* Paper presented at the Ohio College Council of the International Reading Association Conference, Dayton, April 1974.
Introduces a General Teaching Model for teaching reading to college students through specifying quantifiable objectives. As an example, an individualized CAI reading program is described.

217. Huelsman, L.P.; Knief, L.M.; & Tuiten, J. *CMI with a new twist.* Paper presented at the annual meeting of American Educational Data Systems, Phoenix, May 1976.
Presents PROJECT LERN, a four part CMI useful to all instructors including reading course instructors. The parts include 1) routing (or placement) based on internal criteria, 2) tutorial lessons, 3) problem application and feedback, and 4) a monitor (a computerized course outline) to be followed by the instructor.

218. Howe, J. Personal letter, June 10, 1977.
Reports progress at University of Edinburgh in teaching backward children to read using a touch screen device, against which slides are rear projected. Children utter names of pictured objects, learning to associate the uttered sounds with the letters projected on the screen. Correct choices result in information confirming the correctness. Incorrect choices lead to presenting a contrast between the choice made and the correct choice. Six of six children have learned to use word attack skills with the computer and five of six have transferred their skills to the classroom.

219. Blackman, L.S. Personal letter, April 8, 1977.
In 1977, Teachers College, Columbia University, was creating pilot programs in CAI reading, but none were available for distribution at the time of writing.

220. Lopez, A.A. Personal letter, April 5, 1977.
SYYLO was developed by L. Classen with the aid of a small grant from the University of Minnesota foundation. Written in the Minnesota Interactive Language (MIL), SYLLO has five steps: 1) Human teaching that every syllable has a vowel sound; 2) an on-line computer pretest, called a "check-in," tests each of seven tasks with three words and then routes learners to any tasks not mastered; 3) instruction is with worksheet type displays for practice tasks, displayed by the computer after a random choice from a word bank; 4) an on-line checkout test is taken; 5) a game called "Syllo" can be played when the program is completed (or tested out of).

221. Bitter, G.B. Personal communication, September 26, 1977.
Points out that Project READ, a dialogue program teaching third reader level skills to upper elementary and junior high pupils with teletype terminal, was being updated at Arizona State University and was, therefore, unavailable.

222. Hunka, S. Personal communication, October 7, 1977.
Reports little use of AUPER (see Muller #192) in the past four years. Also states that EXPER, a phrase reading program for deaf children, has

had no extensive use in the past four years. However, at the time of writing EXPER was being reviewed for possible use in a school for the deaf and a new program (based on the Distar model) in basic phonics and sound blending was under development with approximately 45 of a projected 160 lessons completed.

Additional References

223. Williams, G. Use of the computer for testing and programing in a reading program, in G. Schick & H. Merrill (Eds.), *Junior college and adult reading programs.* Sixteenth Yearbook of the National Reading Conference, 1967.
224. Roberts, A.D., & Zirkel, P.A. Computer application to instruction. *Journal of Secondary Education*, 1971, *46*, 102.
225. Yett, E. *Computer assisted tutorial and testing system* (CATTS). Pasadena, California: Pasadena City College, 1971.
226. Stolurow, L.M. *Computer assisted vocabulary acquisition: A terminological approach.* Final report. Stony Brook, New York: State University of New York, 1973.
227. *Computer assisted instruction applied tu English spelling. Instructor's manual and imnlementation manual.* Alberta, Canada: Red Deer College, 1973.
228. Spache, G.D. *College adult reading—past, present, and future.* Paper presented at the National Reading Conference, Los Angeles, December 1968.
229. Cole, J.L. *The application of computer technology to the instruction of undereducated adults. Final Report.* Raleigh: Adult Learning Center, North Carolina State University, 1971.
230. Warlick, C.H. Computers in instruction. Austin: Computation Center, University of Texas, 1973.

Chapter 3

COMPUTERS: SCHOOL APPLICATIONS TO READING INSTRUCTION

Most public and private school systems, state departments of education, and intermediate school service agencies have implemented, or are in the process of considering for implementation, microcomputer instructional or management reading projects. Some of these projects will fail or be rejected for various reasons; some will be modified, and many will succeed. Those considering microcomputer based reading instruction or management projects must learn from both the failures and the successes of others as a means of providing for continued refinement of computer services. This learning process normally has not been possible in the past for at least four reasons.

1. Historically, there have been few journals, periodicals, books or other reference sources for reading professionals to examine on subjects related to all types of computer based reading education.

2. Coordinated efforts by the computer industry to inform teachers of the promises and perils associated with computer based reading projects have been few and far between.

3. Diversity in hardware technology and lethargic software development has lead to confusion in the minds of teachers and reading professionals on virtually every question related to all forms of computer based reading education.

4. Teachers question the value of computers as an innovation mostly because they are unsure about the nature of the innovation.

Today, we are beginning to solve some of these problems. This chapter will provide reading educators with sources of information about school projects that have solved or partially solved such problems. The annotated and additional references which will follow, provide a description of mainframe and minicomputer activities as well as a partial description of the tremendous activity generated in school reading programs by the advent of the microcomputer.

Philadelphia Public Schools

Annotated References

231. Farber, I.J. *The development and implementation of a multilevel management information feedback system.* Paper presented at the annual meeting of the American Educational Research Association, Chicago, February 1974.

Describes the Philadelphia school system's development of a multilevel management information feedback system (CMI) to monitor the operation of the reading programs in its eight subdistricts. The major steps involved were: 1) the determination of information needed; 2) the development of noninterruptive information collection procedures; 3) the design of display formats; and 4) the writing of computer programs employing the district's inhouse computer facilities to generate information useful at the same time to classroom, school, and district administration levels.

232. Farber, I.J. Personal Correspondence, October 24, 1977.

Explains that it has been found inadvisable to combine in a single system classroom instructional information with school and system management information. In 1977, a series of instruments (available on demand) were available for computer processing by NCS scanning of response sheets upon which could be recorded any multiple-choice test responses up to 60 items.

Management information about pupil's reading is provided to the system through a set of bar graphs drawn by the computer. Information to the teacher is provided through printouts showing each pupil's answers to each item as either a plus (correct), or as the letter representing the correct answer for that item.

Among the computer processed instruments available to teachers are several levels of the *Sight-Sound Inventory*, the *Phonics Inventory* (initial and final consonants), and the *Informal Reading Inventory for Secondary Schools.*

Also computer processed are Individual Pupil Service Forms which have been piloted for possible future use in keeping track of the reading levels, the reading materials used, the supplementary reading services in which pupils are involved, the time allotted to reading instruction each week, the manner in which the classroom was organized for reading instruction, their Title I eligibility, and the number of days they were absent. This form will probably not be used, however, since one per pupil is required and the processing of 265,000 forms is prohibitive. In the meantime, classroom reading resources are summarized by computer from Classroom Reading Resource Data Forms filled out by the teacher for each reading class.

233. Diamond, J.J. *A report on project GROW: Philadelphia's experimental program in computer assisted instruction.* Philadelphia: Philadelphia School District, Office of Research and Evaluation, August 1969.

Computer assisted instruction (CAI) in developmental reading was operative in four secondary schools in Philadelphia. The achievement of the students in CAI was compared with comparable students in traditionally instructed classes. The results of the standardized reading tests were equivocal. Although the CAI classes performed significantly better than comparable students in traditional classes, an attitude survey constructed for the project indicated that the pupils liked working with the machines, but were frustrated when the system did not function properly. A discussion of the project, including the results of nonstandardized achievement tests and an analysis of the pupils' responses while interacting with the computer, is included.

The project was continued with students in the ninth and tenth grades who are reading below grade level. (According to a printout enclosed by Farber [see previous reference], five secondary schools offered CAI reading instruction to some 37 classes in 1975-1976).

234. Charp, S.A., & Wye, R.A. Computer assisted instruction in a large school system. *Journal of Educational Data Processing*, 1969, *6* (1), 28-39.

Describes the first large school system (Philadelphia) implementation of computer assisted instruction, which included more than 200 hours of reading delivered to four schools. The central processor was (at the time of the writing) a Philco-Ford 102 which was interfaced to eight terminals. The author language used in creating the lessons was INFORM. Units (emphasizing comprehension) were as follows:

- Recognition of sentences
- Recognition and utilization of key words
- Labeling and categorizing concepts
- Seeing the relationship between sentences and sentence order
- Ordering and sequencing ideas and sentences
- Distinguishing general from specific topics
- Finding and understanding supporting details
- Selecting topic sentences
- Drawing sound conclusions
- Following directions

Points out that 254 hours of effort were required to create one hour of CAI, but that efficient use is reducing long range costs per student, and that the school district of Philadelphia was considering formation of a computer services network with neighboring school districts.

Additional Reference

235. Charp, S.A. Computer assisted instruction in reading. *Scholastic Teacher*, 1968, *8* (12), 13, 16.

Chicago Public Schools

Annotated Reference

236. Lilman, G.H. *CAI in Chicago.* Paper presented at the annual meeting of the Association for Educational Data Systems, New Orleans, April 1973.

The Chicago Public Schools' CAI program has involved 12,000 students per day working in basic skills (reading, language arts, math) at over 850 terminals. The coursework was developed by Computer Curriculum Corporation and results warranted expansion of the program to the secondary schools in the fall of 1977. Previous research indicated student gains of at least one month for each month in the program.

Fremont, California, Unified School District

Annotated Reference

237. Eller, L.M. Individualized learning using TV. *Educational Broadcasting*, 1975, *8* (4), 27-30, 42.

Individualized learning using TV controlled by computer has been implemented in the Fremont, California, Unified School District. The system provides TV and computer support (in what appears to be a pilot program) to four participating schools whose locations form a diamond over the area from San Francisco to San Jose and from Fremont to Belmont. (The proximity is necessary because of the microwave television signal sent to some of the schools participating.)

The instructional phase of the program is based on Prescribed Activities for Learning (PAL) with its 138 reading programs. A teacher decides on a specific program selected from the Reading PAL and, depending on the AV facilities at the school, uses a monitor that receives a microwave TV signal from a base station or utilizes a video cassette. For reception of micro TV signals, each participating school has its own tower, receiver disk antenna, down converter, power supply, and an amplifier. TV signals and videocassettes can be used in combination.

Fresno, California, Unified School District

Annotated References

238. Lister, W., & Williams, J. *Fresno reading program with computer assistance.* Paper presented at the Rocky Mountain Regional Conference of the International Reading Association, Salt Lake City, November 1977.

Described the development of a management program which involved stating behavioral goals, developing criterion tests of reading skills, and programing computers to print out recommendations to teachers. High pupil mobility created the need for systemwide management, even though diverse instructional materials are in use.

The first testing is with a locally developed informal reading inventory. This inventory indicates the level at which skills are to be assessed with the system's criterion reference tests. These arrive in classrooms with student names preprinted to insure administration to the proper students. Also provided are skill check tests to be administered and scored by teachers as children practice skills prior to taking a criterion referenced (and computer scored) postassessment.

Children in grade two or above use machine scorable answer sheets. First grade children mark on the tests. Their tests are then converted to "bubblecards" (machine readable) by paid aides. The bubblecards are batch processed during night hours (computer time rented by the school district). Tests and printouts are delivered by the Fresno Unified School District's own internal mailing system. Usually a twenty-four hour turnaround time can be maintained.

This system enables teachers to receive diagnostic-prescriptive information about reading levels and skills of students transferred into their classrooms from another school within the system. The basal readers in use in the system (and for which the computer managed program is designed) are those of the Holt Basic Reading System and the Houghton Mifflin Readers.

239. *Continuum of performance objectives, levels R through VII.* Fresno, California: Fresno Unified School District, mimeo, n.d.

Sketches continuous progress program, outlines procedures used in implementing it, itemizes the skills tested, and provides a flow chart of the system as well as sample printouts, tests, and bubblecards (machine readable answer sheets).

Montgomery County Schools, Rockville, Maryland

Annotated References

240. Dunn, A. (Ed.). *Computer assisted instruction program. A three year report covering July 1, 1971, through June 30, 1974.* Rockville, Maryland: Board of Education, Montgomery County Schools, 1974.

Describes the CAI program begun in 1968. The project was federally funded until 1971. Since that time other sources of funding have contributed. During 1971-1974, an elementary reading curriculum was developed which emphasized decoding skills and related skills such as rhyming.

241. Morgan, C.E. Personal letter, October 25, 1977.

Pointed out that early efforts to program CAI reading were unsuccessful because of unsatisfactory audio support for the computer terminals, and adds that in 1977-1978 a new effort was underway.

242. Bernardo, C.M. *Memo to members of the board of education.* Rockville, Maryland: Montgomery County Public Schools, June 30, 1977.

Describes the development of a system for computer management of the reading program over nine school grades. The system was to make use of standardized tests already required (Iowa Tests of Basic

Skills, the Stanford Achievement Test, and the Maryland Functional Reading Test). It was also anticipated that system-developed cloze tests might be used twice per year as a means of monitoring reading progress of students.

Mineola, New York, Junior High School

Annotated Reference

243. Handler, H. The computer comes to the English classroom: Computerized monitoring of pupil progress in reading. *Educational Technology*, 1975, *15* (11), 34-35.

AIMS, a CMI program developed at the New York Institute of Technology, has been in use at Mineola Junior High School since 1969. The system provides no instruction and is designed to diagnose, prescribe, monitor, and evaluate pupil progress in reading. The program maintains records of student achievement in eleven areas: 1) finding main ideas; 2) making inferences (drawing conclusions); 3) noting and recalling details; 4) recognizing sequences; 5) following directions; 6) finding context clues; 7) finding information—study skills; 8) decoding word analysis; 9) recognizing affixes and roots; 10) recognizing synonyms, antonyms, and homonyms; and 11) using syllabication.

Boston School System

Annotated Reference

244. Innovative implementation of computer aided instruction. In L.A. Harris (Bibliographer) *Title III Pace Projects in reading*, Volume 2. Bloomington, Indiana: Eric Crier Reading Review Series, 1969.

Describes the Boston, Massachusetts, program, designed to develop diagnostic reading programs for elementary and secondary students in urban areas. The program was planned to serve 11,000 students.

New York City Schools

Annotated References

245. The terminal is the best friend I know.... *Reading Newsreport*, 1970, *4* (3), 32-35.

Using an elementary English program designed by H. Wilson at Harcourt Brace Jovanovich, Melvin Mendelsolm (then Director of CAI for New York) suggested that the following year New York City Schools would be using CAI reading.

246. Films on CAI. *Educational Technology*, 1969, *9* (7), 59.

Describes film available from RCA. The film showed a 192 station CAI program serving 16 New York City schools. The consultant was listed as P. Suppes.

Additional References

247. Wilson, H.A., & Fitzgibbons, N.H. Practice and perfection: A preliminary analysis of achievement data from the CAI Elementary English Program. *Elementary English*, 1970, *47*(4), 576-579.

247a. Butler, C.F. CAI in New York City: Report on the first year's operation. *Educational Technology*, 1969, *9*(10), 84-87.

Dallas, Texas, Independent School District

Annotated Reference

248. Students use talking computer in Dallas bilingual program. *Phi Delta Kappan*, 1977, *59* (4), 234.

Describes an ESEA Title VII and Title IV-C program which uses a computerized voice synthesizer to reinforce reading and language programs called ROLL and BOLAR. Students work in groups of five for ten minutes, three times per week.

Eastern Kentucky Development Corporation

Annotated References

249. Brown, H.P. Personal letter, March 29, 1977.

Describes CAI program implemented with teletype terminals in a number of schools in the Eastern Kentucky area. The corporation worked with RCA's computer division and Stanford University. The software was distributed by Harcourt Brace Jovanovich. The program was discontinued in 1972.

250. Mynhier, B. *The impact of federal programs on learning to read in Appalachia.* Paper presented at the annual conference of the International Reading Association, Kansas City, 1969.

Describes ESEA Title III CAI program in 20 counties in Eastern Kentucky.

251. *Reading: Drill and practice teacher's manual.* Ashland, Kentucky: Eastern Kentucky Educational Development Corporation, 1972.

Provides the teacher with directions for using the CAI program to supplement classroom reading instruction. Explains how teachers can call lessons, how students enter the program, and how the teacher is informed of student progress and problems. Gives a complete list of decoding skills, sentence skills, and comprehensive skills practiced by students working at the terminals provided.

New York State Education Department

Annotated References

252. O'Reilly, R.P. *New York state bank of reading objectives.* Paper presented at a joint meeting of the Measurement in Education and American Educational Research Association, New Orleans, February 1973.

The paper presented the rationale, structure, content, and procedures for the computerized bank of reading objectives then being developed for New York state schools. The project was initiated to provide a technical resource which would contribute to planning, design, and evaluation of reading programs. The paper defines the organizing concepts for the project, including a generalized format for writing objectives, a procedure for organizing the generic form of objectives into summative criterion objectives, a structure for scaling reading intent and associating it with objectives.

253. O'Reilly, R.P. Computerized banking as a resource for systematic program development and evaluation in reading. *Educational Technology*, 1973, *13* (9), 38-40.

SPPED (System for Pupil and Program Evaluation and Development) was a research and development project of the New York State Education Department. The SPPED program included both CAM (Comprehensive Achievement Monitoring) and SCAN (Systems Coding Analysis), parts of a comprehensive instructional management system designed to aid several major program development functions in education: planning, design, installation, evaluation and the transmission and use of evaluative information. The bank stores 1800+ specific reading objectives for kindergarten through twelfth grade.

254. Cohen, A.S., & Bednarik, J. *SCAN (Systems Coding Analysis) computerized analysis of reading behaviors.* New York: Random House Educational Systems Division, 1974.

SCAN is a set of instructional reading objectives. This set was developed to coincide with a criterion performance assessment program. SCAN and the computer allow a matching of 1) reading behavior, 2) reading test times, 3) instructional materials, and 4) instructional objectives. This allows efficient and affective matching of student reading behavior with expected or anticipated reading behavior, and with appropriate instructional and assessment materials.

255. Computer tutor. *American Education*, 1976, *12* (5), 4.

Described Tel-Catch, a pilot program then serving homebound school children in New York State. 100 children were enabled to dial the master computer (or central processor) by phone, place the phone on the coupler, type out a lesson request, and get videoscreen "pages" to read and respond to. Teachers were on standby to help with the more than 2,000 lessons available to choose from.

Red Bank, New Jersey, Schools

Annotated Reference

256. Let your fingers do the learning. *Reading Newsreport*, 1972, *7* (2), 26-29.

Operation Bookstrap (simulated CAI) was carried out in 1971-1972 by Red Bank elementary schools with the cooperation of Bell Telephone Laboratories. First and second graders dialed words they didn't know on touchtone telephones. The word was decoded, spelled aloud, and pronounced for the child on the telephone. The project was discontinued for lack of funds.

Billerica, Massachusetts, Schools

Annotated Reference

257. Serlin, J. Good grief! Charlie Brown's computerized! *Reading Newsreport*, 1970, *4* (6), 29-30.

Describes program of computer assisted primary reading at Parker Elementary School. Nearby high school students did the question writing and the programing on their leased IBM 1130. The young pupils answered these questions after off-line reading of their school reading books. Reinforcement messages were given to young subjects when they responded correctly. Encouragement was given and they were urged to try again after an error.

Sierra Vista, Arizona, Schools

Annotated Reference

258. Feugate, J.T. *Computer aided instruction in Sierra Vista, Arizona, elementary schools.* Paper presented at the annual meeting of the Association for Educational Data Systems, Phoenix, May 1976.

Described ESEA Title I program of both CMI and CAI reading. The CAI was a drill and practice program for grades three through six.

Poughkeepsie, New York, Shared Educational Computer System

Annotated Reference

259. Dunwell, S. *Report on WRITE: A CAI course in written English usage.* Poughkeepsie, New York: Shared Educational Computer System, 1972.

An experiment utlizing a CAI spelling and word usage program delivered via teletype terminals to Poughkeepsie, New York, middle schoolers (fifth through eighth grades). The instruction stressed spelling patterns rather than individual words. Results indicated CAI was an effective means of teaching spelling.

Rapides Parish, Louisiana, Schools

Annotated References

260. *Individualized reading instruction for students (IRIS).* Alexandria, Louisiana: Rapides Parish School Board, pamphlet, n.d.

A Title III (ESAA) funded CMI project providing for diagnosis of reading needs, location of materials for treatment, and the monitoring of progress—all with computer assistance.

261. *Individualized reading instruction for student computer managed reading system: Validation report.* Alexandria, Louisiana: Rapides Parish School Board, 1977.

The project provided locally constructed diagnostic tests, computer indexed teaching materials, criterion referenced tests, and periodic summaries of progress for individual students, classes, and schools. The first and second years of the project were used for development and field testing of the various components; the third year was used to implement the program and to investigate its effectiveness. Results from a comparison of 196 pupils from grades three, four, seven, and nine with 143 pupils on control groups are reported for student achievement.

Kansas City, Missouri, Schools

Annotated Reference

262. Taylor, S.S. *A comparison of two public school computer assisted instruction projects.* Paper presented at the annual meeting of the American Educational Research Association, Chicago, April 1972.

Describes short, half-hour, single concept enrichment lessons that allowed a student to bypass a sequence if his pretest performance indicated concept mastery. Developed in Kansas City, these CAI lessons were structured to reduce the redundancy that frequently causes students to progress slowly in programed materials.

Yorktown Heights, New York, Schools

Annotated Reference

263. Reading 1604. In A. Wang (Ed.), *Index to computer based learning.* Milwaukee: Instructional Media Laboratory, University of Wisconsin, 1973.

A listing of a Title III CAI program for word and letter recognition. The presentations were both auditory and visual and involved both upper and lowercase letters.

Additional Reference

264. When computers work overtime. *Reading Newsreport*, 1970, *4* (3), 30-31.

Los Nietos School District of Los Angeles County

Annotated Reference

265. Reading 1743. In A. Wang (Ed.), *Index to computer based learning.* Milwaukee: Instructional Media Laboratory, University of Wisconsin, 1976.

Lists elementary and junior high CAI drill and practice reading programs in Whittier, California, as operational. The program is entitled the ESAA Basic Program.

266. Crandall, N.D. Personal communication, March 25, 1977.

Notes that Los Nietos was using 44 terminals and anticipating increasing the number to 84 for drill and practice in reading, math, and language arts. By so increasing, the system would allow each child 20 minutes per day at the terminal. It is reported that CAI is cost effective and that in the first two years mean CTBS scores rose from the 10th to the 38th percentile. The programs used are those of the Computer Curriculum Corporation (see Chapter 5).

267. CAI gets credit for dramatic achievement gains for minorities. *Phi Delta Kappan*, 1977, *59* (4), 290-291.

Reports project director's report to a House of Representatives panel, and cautions in interpretation urged by a college computer expert.

Multnomah County, Oregon, Intermediate Education District

Annotated References

268. Reading 1744. In A. Wang (Ed.), *Index to computer based learning.* Milwaukee: Instructional Media Laboratory, University of Wisconsin, 1976.

This Portland, Oregon, program is entitled "Parkrose CMI Reading." It provides computer assistance for an elementary school reading management system.

269. Cooper, M.K., & Tobey, G.R. *A computer management support system for IGE.* Paper presented at the annual meeting of the Association for Educational Data Systems, Phoenix, March 1976.

Described the implementation of a CMI system based on the Wisconsin Design for Reading Skills Development in one school in Portland, Oregon.

Los Angeles, California, Schools

Annotated Reference

270. Reading. In H.A. Lekan (Ed.), *Index to computer assisted instruction,* third edition. New York: Harcourt Brace Jovanovich, 1971.

Lists CMI program developed to help manage reading program with Ginn Basal Readers.

Cincinnati, Ohio, Public Schools

Annotated Reference

271. Morgan, M.M. *Computer assisted instruction for the blind and deaf.* Paper presented at the annual meeting of the American Educational Research Association, Washington, D.C., April 1975.

Describes a Title III project in Cincinnati. Special education teachers were trained to prepare CAI lessons and to monitor children trying them out. CAI was found to be beneficial to hearing impaired children. Attitude measures indicated that teachers, students, and parents reacted favorably to CAI use.

Memphis, Tennessee, Public Schools

Annotated Reference

272. Joiner, Lee. Personal communication, December 15, 1977.

CAI in both reading and mathematics was tried in the late sixties. Curricula available from the Computer Curriculum Corporation and from Harcourt Brace Jovanovich were used. The results in math were superb, while the reading results were equivocal. Therefore, the school district decided to use the CAI program for what it taught best—mathematics. In 1977, 64 terminals were in use for mathematics.

Pontiac, Michigan, Schools

Annotated References

273. *INDICOM. (Individual Communication System). Final Report.* Pontiac, Michigan: Waterford Township School District, 1970.

The report is a complete description of the CAI project in reading and mathematics for grades four and five. Rationale, instructional strategy, development and implementation as well as potentials and conclusions are discussed.

274. Hannan, T. Computer assisted instruction—State of the art summary. *Audiovisual Instruction*, 1970, *15* (6), 93-94.

A review of an INDICOM progress report.

Norfolk, Virginia, Schools

Annotated References

275. Gull, R. A successful transition from mini- to microcomputer assisted instruction: The Norfolk experience. *Educational Technology*, 1980, *20*(2), 41-42.

Describes how the Norfolk Public Schools made the transition from time sharing to minicomputer. The article discusses the problems and solutions in such a transition.

276. Tokar, E., & Ford, V. *Effectiveness of an ESAA funded information feedback system on the reading and arithmetic achievement of black and white fifth grade pupils.* Paper presented at the annual meeting of the American Educational Research Association, San Francisco, April 1976.

The authors used a computer system called MIFS (Multiethnic Information Feedback System) to monitor performances in reading and math and to evaluate both the needs of the students and the effectiveness of the instruction. Results indicate the MIFS program significantly increased reading and math achievement.

Pueblo Indian Schools, New Mexico

Annotated Reference

277. Wells, B., & Bell, D. A new approach to teaching reading comprehension: Using cloze and computer assisted instruction. *Educational Technology*, 1980, *20*(3), 49-51.

Pueblo Indian schools of New Mexico have been using a computer assisted instruction program to help their students develop reading skills. The program involves 125 lessons ranging in readability from grades one to seven. The lessons feature a "maze-type" cloze technique presented via a CRT/TTY with the students selecting an answer as they read through a paragraph or series of paragraphs. After all selections have been made, the passage or passages with the selected answers are displayed for the students to reread. Then the CRT presentation changes to multiple-choice questions about the material just read and the student attempts to select the correct answer from the material with the maze choices included. Students are scored on correct maze answers and correct answers to comprehension questions. The program is not speeded and student-written introductions to the lessons are solicited. Students like seeing their own writing on the CRT.

Dillon, Montana, Public Schools

Annotated Reference

278. Bandelier, N. Computer assisted instruction in reading used for kindergartners and first graders in Dillon, Montana, 1979-1980. In D.

Harris & L. Nelson-Heern (Eds.), *Proceedings of the NECC 1981 National Educational Computing Conference.* (ED 207 526)

During the 1979-1980 school year, Dillon, Montana public school kindergarten and first grade students used a Commodore Pet 2001 in computer assisted reading instruction. Thirty programs in vocabulary drill and practice were used. The programs were modifications of "two games appearing in computer magazines" (p. 270). The vocabulary was taken from the Houghton Mifflin basal readers (used in the school). The CAI programs were synchronized with the vocabulary instruction in the readers. A rebus activity was used in some of the kindergarten programs.

Bing Nursery School, Stanford University

Annotated Reference

279. On line: Preschoolers learn using microcomputers. *Classroom Computer News*, 1982, *2*(5), 13-14.

A pilot study at Stanford University's Bing Nursery School found that preschoolers can use microcomputers to develop reading readiness skills. The author reports the study showed that preschoolers are "not intimidated" (p. 14) by the microcomputer and gains in achievement can be expected.

Nursery School, North Texas State University

Annotated Reference

280. Swigger, K.M., & Campbell, J. Computers and the nursery school. In D. Harris and L. Nelson-Heern (Eds.), *Proceedings of the NECC 1981 National Educational Computing Conference.* (ED 207 526)

Children 3-4 years old at the North Texas State Nursery School have been involved in research using several 20 minute computer programs focusing on visual discrimination reading readiness skills. The TI-99/4 microcomputer was used and affective results indicate the young children enjoy using the computer. The program is designed so lack of letter or number knowledge is not necessarily a handicap when using the terminal typing keys.

Great Neck, New York, Public Schools

Annotated Reference

281. Buckley, E., & Rauch, D. *Pilot project in computer assisted instruction in adult basic education students.* Adult Learning Centers, The Adult Program, Great Neck, New York, public schools. Final Three Year Report, 1979. (ED 197 202)

The three year study in this report found CAI in reading "to be effective supplementary learning medium for ABE students" (abstract). Remarkable gains are reported for students using CAI reading in a classroom and learning laboratory situation. Computer Curriculum Corporation provided their Adult Basic Education Program (ABE) for the software. The ABE reading program contains word attack skills, vocabulary skills, literal comprehension, interpretative comprehension, and work-study skills.

Calgary, Alberta (Canada) Schools

Annotated Reference

282. Brebner, A.; Hallworth, H.J.; McIntosh, E.; & Wonter, C. *Teaching elementary reading by CMI and CAI, 1980.* (ED 198 793)

A K-8 CMI reading program with some prescriptive CAI components was initiated by Belvedere-Parkway Elementary School. The CMI program consisted of 329 educational objectives and tests marketed by the Educational Development Corporation. The CAI component featured drill and practice and tutorial programs involving syllabication, roots, affixes, inflectional endings, synonyms, homonyms, word classifications, and compound words. Teachers reported increased reading performance and positive attitudes toward the program and reading.

Mason, Michigan, Capitol Area Career Center

Annotated Reference

283. Danford, J. CMI at Capitol Area Career Center, Mason, Michigan. In H.E. Mitzel (Ed.), *An examination of the short range potential of computer managed instruction.* Proceedings of a conference. Chicago, November 1974. (ED 112 943)

A Univac 70/2 COBOL program analyzes job information and manages instruction. Individuals receive individualized learning packets which spell out the necessary job objectives. Basic skills testing and evaluation for each individual are related to those necessary job related skills, and a program of training is developed.

Waterford School, Provo, Utah

Annotated References

284. Microcomputer based elementary school reading project. *AEDS Monitor*, January/February/March 1982.

This short article announces a microcomputer based elementary reading program to be funded by the Bush Foundation. MECC and the WICAT Institute will help develop and deliver the program.

285. Fisher, W. Personal communication. August 27, 1982.

Waterford School in Provo, Utah, has become perhaps the first nontuition, nonprofit school devoted solely to investigations on the educational potential of the computer.

The WICAT Institute supports the school. From 8 a.m. to 3 p.m. each day 216 pupils attend classes (24 per class, K-8).

The school features a standard curriculum in many areas but not in others, particularly reading, writing, and mathematics. Pupils are involved in experimentation and evaluation of innovative computer software from many sources. In 1982, 25 minutes, 30 minutes, and 20 minutes, respectively, were devoted to reading, writing, and mathematics. The school computer laboratory contains a WICAT System 300 (HYDRA) with 30 work stations, each with a B/W monitor, typewriter style keyboard, lineprinter, and audio.

In 1982 the Waterford staff was working on three projects involving software development. Two of these were in reading:

1. *The Department of Education Reading*

This project, starting its third year, has led to the development of reading comprehension materials in grades four through six. The materials stress inferential comprehension skills and use a "story format" with five different protocols.

2. *Dodge-Bush Foundation Reading*

This project is a cooperative endeavor with MECC (Minnesota Educational Computing Consortium) and has led to the development of an introductory reading program for grades one through three with an audio component for instruction and feedback. The software emphasizes letter and word recognition skills.

Other Public Schools

Annotated References

286. Barber, B. Creating BYTES of language. *Language Arts*, 1982, *59*(5), 472-475.

First grade students use the microcomputer to generate language experience. Some students type their own stories and other less able students talk about their experiences in groups while the teacher types their sentences into the computer. All students get a computer printout of their story to read and use as a basis for skill development lessons.

287. Cummins, R. Microprocessor in reading instruction, diagnostic testing and evaluation. Conference in *Computers in Education*, Missoula, Montana, March 1980.

An examination of problems which hampered the development of CAI in reading (cost, peripherals, speech component). Presents a futuristic version of computer assisted diagnosis and remediation of phoneme and grapheme relationships, fluency, and perceptual problems.

288. Fitzgerald, B. *An analysis of computer assisted instruction in the reading program at Carl Hayden High School.* Doctoral dissertation, Arizona State University, 1974. *Dissertation Abstracts International*, 1974, *35*, 4069-A. (University Microfilms No. 74-20, 129)

289. Miller, Benjamin S. Bringing the microcomputer into the junior high: A success story from Florida. *Phi Delta Kappan*, 1982, *63*(5), 230.

The principal of Miami Lakes Junior High School in Dade County, Florida, tells how he used internal accounts (funds raised by school clubs and activities) to purchase four Apple IIs for a computer lab and the enthusiasm that was generated.

290. Piel, D. *Microcomputers GOTO School*, 1979. (ED 172 776)

Sixth grade students at Bose Elementary, Kenosha, Wisconsin, learned to program the Apple II microcomputer as a way to learn logical thinking. Positive results are reported.

291. Seidel, R.J., & Hunter, B. *Academic computing directory: A search for exemplary institutions using computers for learning and teaching.* Alexandria, Virginia: Human Resources Research Organization, 1977.

The directory, compiled in part from a NSF grant, summarizes many elementary and secondary public school computer managed and computer assisted reading programs. Included are Sierra Vista, Arizona; Los Angeles, Whittier, Atherton, Newport Beach, Palo Alto, East Palo Alto, San Francisco, Redwood City, and Escondido, California; Lakewood, Colorado; Greenville, Delaware; Washington, D.C. Gallaudet College and Kendall Demonstration Elementary School; Chicago, Illinois; Shawnee Mission, Kansas; Alexandria, Louisiana; Westford, Massachusetts; Mason, Pontiac, and Waterford, Michigan; Hopkins, Minnetonka, Bloomington, and St. Paul, Minnesota; Omaha, Nebraska; Teaneck, New Jersey; Albuquerque, New Mexico; Brooklyn, Williamsville, Freeport, Edinger, Guilderland, DeWitt, and Centereach, New York; Dayton, Cincinnati, and Peninsula, Ohio; Portland, Oregon; Memphis, Tennessee; Bryan, Dallas, and Richardson, Texas; Sardy, Utah; Norfolk, Virginia; Seattle, Washington; and Madison, Wisconsin.

292. Thompson, B.J. Computers in reading: A review of applications and implications. *Educational Technology*, 1980, *20*(8), 38-41.

A brief history of computer applications in reading up through 1979. Topics include: computer assisted instruction (drill and practice, tutorial, problem-solving), computer managed instruction, research, and bibliography.

Additional References

293. Fitting, M. Computer use in Santa Clara County schools, 1980. (ED 212 253)

294. Frierl, S., & Roberts, N. Computer literacy bibliography. In J.L. Thomas (Ed.), *Microcomputers in the schools*, New York: Oryx Press, 1981, 131-151.

295. Joiner, L.; Silverstein, B.; & Ross, J. Insights from a microcomputer center in a rural school district. *Educational Technology*, 1980, *20*(5), 36-40.

296. Neufeld, H. Reading, writing and algorithms: Computer literacy in the schools. (ED 211 959)

297. Terzian, P. Microcomputers in public schools: Albany, Schenectady, and Saratoga Counties of New York State, 1981. (ED 212 291)

Chapter 4

COMPUTER ASSESSMENT OF READABILITY AND TEXTBOOK ANALYSIS

Computers can quite easily be programed to count letters, words, lines, sentences, and marks of punctuation. And some computer programs do just that. By counting words per sentence and percentage of hard words, the Fry formula can be applied. Many programs do apply the Fry formula. With the same sort of count and the addition of a constant, the Dale-Chall readability formula can be computed. A few programs do compute it. The Navy Automated Readability Index approximates the Flesch formula estimate and other computer programs also apply the Flesch formula. An Oregon project has developed a program which simultaneously computes four readability coefficients.

By counting letters per word and matching that statistic with syllables counted by humans, computers have derived formulas for predicting letters per syllable and constants to be used to estimate syllables for those formulas requiring a syllable count. For those syntactic components, a computerized measure of syntactic density has been created and tested. And for those interested in comprehension, a computer selection of key words has been designed. Finally, a system for computer abstracting of text has been developed.

Some of these computerized programs use well known computer languages such as FORTRAN. Others, such as TEXAN, are programing languages all by themselves. Very few have actually designed computer readability programs to provide estimates of the reading difficulty of materials which were written for school children. More frequently the programs were created to aid the researcher in classifying materials or generating new materials for studies in reading comprehension.

Since 1978, the readability programers have added a dimension to their works. Some of the programs not only estimate readability but also recommend changes in wording to make passages more readable.

1978 Annotated References

298. Barry, J.B., & Stevenson, T.E. Using a computer to calculate the Dale-Chall formula. *Journal of Reading*, 1975, *19* (3), 218-222.
    Explains rapidity and accuracy of calculating textbook readability levels by computer.
299. Bunde, Gary R. *An effective evaluation between manual and automated readability counting techniques.* CNETS Report Number 5-75. Pensacola, Florida: Naval Education and Training Command, 1975, 33 pp.
    The Automated Flesch Count and the Navy Automated Counter were found to be approximately equal in speed and reliability.
300. Coleman, M., & Liau, T.L. A computer readablity formula designed for machine scoring. *Journal of Applied Psychology*, 1975, *60* (2), 283-284.
    Points out that there is no need to count syllables, since word length in letters is a better predictor than word length in syllables. The formula then generated uses letters per 100 words and sentences per 100 words.
301. Coke, E.U., & Rothkopf, E.Z. Note on a simple algorithm for a computer produced reading ease score. *Journal of Applied Psychology*, 1970, *54*, 209-210.
    Compared Flesch Reading Ease Scores based on syllable counts by humans with computerized scores based on vowels per word, consonants per word, and letters per word (in place of syllables). A correlation of .92 was found between scores based on syllable counts and scores based on vowels per word.
302. Harris, A.J., & Jacobson, M.D. Predicting twelfth graders' comprehension scores. *Journal of Reading*, 1976, *20* (1), 43-46.
    Describes predictive validity of Harris-Jacobson formulas, which are complex and thus require computer processing.
303. Jacobson, M.D., & MacDougall, M.A. *A computerized model of program structure and learning difficulty.* Paper presented at the annual meeting of the American Psychological Association, Washington, D.C., 1969.
    Proposed a computerized system for determining readability or programed materials.
304. Jacobson, M.D., & MacDougall, M.A. Computer management of information and structure in computer supported instructional materials. *Educational Technology*, 1970, *10*, 39-42.
    Readability measures can evaluate both student performance and program structure.
305 Felsenthal, H. *Readability: Computer utilization.* Paper presented at the annual conference of the International Reading Association, Denver, May 1973.

Describes the development of TEXAN (Textual Analysis of Language Samples) at Purdue, and the variables TEXAN measures. Estimates were generally close to expected readability levels, but some wide variations were noted. Syllable counts were estimated by dividing average word length by 3.1127 (a constant).

306. Hopkins, C.J., & Moe, A.J. *The validation of a synthetic syllable count appropriate for computer determined readability estimates.* Paper presented at the annual conference of the International Reading Association, New York, May 1975.

Letters-per-syllable constants were derived for use in place of syllable counts in readability formulas.

307. Herndon, M.A. An approach toward computer control of redundancy in textual materials. *Journals of Reading Behavior*, 1976, *8* (3), 259-271.

Describes progress of RDE, a computer program for Redundancy Detection and Editing. With continued progress, the program may offer a less arduous task for partially sighted individuals and foster (less redundant) reading for others.

308. Joos, L.W. *Computer analysis of reading difficulty.* Paper presented at the annual meeting of the Association for Educational Data Systems, New Orleans, April 1973.

Describes an automation of the Dale-Chall Formula for Estimating Reading Difficulty.

309. Klare, G.R. Automation of the Flesch Reading Ease-Readability Formula with various options. *Reading Research Quarterly*, 168-1969, *4* (4), 550-559.

Gives options in computerizing the Flesch Reading Ease Formula and suggests best choices.

310. Koethe, M.E., & Coke, E.U. *A scheme for text analysis using FORTRAN.* Paper presented at the annual meeting of the American Educational Research Association, New Orleans, February 1973.

A discussion of the development of a program which measures complexity of text in word length, sentence length, key word occurrence, and certain style indicators. The uses of such a program are 1) grading essays, 2) identifying sources of response bias in tests, 3) aiding editors, and 4) aiding researchers in establishing text parameters for research in communication.

311. Mockovack, W.P. *The application and evaluation of PLATO IV in AF technical training.* Lowry AFB, Colorado: Technical Training Division, United States Air Force, 1974.

Describes PIRL readability formula and gives results of comparison with other formulas.

312. Moe, A.J., & Arnold, R.D. Computer assisted readability levels of twenty-five Newbery books. *Reading Improvement*, 1975, *12*, 59-64.

Used computerized versions of the Lorge and the Fry Readability Formulas to estimate readability of Newbery books.

313. Stolurow, L.M., & Klare, G.R. *Project CREATES (Combined Resources for Editing Automated to Enlighten Students).* First Annual Report,

1968-1969. Cambridge, Massachusetts: Harvard University, Computation Laboratory. (ED 032-778)

Two major projects in CREATES related to reading, known as TREE and CAIBLS. TREE encompasses the development of computer aided revisions of adult basic education materials. CAIBLS is the development and implementation of basic language skills and reading materials.

314. Thomas, G.; Hartley, R.D.; & Kincaid, J.P. Test-retest and inter-analyst reliability of the Automated Readability Index, Flesch Reading Ease score, and the Fog count. *Journal of Reading Behavior*, 1975, *7* (2), 149-154.

Six analysts applied three computerized readability formulas to derive scores which were then analyzed for reliability and time requirements. All were highly reliable. The Flesch took the greatest amount of time and the Automated Readability Index was easiest to program.

315. Watkins, C.E. READABILITY. A program available from Project CONDUIT, Oregon State University, Corvallis, Oregon.

This program, written in FORTRAN for use with CDC 6400 processor, simultaneously calculates four readability estimates—Flesch, Dale-Chall, Farr-Jenkins-Patterson, and Danielson-Bryan. It is intended for use with communications research.

1978 Additional References

316. Edmundson, H. New methods in automatic abstracting. *Journal ACM*, 1969, *16* (2), 264-285.

317. Rush, J.; Salvador, F.; & Zamora, A. Automatic abstracting and indexing. Production of indicative abstracts by application of contextual inference and syntactic coherence criteria. *Journal of the American Society for Information Sciences*, July-August 1971, *22* (4), 260-274.

318. Carroll, M.N., & Roeloffs, R. Computer selection of key words using word frequency analysis. *American Documentation*, 1969, *20* (3), 277-233.

319. Fang, I.E. By computer Flesch's Reading Ease Score and a syllable counter. *Behavioral Science*, 1968, *13* 249-251.

320. Felsenthal, N.A., & Felsenthal, H. *Utilizing the computer to assess the readability of language samples.* Paper presented at the annual meeting of the American Educational Research Association, Chicago, April 1972.

321. Gillman, D.A., & Moreau, N.A. Effects of reducing verbal content in CAI. *AV Communication Review*, 1969, *17*, 291-298.

322. Luhn, H.P. The automatic derivation of information retrieval encodements from machine readable texts. *Documentation and Library Science*, 1959, *3*, 1021-1028.

1982 Annotated References

323. Angier, N. Bell's letters. *Discover*, 1981, *2*(7), 78-79.

Describes Writer's Workbench system developed by Bell Laboratories personnel and gives examples using "The Gettysburg Address" and "A Tale of Two Cities," original and edited.

324. Braby, R., & Kincaid, J.P. Computer aided authorizing and editing. *Journal of Educational Technology Systems*, 1981-1982, *10*(2), 109-124.

Describes TAEG (Navy's Training Analysis and Evaluation Group) efforts to develop programs helping authors write simply. Authoring routines automatically format and compose text and merge stored graphics with it. Editing routines 1) "flag" uncommon words, 2) suggest substitutes for awkward or difficult words and phrases, and 3) indicate the readability level.

Describes how 154 pages of camera-ready worktext was generated in about two hours of author time.

The readability formula used is the Flesch-Kincaid Formula which is the standard used by the Department of Defense.

325. Butz, R.; Gunsbalan, L.; Oostergaard, E.; Kaiser, J.; & Burgess, C. *VRP: Reading power in the content areas.* Minneapolis: The EXCHANGE, University of Minnesota, 1979.

A training manual for content area reading teachers, it includes a description of the STAR readability program (computerized) developed by General Motors and the VRP staff. The program yields a Flesch index and a Dale score.

326. Carlson, Ronald. Reading level difficulty. *Creative Computing*, 1981, *6*(4), 60-61.

Describes and lists computerization of Fog Index (Robert Gumming's).

327. Danielson, W., & Bryan, S. Computer automation of two readability formulas. *Journalism Quarterly*, 1963, *40*, 201-206.

Finding that the Farr-Jenkins-Patterson version of the Flesch formula was unwieldy when programed on the UNIVAC 1105, the authors developed their own computerized formula.

328. Frase, L. *Using the computer in analyzing texts.* Paper presented at the NCRE sponsored session of the annual conference of the American Educational Research Association. New York, March 1982.

Discussed his work in computer assessment of readability and computer assistance to writers. Explained WRITER'S WORKBENCH SYSTEM (six programs):

1. PARTS (checks readability and 54 rules)
2. STYLE
3. PROSE
4. PROOFER
5. SEXIST
6. CHUNK

329. Goodman, Donald, & Schwab, Sandra. Computerized testing for readability. *Creative Computing*, 1980, *6*(4), 46, 48, 50-51.

Describes development of "Wanda Wangs" version of the Flesch Readability Formula *Wang 2200*. Prints out (lists) the program.

330. Irving, S.L., & Arnold, W.B. *Readability index.* Freeport, New York: Educational Activities, 1980.

A readability estimating program available on cassette tape for loading in a microcomputer in any classroom.

331. Jerman, Max. READAN II. Portland, Oregon: Bertamax, 1978.
Generates approximation of Dale-Chall and Flesch, Fog, and Smog as well as an average of first three. Runs on TRS-80, Mod 1, Level 2, 16K (tape). Can be purchased from Radio Shack.

332. Judd, D.H. Avoid readability formula drudgery: Use your school's microcomputer. *Reading Teacher*, 1981, *35*(1), 7-8.
Gives sources of commercially available microcomputer reading programs.

333. Keller, P.F.G. Maryland micro: A prototype readability formula for small computers. *Reading Teacher*, 1982, *35*(7), 778-782.
Discusses flaws in earlier microcomputer readability formulas and describes the development of a new one.

334. Kincaid, J.P.; Aagard, J.A.; O'Hara, J.W.; & Cottrell, L.K. Computer readability editing system. *IEEE Transactions on Professional Communication*, 1981, *PC-24*(1), 38-41.
CRES, as this system is known, was designed to assess readability and suggest wording changes to ease the readability of Navy Training Manuals.

335. Kincaid, J.P.; Aagard, J.A.; & O'Hara, J.W. *Development and test of a computer readability editing system (CRES)*. Technical Report No. 83. Orlando, Florida: U.S. Navy Training and Evaluation Group, 1980 (mimeo).
The complete report of the development and testing of the system for improving the ease of reading Navy Manuals.

336. Kincaid, J.P.; Braby, R.; & Walfeck, W.H., II. *Computer aids for authoring tests*. Paper presented at the 23rd Annual Conference of the Military Testing Association, Alexandria, Virginia, October 1981.
Presents a modified version of the CRES, listing 14 performance features and gives a printed version of an application.

337. Klass, P.J. Software augments manual readability. *Aviation Week & Space Technology*, January 11, 1982, 106.
Describes Navy software used for evaluating (Flesch-Kincaid formula) readability and for improving writing. Also refers to work at Bell Laboratories.

338. Moe, A.J. *Analyzing text with computers: The state of the technology*. Paper presented at the annual meeting of the National Reading Conference, San Antonio, Texas, November 1979.
Excellent review of programs for computerizing readability estimates.

339. Moe, A.J. Analyzing text with computers. *Educational Technology*, 1980, *20*(7), 29-31.
Describes the types of text analysis which can be performed by computer, and discusses several examples.

340. Noonan, Larry. Reading level determination. *Creative Computing*, 1981, *7*(3), 166-168, 170, 172-173.
A translation of Ronald Carlson's "Reading Level Difficulty" (Creative Computing, 4/80) into PET Basic.

341. Nottingham, R.B. Fog index. *Creative Computing*, 1981, *7*(4), 152, 154.

Developed computerized Fog Index based on theorem that

"Any word having three or more vowels (a, e, i, o, u, or y) has three or more syllables if:

Double vowels are counted as one

Final *e* and final *ed* are not counted except in the case of *ded, ted* and *le*. . . ."

then lists program in R/S BASIC. (only 31 lines)

342. Schuyler, M.R. A readability formula program for use on micrcomputers. *Journal of Reading*, 1982, *35*(6), 572-589.

Discusses computerized readability and gives complete listing of an Apple II program generating several different readability estimates.

343. Standel, T.C. Critically speaking. *Reading Teacher*, 1978, *32*(2), 222-223.

Section completely devoted to review of the readability analyses by Britton and Lumpkin. Says the analyses are useful but their explanations are not.

344. Walker, N., & Boillot, M. A computerized reading level analysis. *Educational Technology*, 1979, *19*(1), 47-49.

A Pensacola junior college computerized reading level analysis to meet six criteria: 1) The reading level would be correlated with a standard; 2) valid determination of reading level over a wide grade range; 3) no special knowledge or training required; 4) low cost; 5) the program useable by a number of different computers; 6) the procedures would be simple. The program was written in FORTRAN to derive the Fry and Flesch formulas.

1982 Additional References

345. Barry, J.B. Computerized readability levels—their need and use. *Journal of Educational Data Processing*, 1979, *16*, 10-22.

346. Britton, G., & Lumpkin, M. *Readability analysis—1976, Reading Basics Plus (1-8), Harper & Row.* Corvallis, Oregon: Britton, 1978.

347. Britton, G., & Lumpkin, M. *Readability analysis—1977, Holt Basic Reading System (1-8), Holt.* Corvallis, Oregon: Britton, 1978.

348. Britton, G., & Lumpkin, M. *Readability analysis—1975, Reading Perspectives (1-6), Heath.* Corvallis, Oregon: Britton, 1977.

349. Britton, G., & Lumpkin, M. *Readability analysis—1975, Merrill Linguistic Reading Program (1-6), Merrill.* Corvallis, Oregon: Britton, 1977.

350. Britton, G., & Lumpkin, M. *Readability analysis—1975, Keys to Reading (1-6), Economy.* Corvallis, Oregon: Britton, 1977.

351. Britton, G., & Lumpkin, M. *Readability analysis—1976, Houghton Mifflin Reading Series (1-6).* Corvallis, Oregon: Britton, 1977.

352. Britton, G., & Lumpkin, M. *Readability analysis—1976, Reading Unlimited (1-6), Scott, Foresman.* Corvallis, Oregon: Britton, 1977.

353. Britton, G., & Lumpkin, M. *Readability analysis—1976, Reading (1-6), Ginn.* Corvallis, Oregon: Britton, 1977.

354. Fox, S.E. Syntactic maturity and vocabulary diversity in the oral language of kindergarten and primary school children. Elementary.

355. Gerbens, A. Read any good books lately? *Kilobaud Computing*, 1978, *14*, 104-106.
356. Helm, C.E., & McIver, C. Automated sentence analysis for language instruction. *Computers and the Humanities*, 1974, *8*, 239-245.
357. Irving, S., & Arnold, B. Measuring readability of text. *Personal Computing*, 1979, *3*, 34, 35.
358. Kidder, C.L., & Golub, L.S. Computer application of a syntactic density measure. *Computers and the Humanities*, 1976, *10*, 325-331.
359. Klare, G.R.; Rowe, P.P.; St. John, M.G.; & Stolurow, L.M. Automation of the Flesch Reading Ease readability formula with various options. *Reading Research Quarterly*, 1969, *4*(4), 550-559.
360. Kucera, H., & Francis, W.N. *Computational analysis of present day American English.* Providence: Brown University Press, 1967.
361. Moe, A.J., & Hopkins, C.J. *Parsing word strings from text with a computer: Implications for reading instruction.* Paper presented at the annual meeting of the International Reading Association, Houston, May 1978.
362. Pepinsky, H.B. A computer assisted language analysis system (CALAS) and its applications (ED 162 663), 1978.
363. Ratkowsky, D.A., & Hantrais, L. Tables for comparing the richness and structure of vocabulary in texts of different lengths. *Computers and the Humanities*, 1975, *9*, 69-75.
364. Rush, J.E.; Pepinsky, N.M.; Landry, B.C.; Strong, S.M.; Valley, J.A.; & Young, C.E. *A computer assisted language analysis system.* Columbus, Ohio: Computer and Information Science Research Center, Ohio State University, 1974.
365. Rush, R.T. *A program for estimating the readability of English language texts.* Unpublished paper, Purdue University, 1979.
366. Selden, R.W. *Use of linguistic string analysis to explore frequency phenomena in the recognition of syntax.* Paper presented at the annual meeting of the National Reading Conference, St. Petersburg, Florida, December 1978.
367. Shamo, G.W. Predicting syllable count by computer. *Journalism Quarterly*, 1975, *52*, 344-346.
368. Strong, S.M. An algorithm for generating structural surrogates of English text. *Journal of the American Society for Information Science*, 1974, *25*(1), 10-24.
369. Woods, M.L., & Moe, A.J. *Analytical reading inventory.* Columbus: Charles E. Merrill, 1977.

Chapter 5

SOURCES OF COMPUTER SERVICES

In 1978, schools and colleges made use of computer time as it was available. As was pointed out earlier, some public schools used the computer facilities of banks, trucking companies, or nearby colleges to process their data and/or diagnose and prescribe for instructional needs. For schools and school districts without available expertise to computerize their own instructional programs or instructional management systems, a number of companies offered computer programs or computer time (or both) for a price.

At least four kinds of companies have been marketing computer assisted or computer managed reading systems: 1) book publishers who have long served the reading materials needs of schools, 2) test publishers, 3) experts in computer programing and systems development, and 4) manufacturers of computers. (As the reader will soon note, sometimes two or more of the foregoing are combined in one company.)

In 1982, the presence of microcomputers in many schools led many companies to create special divisions for publishing and marketing computer programs. Among the most prominent publishers were Creative Computing Press, Datacommand (division of Imperial Learning), Educational Activities, Micro-Ed, Milliken, Milton Bradley, Random House, Scholastic, Science Research Associates, Scott, Foresman, and Teaching Tools. The products of these organizations have become so extensive that in this revised edition a new chapter (Chapter 9) had to be created to describe them. The 1982 references added to this section, therefore, include only those relating to companies whose products were listed in the original edition of this book.

Book Publishers

Book publishers are aware of the possibilities and have explored CAI and CMI with many school districts. Tom Beall, a consultant for American Book Company, pointed out that he had worked with the Minneapolis schools on Project PYRAMID, which was to have become a computerized management system but stopped short of computerization.

Addison-Wesley tried publishing the *Ransom Diagnostic and Prescriptive Reading Program* (a CMI system) but gave up and withdrew the program from the market. At the time of the writing of the original edition, the extent of Addison-Wesley's involvement with computers was hiring computer companies to run readability estimates on stories being considered for inclusion in their readers.

Harcourt Brace Jovanovich developed and marketed two CAI reading programs between 1967 and 1971. One of these was *CAI Elementary English*, a drill and practice program designed to supplement basal reader programs in grades four, five, and six. Teachers at any of these three grade levels could select from a 320 lesson sequence those topics fitting their lesson plans and direct the computer to present those lessons to the students. The other program was *CAI Remedial Reading*, a three level sequence of 180 lessons per level for middle and junior high school pupils reading at least second reader level. After initial pretesting, the students were branched into the lessons for their ten to twenty minute daily sessions at the terminals.

Excellent results were achieved with these two programs at several sites. Among those school systems using the Harcourt Brace Jovanovich software (programs) were New York City, Cincinnati, Memphis, Macomb (Mississippi), and Waterford Township (Pontiac, Michigan). More than 3,000 students were on-line with the English program and nearly 1,000 made use of the remedial reading program. However, even though software costs were reduced to only 7.5 cents per student contact hour, the installation and maintenance costs for computer hardware were high and Harcourt Brace Jovanovich ceased marketing these programs.

For some time, the Lippincott Company worked with schools in Richmond and Roanoke, Virginia, to develop a CMI program for those two districts. However, differences in school district needs and differences in computing machinery hindered progress there.

Prentice-Hall Developmental Learning Centers for a time were merchandising the products once marketed by the Responsive Environments Corporation. One of these is the Edison Responsive Environment (ERE) or Talking Typewriter, a computerized electric typewriter with jumbo sized type, microphones, speakers, and a projection screen. This device was automated by Richard Kobler to take advantage of a methodology developed by O.K. Moore, who used an electric typewriter, a tape recorder, and a slide projector to teach his two year old daughter to read.

There are three phases in the operation of the machine. In Phase I, the machine acts like any other electric typewriter. In Phase II, the typewriter responds to the pressing of a key with a one second sound recording (the keyvoice) which may give the letter name, the phoneme it represents, or any other information which can be imparted in one second. Phases I and II are free phases: the child can press any key. In Phase III, the machine is controlled by computer programing so that no key can be depressed until it is appropriate to the program for it to be depressed. This locked key feature may be used in conjunction with the keyvoice to provide simultaneous oral and visual stimuli in complex instructional combinations.

The results of using the ERE have been generally favorable whether the target populations were preschoolers, adult illiterates, or poor readers in the intermediate grades. Recently, a method called Oralographic Instruction has been devised for presentation by the ERE. In this 60 lesson program, the student is presented with letter-sounds and symbols which he learns to blend into words. These words are then printed for the student to hear, read (and record), and write for comparison with the machine model. These 60 lessons provide from 120 to 200 hours of instruction.

1978 Annotated References

370. Green, D.R. *Learning to recognize words and letters on a CAI terminal.* Paper presented at the annual conference of the International Reading Association, Boston, April 1968.

An IBM 1050 AV computer system was used to teach four-year-olds word and letter recognition. Tapes and slides were also used. In one experiment sixteen disadvantaged children explored the (typewriter) keyboard for six sessions and then were given matching tasks using words only. In a second experiment, ten children were trained in words only and ten in letters only. No differences were found in word and letter programs, but boys did better than girls in both experiments. In a third experiment with middle class children, there were no sex differences, but letter programs were better than word programs. The author believed the CAI program was too slow to react to student response but that it was good for boys.

371. Reading 1609. In A. Wang (Ed.), *Index to computer based learning.* Milwaukee: Instructional Media Laboratory, University of Wisconsin, 1973.

A very brief description of the Remedial Reading program (once marketed and still owned by Harcourt Brace Jovanovich) as used by the Eastern Kentucky Development Corporation, a public school consortium.

372. Serlin, J. Two for one. *Reading Newsreport*, 1970 *5* (1), 18-22.

Describes the development of the Ransom Diagnostic and Prescriptive Reading Program in Fresno and Los Angeles, California, schools prior to the computerizing of the program and its short-lived marketing by Addison-Wesley.

373. Moore, O.K. Autotelic responsive environments and exceptional children, in O.J. Harvey (Ed.), *Experience Structure and Adadptability.* New York: Springer, 1966.

Describes the talking typewriter as a responsive environment for a young child who types on a color coded keyboard with fingers which have fingernails painted to match fingers to the colors of the keyboard.

374. Frazier, R.I., & Zaslav, S.S. An automated and nonautomated system of teaching. *Reading Teacher*, 1970 *24* (2), 115-119.

Describes evaluation of an 18-station Edison Responsive Environment system by Prince George's County, Maryland, Board of Education. Twenty-two second and third grade children, who were at least a year retarded in reading, were taught Dolch words and other words from the school's basal readers. The 11 members of the control group used a nonautomated electric typewriter. The ERE group (N = 11) gained two years in reading test norm scores while the control group gained one.

375. Richardson, E., & McSweeney, J. An analysis of the ERE "Talking Typewriter" as a device for teaching beginning reading skills. *Educational Technology*, 1970, *10* (4), 81-89.

An evaluation of the technology of the machine itself and of its programing for teaching reading. An excellent description of the device is included. The authors base their conclusions on experience with the device at P.S. 174 in Harlem (New York City), where it was used in conjunction with a project directed by Lamar Gotkin.

376. Schulman, R., & Steg, D. *Remarks on the possible economic significance of early childhood educational technology.* Paper presented at the annual meeting of the American Orthopsychiatric Association, New York, May-June 1973.

Reported that gains using the Edison Responsive Environment were twice those made by other young children not using the ERE.

377. Steg, D.R. *Effects of individual programed instruction of initial reading skills and language behavior in early childhood.* Paper presented at the annual conference of the International Reading Association, Boston, April 1968.

Twenty seven three- and four-year-old children from lower and middle class homes were taught with the Edison Responsive Environment computerized typewriter. First they learned to name letters, then to type words and stories. At the end of five months, all twelve pre- and posttested children could name all upper and lowercase letters and could type their own names. There was no difference in language development or in primary reading skills, even though the middle class IQ mean was 17 points above the lower class mean IQ.

378. Steg, D.R., & Schenk, R. Intervention through technology: the "Talking Typewriter" revisited. *Educational Technology*, 1977, *17* (4), 45-47.

Describes systematic use of the ERE at Drexel University's Early Childhood Center from 1967 to 1977. Reports studies in which disadvantaged children maintained early gains from using the Talking Typewriter.

379. Ratekin, N. *The effect of oralographic instruction on the reading achievement of disabled learners.* Paper presented at the annual conference of the Association for Children with Learning Disabilities, Washington, D.C., March 1977.

Midyear results of the sixty-lesson oralographic (phonic, sound-blending) method which can be presented by either the "Talking Typewriter" or the "Talking Page" with the "Voice Mirror." The test scores for thirty one learning-disabled children who completed the program were randomly selected from those tutored or taught in the usual small groups for LD children. The experimental children led their controls by approximately one-half year.

380. Ratekin, N. *The effect of oralographic instruction on the reading achievement of disabled learners: A final report.* West Orange, New Jersey: Prentice-Hall Developmental Learning Centers, 1977.

An end of year report on the project described above. Forty-five experimental subjects made greater gains than did forty-four control subjects.

1978 Addtional References

381. *Bibliography of materials published about the Edison Responsive Environment Learning System: The talking typewriter.* New York: Responsive Environments Corporation, n.d. (ED 028 648)

382. Long, S. Personal telephone conversation, November 18, 1977.

383. Fitzgibbon, N.H. Personal correspondence, November 15, 1977.

384. Pines, M. What the talking typewriter says. *New York Times Magazine*, 1965, *23* 74-79.

385. Goodwin, M.S., & Goodwin, T.C. In a dark mirror. *Mental Hygiene*, 1969, *53*, 550-563.

386. Steg, D.R. *Early intervention through technology: A seventh year report, 1968-1975.* Paper presented at the annual conference of the International Reading Association, Anaheim, May 1976.

387. D'Annunzio, A. *The effects of the talking typewriter on psycholinguistic and perceptual growth in early childhood.* Paper presented at the annual conference of the International Reading Association, Anaheim, May 1970.

388. Ridgeway, J. Computer tutor. *New Republic*, 1966, *154*, 19-22.
389. Martin, J.H. *Freeport Public Schools' experiment on early reading using the Edison Responsive Environment instrument*. New York: Responsive Environment Corporation. n.d. (ED 022 586)
390. Sanderson, B.A., & Kratochvil, D. *The Edison Responsive Environment learning system, or the talking typewriter, developed by Thomas A. Edison Laboratory, a subsidiary of McGraw Edison Company*. Palo Alto, California: American Institutes for Research in the Behavioral Sciences, 1972. (ED 059 606)
391. Bender, M.L. *A voluntary prekindergarten language development and reading program for the entire four-year-old population of a city*. Final report. Mt. Vernon, New York: Mount Vernon Public Schools, 1968. (ED 020 855)
392. Israel, B.L. *Responsive environment program: Brooklyn, New York: Report of the first full year of operation*. New York: New York City Board of Education, 1969. (ED 027 742)

Test Publishers

Test publishers make available to their customers a variety of computer printed scores and reports. Most modern testing companies can produce printouts of results for each child, as well as class summaries for the teachers, school summaries for principals, and system summaries by grade level. Measurement Research Corporation of Iowa City has scored and processed results for both Houghton Mifflin and Harcourt Brace Jovanovich. TRACER, a newly-purchased subdivision of McGraw-Hill, has been assigned the job of computerizing the management of materials developed by McGraw-Hill's California Test Bureau (CTB).

CTB has developed ORBIT, a list of 335 objectives in reading and communication skills. ORBIT (Objectives Referenced Bank of Items and Tests) is made available to school officials who choose the objectives appropriate to their own instructional programs. For each objective chosen, the computer prints four multiple-choice items which make up tests to be given to the school district's pupils. A computer scoring and reporting system is available to provide reports at classroom, school, district, and individual pupil levels.

A subsidiary of IBM company, Science Research Associates (SRA) markets MASTERY: An Evaluation Tool, part of the SRA *Criterion Referenced Measurement Program*. The reading portion of MASTERY (SOBAR reading) was developed by the Center for the Study of Evaluation at UCLA.

School personnel can select reading objectives from either or both of two catalogs (K-2 and 3-9). Once objectives are selected, the computer constructs customized tests of three items per objective. The SRA scoring service provides individual student profiles, list reports (for grouping by skill), group reports (students' performance by objective), and mastery distribution reports (mastery of objective is three correct items). Teachers may use these reports with the *SRA Learning Cycle Guide: Reading K-3* or the *SRA Learning Cycle Guide: Reading 4-8* to match materials to each of the objectives assessed. Then MASTERY can be used for postassessment. SRA's newer offerings are listed in Chapter 9.

Educational Progress, a division of Educational Development Corporation, markets *Individualized Criterion Referenced Testing* (ICRT). School personnel administer approximately forty tests which are available for grade levels 1-8. Tests are color coded by grade level. Students mark on computer cards which are mailed to the company. Printouts mailed back to the school have three sections entitled "You are able to . . . ," "You need to review how to . . . ," and "You need to learn how to . . . ." Under each title is printed the objectives which are appropriate for that title for the particular student. For those objectives listed in the latter two sections, appropriate lessons from the *Audio Progress Reading Laboratory* and *Clues to Reading Progress* are listed along with lessons from many other programs named by the buyer (school). Also available are class, building, and district summary reports for teacher and administrator use.

The Center for Educational Assessment is a division of the Economy Company which has developed a computerized diagnostic and prescriptive program for early childhood education (ages four to seven). ACEPT (Assessing Children for Early Prescriptive Teaching) defines goals; provides tests; and writes prescriptions in the cognitive, social-emotional, and perceptual-motor areas.

Teachers, aides, paraprofessionals, and parents may be trained to give the test. The test administrator marks responses on the score sheet. The marked score sheets are then mailed to the center where the computer scores each test and prints out 1) a prescriptive activity sheet for each child (one for the child's teacher and one for his parents), 2) a class profile sheet for the teacher, and 3) a class record. The company guarantees that prescriptions will be returned to the school in no more than seven days from the date of mailing. The prescription may include 30 to 55 tasks.

1978 Annotated Reference

393. Yawkey, T.D., & Lewis, L. ACEPT: *Assessing children for early prescriptive teaching.* Oklahoma City: Center for Educational Assessment, Economy Company, 1976.

A 150-item, criterion referenced, individually administered test of pointing, acting-out, answering questions, matching, imitating, repeating after, and identifying pictures. The score sheet is marked by blackening one of three ovals after each item (yes, no, no response) with a number two pencil.

1978 Additional References

394. Seeds, B. Personal letter, November 18, 1977.
395. *ORBIT: Objectives Referenced Bank of Items and Tests* (brochure). Monterey, California: 6CTB/McGraw-Hill, 1975.
396. MASTERY. Brochure 2-4129. Chicago: Science Research Associates, 1976.
397. Eldredge, J.L. *SRA Learning Cycle Guide: Reading K-3.* Chicago: Science Research Associates, 1977.
398. Eldredge, J.L. *SRA Learning Cycle Guide: Reading 4-8.* Chicago: Science Research Associates, 1976.
399. *Educational Progress Presents . . . Individualized Criterion Referenced Testing* (Brochure 29-00034). Tulsa, Oklahoma: Educational Progress, n.d.

Computer Programing and Systems Development Companies

Some companies have been formed to market computing expertise and information. ENTELEK (Newburyport, Massachusetts), Technica (Salt Lake City), National Computer Systems (which markets WIS/SIM), ENTRAN (Milwaukee), BASIC Timesharing (Cherry Hill, New Jersey), Minicomputer Systems (Elmsford, New York), Educational Research Associates (Palo Alto, California), TimeShare Corporation (West Hartford, Connecticut), QUICKTRAN (at centers in ten large cities), MITRE Corporation (McLean, Virginia), Courseware (San Diego), ARIES Information Systems (Milwaukee), Bolt, Baranek, and Newman (Cambridge, Massachusetts), and Computersharing (Philadelphia) are a few of the companies.

In the area of computer assisted instruction, the company most often referred to is the Computer Curriculum Corporation of Palo Alto. This company markets nine CAI drill and practice reading courses: Basic Reading, Audio Reading 1 and 2, Reading, Grades 3-6, Reading 7-8, Adult Reading Skills, Reading for Comprehension, Survival Skills, English as a Second Language, and Critical Reading Skills. Since

Patrick Suppes (Stanford) is president of the company, the programs are strongly influenced by the late 1960s research and development activity of the Institute for Mathematical Studies in the Social Sciences.

At the lowest level is Audio Reading 1 and 2, which uses synthesized speech to teach words. Reading, Grades 3-6, consists of presentations of simple sentences (with as few as two words per sentence), each containing a blank and each followed by three words. The student selects the word and is immediately reinforced for a correct choice. The sentences are said to be of 2.5 to 3.5 level of difficulty. If the student does not respond in 60 seconds, the word *time* appears on the screen or printout and the item is scored as incorrect.

The teacher sets the grade level (to the nearest half grade) at which a child is first to be taught by the computer. During the first ten lessons the computer adjusts upward and/or downward in each of the five strands of the program to find the correct level. After the tenth lesson, the computer presents items from each strand to each student in each lesson. The items are randomly selected from those available at the appropriate level for that particular strand.

When the student has tried all the items at a particular level in any strand, he is moved forward to the next level of that strand *if* he has made no mistakes or only one mistake. If he made one mistake, he moves up a level, but the missed item will be presented again at that higher level. If he missed two items, he will not move up; the missed items will be re-presented in random order. If he missed three or more items, he will move back and will be presented items from the level below the one in which he had been working in that particular strand.

The five strands are described and a typical item for each part of a strand follows.

Strand A. Word Attack

Letter Discrimination

It's__________ for the movie to start.

tim   time

Contractions

He's in the kitchen.

He__________ in the kitchen.

is   it

Compounds

A sunburn is a burn caused by the__________.

sun   moon   heat

Prefixes

The color of your hair is determined before you are born.

The color of your hair is__________

prejudiced predetermined precooked

Suffixes

We had a lot of snow here last winter.

Last winter was very__________.

foggy snowy rainy

Root Words

That was not really a giant ant in the movie.

The giant ant in the movie was not__________.

real red rented

Strand B. Words

Vocabulary

The lofty building blocked out the sun.

"Lofty" means__________.

very high made out of glass

Homonyms

An octopus has a large head and __________arms.

ate eight

Words With More Than One Meaning

Even the handle of the pan is too hot to touch. In this sentence sentence, "handle" means__________.

hold or touch with your hands

the part made to be held

Strand C. Literal Comprehension

Transformations

Our school was struck by lightning.

__________stuck our school.

Categories

Which word names a taste?

cave sour typewriter

Questions and Answers

Wilson has to wear glasses all the time.

What does Wilson have to wear?

Sequence of Events

Barbara woke up__________. Then she woke Albert up.

last while first

Likeness and Difference

I had a nickel and a penny. Roberta had a dime and a penny.
Who had a dime?

Strand D. Interpretive Comprehension

Synonyms

The noisy crowd ran through the street.
The crowd was very__________.

quiet gentle loud

Antonyms

Mark's shoes are loose.
His shoes are not__________.

tight loud easy

Fact and Opinion

That man's fur coat looks strange.
This is__________.

a fact an opinion

Primary Inference

Patricia likes to run in the snow. She likes__________.

time winter spring

Character Study

Phoebe quickly changed her answer when the teacher frowned.
Phoebe was__________.

anxious to be right in a daze

Slanted Writing

Stan borrows from people without paying them back.
Stan thinks everyone should share what they have.

Which sentence makes Stan sound good?

Cause and Effect

A big dog scared Phyllis out of the park.
Phyllis left the park because__________.

her father told her to she is afraid of big dogs

Analogies

Catch is to miss as win is to __________.

prize sit lose

More Interesting Writing

Which sentence is more interesting?

Sandy smacked her lips as she ate the snails.
Sandy enjoyed eating the snails very much.

Metaphors

The cold wind knifed through Alice's thin coat.

The cold wind went through Alice's thin coat like a________.

Strand E. Work Study Skills

Alphabetizing

________ comes first alphabetically.

Lounge   Mercy   Prairie

Guide Words and Letters

The word________comes between the words "blind" and "bring" in the dictionary.

butter   bottom   beach

Finding Information

To find out if it will be windy tomorrow, you would look in

____

an encyclopedia   an atlas   a newspaper

Whenever teachers wish, they may call for student and class performance information. The computer will give each student's placement in each of the five strands (if the student has completed a strand, it is so indicated with the word TOP), the amount of time the student has spent on the program, the number of time-outs for each student, and which used the program on the day of the report.

"Reading 7-8" is a drill and practice program of only two strands, vocabulary and reading comprehension. The vocabulary strand presents practice on 2,250 words at each grade level. The presentations range from providing a definition to using the word in a minimal context requiring the student to understand the word's meaning. The comprehension strand has two texts for off-line reading. Each contains 150 passages. After reading the text passages, students respond to computer presented questions. Teachers have the option of assigning neither or both strands.

The "Adult Reading Skills" program may also be classified as drill and practice. It is designed around the same five strands as the "Reading, Grades 3-6" program. It begins with single sentence items and builds to five line paragraphs accompanied by sets of questions in Strands C and D. The subject matter is oriented toward young adults, and much of it deals with consumer education.

"Reading for Comprehension" and "Critical Reading Skills" are higher level programs. The former is designed to provide ten minutes of drill and practice daily for grade levels 3.0 to 6.9. It emphasizes content area vocabulary (approximately 300 words per grade level) and paragraph reading, requiring more discrimination in choosing answers than its predecessors. The latter program ("Critical Reading Skills") is for students reading above the sixth reader level. The program concentrates on vocabulary development and comprehension through off-line reading of passages in a text written to accompany the computer program.

In computer managed instruction (CMI), a large number of options have become available to school personnel. AIMS (Automated Instructional Management System) was developed by the New York Institute of Technology. CAM (Comprehensive Achievement Monitoring) was jointly developed by Stanford University and the University of Massachusetts. IMS (Instructional Management System) was jointly developed by the Systems Development Corporation and the Southwest Regional Laboratory for Educational Research and Development. TAG (Teachers' Automated Guide) was developed by the Portland, Oregon, Schools.

Four components are common to these CMI programs. Each contains a description of the instructional sequence or course of study, frequent tests based on performance objectives, computer scoring and reporting, and computer made prescriptions. CAM and IMS require the definition of very small objectives and the testing of pupils as often as twice a week. Similar to CAM and IMS in this respect are PREP, of General Learning Corporation; TIES (Total Information for Educational Systems), a computer network of Minnesota High Schools; and SPPED (System for Program and Pupil Evaluation), of the New York State Education Department. TAG emphasizes the careful coding of materials to tested objectives so that teachers can easily retrieve the prescribed materials for assignment to their pupils.

A CMI program slightly different from the others is PLAN (Program for Learning in Accordance with Needs), developed by the American Institute for Research, Westinghouse Learning Corporation, and several participating schools. PLAN allows the learner to choose from a "menu" of activities prescribed by the computer.

PLAN is marketed by Westinghouse Learning Corporation of Iowa City, Iowa. The basic organizational component in PLAN is the TLU ("Teaching Learning Unit"), which includes objectives, activities to meet the objectives, and tests to determine whether objectives have been met. Completing a TLU usually takes two to three weeks. Students can choose the order in which they do the activity within a TLU.

The activities are presented in materials listed in *The PLAN Materials List: Levels 1-8,* published by a variety of publishers. These materials are prescribed as part of TLU's recommended by computer printouts which teachers receive every morning. At the end of each day, pupils fill out cards indicating where they are in their present TLU. This enables the computer to batch process the data overnight and provide the teacher with a complete report on each pupil's progress, the materials and activities of the day, test results, and names of students needing special attention. The aim is to allow teachers more time for individualized instruction by providing computerized clerical work.

The central computer, an IBM 370/155, is located in Iowa City. Most schools subscribing to PLAN have terminals capable of reading cards marked by students and of printing out the computerized prescriptions and summaries. In 1970, some 30,000 pupils in 79 schools were involved. Data for more recent years have been unavailable.

A CMI program similar to PLAN is LMP (Learning Management Program) marketed by the Learning Unlimited Corporation of New Canaan, Connecticut. To enter the program, the student takes a diagnostic test which is mailed to the nearest data processing center. There the test is computer scored and a prescription is mailed back to the school on the next day. This prescription names a sequence of modules which the student is to complete at his own speed. If the school has a computer terminal, an interim (abbreviated) prescription will be available 24 hours after he takes the test. This prescription is to be followed until the detailed prescription arrives.

Each module has pretests, posttests, and progress check tests. The teacher decides whether (and when) to give the tests. A student who scores less than 80 percent on a pretest earns an *E* and enters the module. If he scores 80 percent or more, he earns an *NM* and proceeds to the next module. After he has completed some of the work in the module, the teacher may give him a progress check test which is a minitest for informal progress assessment. When the student has completed all the lessons in a module, or when he challenges, he is given the posttest, which is then scored by school personnel. Results are mailed to the LMP data processing center where weekly or biweekly reports are printed out and sent to the schools.

The materials listed in the prescriptions have been selected from a variety of publishers and some have been developed for LMP by Learning Unlimited. On the prescription sheet, modules are listed by an LMP identification number. Working in a reading laboratory or reading center, students find a Module Plan sheet or booklet which lists several materials and some activities (usually questions to be answered) to be completed with each of these materials. They contract with their center teacher to accomplish a module in a certain time period and may be awarded points for succeeding. Another CMI program similar to (and adapted from) PLAN is TRACER, which was implemented in the Jordan, Utah, schools in 1977-1978 with the services of WICAT and support from Title IV ESEA. This project involved more than 250 teachers.

A 1982 view of computer managed reading instruction is included as part 8 of Chapter 9 in this, the revised edition.

1978 Annotated References

400. Chaffee, P. Students jump grades in contract learning. *The Grand Rapids Press*, April 13, 1972.
Describes success of LMP with Dominic Mattone's fourth through eighth grade classes at St. Andrew's-St. Joseph's Elementary School in Grand Rapids, Michigan.

401. Flanagan, J.C. *The role of the computer in PLAN.* Washington, D.C.: American Institutes for Research, 1970.
Describes computer management of educational activities.

402. Follettie, J.F. *Achievement information monitoring in schools (AIMS): Larger straws in the winds of change.* Professional paper Number 36. Los Alamitos, California: Southwest Regional Educational Laboratory, 1976.
Describes AIMS as consisting of a CPE (districtwide comprehensive proficiency report, CRES (criterion referenced exercises), and delivering ISI (instructional status information) by an SSE (school sited electronics system).

403. *Language arts materials catalog, school year 1977-1978.* New Canaan, Connecticut: Learning Unlimited, 1977.
A list of materials needed to implement LMP in a school. Prices and suggested quantities are listed and each item is ranked as strongly or mildly recommended consumable or nonconsumable.

404. *Learning management program: Management training manual.* New Canaan, Connecticut: Learning Unlimited, 1975.
Contains six modules to be used in a two-day seminar for teaching teacher to participate in LMP.

405. *PLAN School Directory.* New York: Westinghouse Learning Corporation, 1970.
A list of locations of the various PLAN programs in four subject areas.

406. *PLAN Materials List (0800-17).* New York: Westinghouse Learning Corporation, 1973.
A two part list of materials referenced in PLAN TLUs. One list is materials available from publishers. The other is of materials which "can be scrounged from the community." The reading materials are largely programed, linguistically based, and/or self correcting.

407. *A proposal to study the effects of a "Computer Learning Culture" in changing the behavior and self-image of predelinquent and delinquent youths.* New York: WICAT, 1977 (mimeo).

Includes description of a pilot CAI project in which delinquent and predelinquent youths, aged 12-16, learned from CAI for an hour daily for 18 weeks. Those succeeding in using CAI became the tutors who helped new students learn to use the equipment. Attendance, grades, and reading scores increased while vandalism decreased.

408. Seaman, D. Computerized reading programs bring individual instruction. *Johnson City Press-Chronicle*, February 1, 1976.

Explains project COMRAD a CMI project in seven eastern Tennessee elementary schools. The system used is LMP.

409. Shanner, W.M. *PLAN. A system of individualized instruction utilizing currently available instruction materials.* New York: Westinghouse Learning Corporation, 1967.

Explains PLAN as an information system for student data control and feedback to the teacher. It requires specific instructional objectives, activities, and measures.

410. Steen, M.T., & Lipe, D. *Teacher behavior in PLAN and control classrooms using the PLAN Teacher Observation Scale.* Paper presented at the annual meeting of the American Psychological Association. Miami Beach, September 1970.

Found that teacher role changed with PLAN. Teachers spent more time studying diagnoses and discussing activities with students and spent less time imparting information. Students spent more time planning their work and working alone.

411. Steen, M.T.; Lipe, D.; & Quirk, T.J. The development of the PLAN SOS: A student observation scale for individualized instruction. *Psychology in the Schools*, 1972, *9*, 37-88.

Describes the development of the scale used in the above study.

1978 Additional References

412. Bureau of School Research. *Comprehensive achievement monitoring: A technique for instructional monitoring.* Albany, New York: New York State Education Department, 1971.

413. Coulson, J.E. *Progress report for the instructional management system: A report to the Southwest Regional Laboratory for Educational Research and Development.* Santa Monica, California: Systems Development Corporation, 1968.

414. Easter, J. *Comprehensive achievement monitoring in the Sequoia Union High School District.* Paper presented at the Symposium of the California Educational Data Processing Association, December 1972. (ED 084-818)

415. Flanagan, J.C. Individualizing education. *Education*, 1970, *90*, 191-206.

416. Flanagan, J.C. Project PLAN: Basic assumptions, implementation, and significance. *Journal of Secondary Education*, 1971 (a), *46*, 172-8.

417. Flanagan, J.C. *The* PLAN *system for individualizing education.* Special report of the National Council of Measurement in Education, 1971 (b). (ED 051-296)
418. Gorth, W.P.; O'Reilly, R.P.; & Pinsky, P.D. *Comprehensive achievement monitoring: A criterion referenced evaluation system.* Englewood Cliffs, New Jersey: Educational Technology Publications, 1975.
419. Kooi, B.Y., & Geddes, C. The teacher's role in computer assisted instructional management. *Educational Technology*, 1970, *10* (2), 42-45.
420. Liberman, H. Project PLAN: An individualized learning system. *Audiovisual Instruction*, 1970, *15* (6), 84.
421. Schiller, H., & Fredrickson, J. Computer managed learning. *Reading Newsreport*, 1969, *3* (6), 18-22, 64.
422. Sorenson, P. Program for learning in accordance with needs. *Phi Delta Kappan*, 1970, *52*, 180-181.
423. Thompson, W. Personal correspondence, November 18, 1977.
424. Wright, C.F. Project PLAN progress report. *Education*, 1970, *90*, 261-269.

Manufacturers of Computers

Manufacturers of computers make every effort to assist their buyers in making maximum application of their hardware. Control Data Corporation markets the complete PLATO IV program which includes both the necessary hardware (central processor, interface, terminals, and adjunct devices such as printers, random access audio devices, touch panels, and microfiche projectors) and the software (developed at the University of Illinois, the University of Delaware, and the University of Ottawa and field tested by Florida State University).

Control Data Corporation (CDC) has developed and marketed the Basic Skills Learning System, which includes an extensive reading curriculum. Its components include Making New Words, Understanding New Words, Understanding What You Read, Thinking About What You Read, Judging What You Read, Practical Reading, and General Reading.

These components can be accessed either through terminals connected to the CDC PLATO network or by use of disks inserted in a disk drive unit connected to the terminal. The lessons usually present information through both text and pictures or diagrams before requesting students to respond by pressing a key or some location on the PLATO terminal screen. The lessons have been quite successful in adult learning centers, prisons, and juvenile detention homes where adults and young adults need retraining in reading.

Sperry Univac has developed curricula for schools for the deaf, using its own author language, ASET. The MITRE Corporation, in cooperation with Brigham Young University, has developed TICCIT (Time Shared, Interactive, Computer Controlled, Information Television) which has been used at Phoenix Community College and at the Alexandria campus of Northern Virginia Community College (both demonstration sites).

Hewlett-Packard publishes a newsletter for its Users Group who share ideas and applications about educational computing. In addition, the company maintains the HP Contributed Program library (in five volumes) which contains more than 500 education programs, some of which are for reading and/or vocabulary development. Hewlett-Packard markets Adult Skills programs leading to the General Educational Development (GED) Curriculum which is preparation for the GED High School Equivalency Examination.

The HP Adult Reading Skills program is very similar to that marketed by the Computer Curriculum Corporation. It has the same five strands, the same random selection of items at a given level within a strand, and the same standards for moving from one level to another. One difference is that the classes of items within each strand are not identical.

1978 Additional References

425. *Educational user services:* Helping educators help themselves (brochure). Santa Clara: Hewlett Packard, 1975.
426. *HP application brief: Adult skills programs* (brochure). Santa Clara: Hewlett Packard, 1973.
427. Jones, M.C. *TICCIT courseware delivery system.* McLean, Virginia: Hazeltine, 1976 (b).
428. Johnson, G.W. *Don't program your world—PLAN it.* Paper presented at the Second Annual Plains Regional Conference of the International Reading Association, St. Louis, February 1975.
429. Jones, M.C. *TICCIT mailbox communication.* McLean, Virginia: Hazeltine, 1976 (b).
430. Passman, B.M. Personal communication. May 12, 1977.
431. Rahmlow, H.F. *Use of student performance data for improvement of individualized instructional materials.* Proceedings of a symposium. Washington, D.C.: American Psychological Association, 1969. (ED 032-792)
432. Rappaport, W., & Olenbush, E. *Tailor made teaching through TICCIT.* Bedford, Massachusetts: Mitre Corporation, 1975.

1982 Annotated References

433. Advanced, remedial students served by PLATO system. *Application report: Control Data Corporation.* Minneapolis: Control Data Corporation, n.d.

Describes one Minnesota school's (916 Area Vo-Tech Institute) effort to update its 100 courses of study using the CDC PLATO system.

434. Fehner, A. Computers in the classroom. *PLATO Password,* 1981 (Winter Quarter), 28-32.

Anecdotal report of use of PLATO Basic Skills Program in Burnet Elementary School in San Antonio. Classrooms involved have multiple terminals.

435. Macken, E., & Suppes, P. Evaluation studies of CCC elementary school curriculums, 1971-1975. *CCC Educational Studies,* Vol. 1, No. 1. Palo Alto: Computer Curriculum Corporation, 1976.

Describes elementary studies (in Freeport, New York; Fort Worth and Houston, Texas); studies of deaf (in Florida, Oklahoma, and Texas); and handicapped (in Dalton, Illinois; Isleta, New Mexico; Meridan, Mississippi; San Dinas, California; Gulfport, Mississippi; Los Nietos, California; Seattle, Washington).

Report concludes that carefully organized computer drill and practice in basic skills can increase student gains.

436. Poulsen, G., & Macken, E. Evaluation studies of CCC elementary school curriculum, 1975-1977. *CCC Educational Studies,* Vol. 1, No. 2. Palo Alto: Computer Curriculum Corporation, 1978.

Summarizes 1975-1977 reports of math and reading projects conducted in multiple locations using CCC curricula (13 locations—most used "Reading, Grades 3-6"). Concludes that ten minutes daily (or 1500 minutes per year) can lead to 1.2 grade levels of progress on standard tests.

437. The promise of technology. In P.B. Mann (Ed.), *R & D: Research and development at ETS.* Princeton, New Jersey: Educational Testing Service, 1981.

Using "Computerized Adaptive Testing" (the computer selects items to present, based on responses to first few items), verbal aptitude was measured as accurately as it could be measured with much longer conventional tests.

438. Ragosta, M.; Holland, P.W.; & Jamison, D.T. Computer assisted instruction and compensatory education: The ETS/LAUSD study. Project Report No. 20. Washington, D.C.: The program on teaching and learning, U.S. National Institute of Education, June 1982.

Students in grades four and six made significant gains in reading with use of the Computer Curriculum Corporation's programs during the first year only. Later results were not impressive.

The report summarizes earlier CAI research also. A pattern of good results with CAI math and less positive findings for CAI reading and language arts was shown.

1982 Additional References

439. Aubrey, S. *Teacher's handbook for audio reading, grades 1 and 2.* Palo Alto: Computer Curriculum Corporation, 1981.
440. Bork, Alfred. Learning—not hardware—is the issue. *Electronic Education*, 1982, *1*(2), 12, 14, 25.
441. Newcomb, Steven. PLATO's "finest, most expensive." *Electronic Education*, 1982, *1*(2), 12, 14.
442. Newcomer, N.J.; Hamilton, M.; & Carter, L.C. *Teacher's handbook for reading for comprehension* (revised edition). Palo Alto: Computer Curriculum Corporation, 1981.
443. Perron, J.D. *Teacher's handbook for basic reading.* Palo Alto: Computer Curriculum Corporation, 1980.
444. Tingey, B. (Ed.). *Teacher's handbook for critical reading skills* (revised edition). Palo Alto: Computer Curriculum Corporation, 1979.
445. Tingey, B.; Ager, M.; Know-Seith, B.; Parker, R.; Seeburger, E.; Sodman, S.; & Walberg, F. *Teacher's handbook for survival skills.* Palo Alto: Computer Curriculum Corporation, 1981.

Chapter 6

RECOMMENDED USES OF COMPUTERS IN THE READING PROGRAM

Numerous suggestions for using computers to improve reading instruction and reading achievement are found in the literature of computer assisted and computer managed instruction. Many of these suggestions have been put into practice and verified on a small scale as part of one or another research project. For example, computers have already been used to diagnose reading problems and prescribe remedial materials. Furthermore, computers have already been used to generate word lists, to record words dictated by children being taught with the language experience approach, and to model the reading process.

In this chapter, many additional uses of the computer are advanced. Among these are motivational games, simulation of the informal reading inventory, test generation from an item bank, and translation of print into braille. These not only have been proposed but also have been accomplished. Also included in this chapter are articles describing a national system for keeping educational and medical records for children of migrant workers.

The suggestions added in 1982 deal with the same topics, but often with greater specificity. Many of the recommendations were made by classroom teachers using computers in their classrooms, others were made by reading specialists or clinicians who have learned the capabilities of computers and their software. Many dealt with methods and/or programs for using computers to help learning disabled and handicapped children learn reading and other basic skills. A few recommended particular programs (such as word processing) and some recommended that teachers develop their own software. A few recommended training poor readers in programing as a type of remedial reading instruction.

A number of recommendations included descriptions of how to get computers into schools and classrooms and/or how to influence faculty perceptions and win acceptance of computers. The remainder dealt with library applications of microcomputers.

What is astonishing about these articles is not their topics, but their sheer numbers. These 1979-1982 articles considerably outnumber the pre-1979 testimonials, recommendations, and reports.

1978 Annotated References

446. Ahl, D. Computers in language arts. In O. Lecarme and R. Lewis (Eds.), *Computers in education.* Amsterdam: North-Holland Publishing, 1975.

Recommends computer aided writing stimuli which generate highly motivating reading matter. Describes BUZZWORD (1 and 2), MADLIB (1 and 2), and the writing of poetry by computer.

447. Burns, E. Simulating psychoeducational data. (ED 124-109)

Describes a computer program written in FORTRAN IV to simulate data in reading and three other areas and enhance the user's diagnostic skills.

448. Davison, F.C. The state of the university address. *Columns*, 1977, 5, 3-6.

Reports availability, at the University of Georgia, of computer programs which translate print into braille.

449. Johnson, D.B. Computer frequency control of vocabulary in language learning reading materials. *Instructional Science*, 1972, *1*, 121-131.

Proposes a set of frequency groups and an algorithm for making frequencies with an IBM 360 computer. Gives a sample of the technique applied to a Russian textbook.

450. Kinkaid, J.P. Use of the automated readability index for evaluating peer-prepared materials for use in adult reading education. Statesboro, Georgia: Georgia Southern College, 1973. (ED 068-814)

The automated readability index (ARI) was used to create three versions (each at a different reading level) of stories dictated by black adults. The two easier versions were readily comprehended by high school remedial reading students. Graduate students in reading and black trainees in a funded project rated the stories as being highly interesting.

451. Miller, W. How the MSRTS contributes to the educational continuity of the migrant child. In J.P. Nix, H.B. Bullock, & S. Underwood (Eds.), *Proceedings of the Fifth Annual Eastern Stream Conference on Migrant Education.* Atlanta: Georgia State Department of Education, 1974.

Points out that 8,000 school districts are attached to 137 MSRTS terminals in 44 states and that 90,000 children are on the inactive lists at the data bank. Enters a plea for teachers to continue to feed in student data and make use of the system.

452. Pfiel, M.P. New data processing network tracks child's full scholastic and health history. *American Education*, 1970, *6* (5), 4-6.

Describes the Migrant Student Record Transfer System (MSRTS) then operational in seven southern and western states and being readied for use in more states. Funded by a portion of the 1969 Title I migrant projects appropriation, the computer bank employed is that of the University of Arkansas Medical Center. Eighteen terminals were connected in 1970 and a total of 300 were anticipated by 1971. When migrant children entered a participating school, the school secretary could call the terminal operator using the student's ID number and request such things as the student's reading and math levels and any chronic ailments.

453. Plattor, E.E., & Woestehoff, E.S. *The application of computer technology to education diagnosis*. Paper presented at the annual conference of the International Reading Association, Boston, April 1968.

Details seven steps in employing the computer for educational diagnosis: 1) identifying categories requisite to educational diagnosis, 2) specifying category variables, 3) selecting instruments, 4) organizing data storage, 5) developing a computer program library to execute diagnostic procedures, 6) specifying data presentation format, and 7) translating data into instructional sequences.

454. Roe, M.H., & Aiken, R.M. A CAI simulation program for teaching IRI techniques. *Journal of Computer Based Instruction*, 1976, *2*, 52-56.

A computer simulated workshop (RDLAB) was used to teach informal inventory (IRI) techniques to college students. First the computer simulated an instructor, guiding students in constructing an IRI. Then it simulated both a pupil to be tested with the IRI and the instructor guiding the student in assessing the simulated pupil.

455. Shoemaker, D.M., & Osburn, H.G. Computer aided item sampling for achievement testing: A description of a computer implementing the universe defined test concept. *Educational and Psychological Measurement*, 1968, *29*, 165-172.

Describes the creation of a set of tests for repeated measures by sample from a large body of test items.

456. Troxel, D.E. Automated reading of the printed page. *Visible Language*, 1971, *5*, 125-144.

Explains automated reading in print leading to character codes which can be processed to produce braille, spelled speech, or synthesized speech.

1982 Annotated References

457. Abey, C. *Teaching basic skills: An electronic alternative for remedial students*. Paper presented at the Seventh Annual Conference of the Georgia Council of the International Reading Association. Atlanta, Georgia, March 1982.

Describes Abey's program for using "Speak 'N' Spell" devices for her intermediate grade Title I reading program.

458. Blanchard, J.S. Computer assisted instruction in today's reading classrooms. *Journal of Reading*, February 1980, *23*, 430-433.

Explains briefly the terms computer assisted instruction (CAI) and computer managed instruction (CMI). Three types or combinations of types of computer assisted instruction are described: drill-and-practice, dialogue or inquiry, and tutorial. The term "frame-based" is discussed as well as two additional types of CAI systems, "expert-based" and "learner-based." A brief history of computer based reading programs is presented, beginning with the 1964 Palo Alto program. Bilingual reading programs and reading programs for the handicapped also are described.

459. Foley, K.M. *The mighty micro—A reading teacher's backup brain, small group support, and accuracy.* Paper presented at the 26th Annual Convention of the International Reading Association. New Orleans, May 1981.

Describes introduction of computers into the author's Title I reading classroom. Displays simple programs used with her pupils and her own library book management program.

460. Foley, K.M. *So it's not a joystick?!! What's a teacher to think next?* Paper presented at the 27th Annual Convention of the International Reading Association. Chicago, April 1982.

Describes the author's experiences as a classroom remedial reading teacher using microcomputers with groups of two to four kids each in her classroom. Recommends that pupils learn programing. Recommends not putting computers in carrels (children leave wastepaper behind the computer—in the carrel).

461. Goldenberg, E.P. *Special technology for special children: Computers as prostheses to serve communication and autonomy in the education of handicapped children.* Baltimore, Maryland: University Park Press, 1979.

Describes use of LOGO system to enable students to generate sentences (when interfaces allowed bypassing handicaps).

462. Hansen, C. Computer countdown. *Creative Computing*, 1980, *6*(9), 96.

Describes how Minnie P. Blair Middle School initiated pupils and teachers to their 3 PET-2001 computers in "Captain Commodore's Cubicle" with "Star Passes," posters, etc.

463. Harris, L. Which way did it go? *Classroom Computer News*, 1982, *2*(5), 35-36.

Use of Big Trak and an Apple II for teaching directionality to first graders.

464. Hines, Theodore C.; Winkel, Lois; Collins, Roseann W.; & Harvey, Francis A. *Library applications of microcomputers.* Unpublished paper. Library Science/Educational Technology Department, School of Education, University of North Carolina at Greensboro (n.d.).

Recommends 31 uses for microcomputers in libraries and gives advice on how to get started. Faculty members at UNC-Greensboro have programs which execute all 31.

465. Howe, J.A.M. Using technology to educate pupils with communication difficulties. *T.H.E. Journal*, 1978, *5*(5), 36-39.

Describes teaching special education children with their own dialect of LOGO, and by using sentence generating programs. Tells of success with a dyslexic and details several Australian efforts.

466. Joyce, P. *Student programers make better readers.* Paper presented at the 26th Annual Convention of the International Reading Association. New Orleans, May 1981.

Experience based testimony on the impact of learning to program on improvement in reading performance.

467. Judd, D.H. *A microcomputer role in the language experience approach to teaching reading.* Paper presented at the 27th Annual Convention of the International Reading Association. Chicago, April 1982.

Describes microcomputer potential as device for presenting, storing, and retrieving language experience stories by young children.

468. Judd, D.H., & Walker, J.E. Use of microcomputer to enhance the language experience approach to teaching reading. *Ohio Reading Teacher*, 1982 (in press).

Points out advantages of microcomputer for LEA (according to 10 of 47 teachers in a microcomputer workshop).

469. Jurrens, Gerald J. Letter to the editor. *NEA Reporter*, 1981, *20*(1), 14. "Microcomputers are not goblins, waiting in the wings to devour teachers' jobs."

A former ESL teacher now in data processing teaches adults to use computer products. Referring to his children (3 & 7), he says, "...problem solving (at the computer) together has enhanced our relationship with each other."

"Teachers who fail to adapt to the changing complexity of the world, and the demands that increased sophistication have placed upon young people, will find themselves ridiculed and scorned, less respected even than now."

470. Kosel, M. *Designing mathematics applications on microcomputers.* Paper presented at the University of Montana Conference on Computers in Education. Missoula, Montana, March 1980.

Discusses points of importance for designers of educational computing programs. Says readability of program should be two grade levels less than the grade level for which the program is intended. Some authors suggest increasing the reading level of positive responses (after correct answers to drill items are entered), since students "tend to decode new words which praise them."

471. Maller, P. Indians told language by computer. *Green Bay Press-Gazette*, July 19, 1981.

Describes funded program designed to teach speaking and reading of Ojibwe to Wisconsin Chippewas (using PLATO computer programs).

472. Homework: A training solution. *Human Development News*, August 1981, 1-2.

Describes programer training offered to handicapped persons in their homes (even in their beds) by PLATO terminal training programs.

473. Martin, J. Computers: Future shock in Georgia schools. *Georgia Alert*, 1982, *13*(3), 16-20.

Describes implementation of computer by Frank Barber (Dekalb), who has 40 teachers per quarter in his computer learning lab. B.J. McClendon (Principal of Peach County High School) was given $10,000 for computers by Blue Bird Body Company in Fort Valley (and promised more). "Computer Moms" in six Dekalb schools.

474. Mason, G.E. Computerized reading instruction: A review. *Educational Technology*, October 1980, *20*, 18-22.
Discusses the three early successful attempts to teach reading provided: Stanford University program, PLATO system, and TICCIT. Several computer based reading programs are described including DOVACK and the Talking Typewriter. Computer based college reading programs and computer reading programs marketed to elementary and secondary schools are also discussed.

475. Mason, G.E. The computer as a teacher of the disabled reader. *Journal of Research and Development in Education*, 1981, *14*(4), 97-101.
Describes how reading clinicians are using computers in diagnosing and teaching clinic patients.

476. Mason, G.E. *The micro from a university point of view*. Paper presented at the 27th annual convention of the International Reading Association. Chicago, April 1982.
Describes need for research about the computer as a vehicle for displaying printed text. Gives results of a survey of special interest group (microcomputers and reading) members on uses of computers in their reading programs.

477. Mason, G.E., & Blanchard, J.S. Computerized reading in the eighties. In E.K. Dishner; T.W. Bean; & J.E. Readence (Eds.), *Reading in the content areas: Improving classroom instruction*. Dubuque, Iowa: Kendall/Hunt, 1981.
Suggestions on using CAI for content area reading instruction.

478. Mason, G.E., & Blanchard, J.S. Reading teachers put the computer to work. *Classroom Computer News*, 1982, *2*(5), 44-45.
Describes the work of two reading teachers who learned to use micros in their classrooms.

479. McClellan, J., & Griffin, H. Imitation bacon bits, onions aside. *Electronic Education*, 1981, *1*(4), 14-15.
Describes 1978-1979 spice selling campaign (Ft. King Middle School, Ocala, Florida) leading to $10,000 profit and purchase of 15 4KTRS-80 Level I machines. Soon all machines expanded to Level II, 16K, and 6 Ataris purchased for 1981-1982.
"Maintenance is a struggle." School now has separate account for micro maintenance. Money for maintenance comes from teacher-written manual of "helpful hints" and "try" and "no try" methods for teachers who were planning to introduce 12 and 13 year olds to the world of computers.

480. McKean, K. Computers, fiction, and poetry. *BYTE*, 1982, *7*(7), 50-53.
Explores computer assisted literature: Its history and current developments. Examples of computer generated poetry are provided as well as computer generated narrative prose.

481. Microcomputer based elementary school reading project. *AEDS Monitor*, 1982, *20*(7, 8, 9), 27.

Describes goals of MECC Special Projects' R & D project with WICAT funded by the Bush Foundation. Topics in the reading curriculum include letter skills, sight word recognition, phonics, and vocabulary skills as well as inference, information evaluation, and nontextual reading skills.

482. O'Donnell, H. ERIC/RCS computer literacy, part I, an overview. *Reading Teacher*, 1982, *35*(4), 490-493.

Resources in Education (ERIC/RCS) and Current Index to Journals in Education (CIJE) form the nucleus for a review of computer applications in education.

483. O'Donnell, H. ERIC/RCS computer literacy, part II: Classroom applications. *Reading Teacher*, 1982, *35*(5), 614-617.

Resources in Education (ERIC/RCS) and Current Index to Journals in Education (CIJE) provide sources for a review of early computer applications in reading (CAI and CMI).

484. Peterson, C.M. Minicomputers for mini-kids. *The Computing Teacher*, 1980-1981, *8*(7), 28.

Describes how a computer was first employed in the back room of an elementary school library. Goes on to relate how six commands allow intermediate grade students to program a level II TRS-80.

485. Small computers get big results in Dallas. *Mechanix Illustrated*, 1981, *11*(3), 54-55.

Robert Mendro is principal planner. "First math—then reading." More than 700 TRS-80 Model I's in DISD (Dallas Independent School District) classrooms, but using TI-99/4 for math and early reading because of its excellent audio. Staff has cross-referenced all the CAI to local texts. Teachers can write CAI prescriptions. Elementary schools have computer labs with 4 to 12 per lab. High schools have Apple for science and computer literacy.

486. Stevens, D.J. How educators perceive computers in the classroom. *AEDS Journal*, 1980, *13*(3), 221-232.

K-12 teachers, student teachers, and faculty of a college of education (Nebraska) favored computer literacy instruction in schools but didn't feel qualified to give it.

487. Stone, Deborah. Computers at an alternative school. *Creative Computing*, 1980, *6*(9), 46-47.

Twenty students (ages 8 to 18) on a farm converted to a school for students having trouble in school. Four teachers living there. Started with "Lunar Landing" game on SOL and Sorcerer. First bought Apple. Only one repair after 1½ years. Later obtained TRS-80. Machines in lockable room. Some kids go alone. Others must have company along. Kids loved *Breakout* which came with original cassette driven Apple. And they loved modifying it. *Animals* game (on disk) also very popular.

"One of the charms of the situation has been that the faculty knew absolutely nothing about the computer, and weren't even too interested. Aside from the one parent who got us started. . .teaching about the machine has by default been left to the students who understood it. The kids have been free to do it on their own.... Our experience with computers at High Valley has been positive and enjoyable, and has shown the adaptability of computers to the alternative school setting" (p. 47).

488. Sturdivant, P. *Computer managed instructional support can make an impact on reading improvement.* Paper presented at the conference of the Association for the Development of Computer Based Instructional Systems, San Diego, California, February 1979.

489. Tennis, Jean G. The computing diary: Journal of a first-year computer user. *Electronic Learning,* 1981-1982 (a section in each issue, starting with November, December).

Tennis describes the decision to get an Apple, learning to operate it, taking it to school, getting her pupils and fellow teachers involved with it, and eventually becoming the area computer education expert and giving speeches and teaching inservice sessions.

490. Townsend, B., & Hale, D. Coping strategies for resistance to microcomputers. *T.H.E. Journal,* 1981, *8*(6), 49-50, 52.

Explains strategies for dealing with opposition to micro use by 1) faculty, 2) administration, and 3) students.

491. Vickery, C.A. *Integrating microcomputers into the junior high potential English program.* Paper presented at the 26th annual convention of the International Reading Association, New Orleans, April 1981.

492. von Feldt, James R. *An overview of computer assisted instruction (CAI) at the National Technical Institute for the Deaf.* Presented at the annual convention of ADCIS, February 1979.

Explored 4 alternatives: 1) Large scale timesharing and dedicated systems such as PLATO, 2) Intermediate to small timesharing and dedicated systems such as CCC and TICCIT, 3) Small scale special purpose system such as DAVID, 4) General purpose microcomputers such as TRS-80, PET, Apple, IMSI, Horizon, and Compucolor.

493. Wallace, D. Frogs in sleeping bags? Sure, but the real fun is in the software at Denison Bollay's Computer camps. *People,* 1982, *18*(2), 61-62.

Has one camp north of Santa Barbara, one at Lake Tahoe, and one in upstate New York. Allows kids only three to six hours per day at the machines.

494. Wilson, Gay, & Hammond, John. *Instructional technology: End-of-year status report.* Dallas, Texas: Dallas Independent School District, 1981.

Five major developmental programs going on. 1) Title VII bilingual language instruction program, 2) Microcomputer mathematics program, 3) Title IV-c higher order computer assisted math skills program, 4) Microcomputer reading program, 5) Title IV-c higher order computer assisted reading program.

495. Yerger, B. A homemade "computer" for reinforcing reading skills. *Reading Teacher,* December 1979, *33,* 313-316.

Describes a simple, inexpensive method for converting a cassette tape recorder into a "computer" that can be used to reinforce reading and math skills. Works on the principle of completing an electrical circuit by making a metallic connection. Many variations of reading and math activities can be applied with this computer, and motivation for such a device runs high.

496. Zsiray, S.W., Jr. Using the microcomputer to develop library media/information research skills. *Computing Teacher*, 1982, *9*(9), 15-19.
Describes use of gifted middle school children to create CAI reference skills program for the school and lists program called "Abridged *Readers' Guide*."

497. Zucker, Andrew A. The computer in the school: A case study. *Phi Delta Kappan*, 1982, *63*(5), 317-319.
Describes use of PDP 11/40 (32K) DEC mini installed in 1975-1976 at Milton Academy in Massachusetts. Reading teachers in grades 3-6 used *Maze* which produces one-of-a-kind printouts for completion by pencil. Had to terminate access at 4 PM so students would do other things besides "play" with computer. Lower school teachers used computer-printed large block letters for posters.

1982 Additional References

498. Boettcher, J.V. *Developing comprehension skills via computer in an elementary classroom.* Paper presented at the 26th Annual Convention of the International Reading Association, New Orleans, April 1981.

499. Daniel, D. *MECC and micro.* Paper presented at the 27th Annual Convention of the International Reading Association, Chicago, April 1982.

500. Dworkin, Y., & Dworkin, N. *Computers in reading instruction.* Paper presented at the Sixth Southeastern Regional Conference of the International Reading Association, Norfolk, Virginia, November 1980.

501. Fech, E.B. *Present day computer materials and use in instruction in general and reading instruction in particular.* Paper presented at the 27th Annual Convention of the International Reading Association, Chicago, April 1982.

502. Geoffrion, L.D. The ability of hearing impaired students to communicate using the TTY system. *Volta Review* (in press).

503. Geoffrion, L.D. *Using computers to develop elementary reading and writing skills.* Paper presented at the 27th Annual Convention of the International Reading Association, Chicago, April 1982.

504. Gibbs, D. *Reading and the microcomputer.* Paper presented at the Seventh Southeastern Regional Conference of the International Reading Association, Orlando, February 1982.

505. Hirschbuhl, K. *A computer in a reading clinic.* Paper presented at the 23rd Annual Convention of the International Reading Association, Houston, Texas, May 1978.

506. Judd, D.H. Word processing and the microcomputer: Creative uses for administration. *Educational Computer Magazine*, November-December 1981, *1*, 18-19.

507. Judd, D.H. *Partners in education: Instructional uses of the microcomputer.* Chicago: Follett, 1981.

508. Judd, D.H. Learning to program really isn't necessary or BASIC isn't basic anymore! *Educational Computer Magazine*, September-October 1981, *1*, 10-11.

509. Judd, D.H. Administrative decision tools: A microcomputer reality available now. *Educational Computer Magazine*, July-August 1981, *1*, 6-7.

510. Judd, D.H. Microcomputer classroom use patterns. In Diana Harris & Laurie Nelson-Heem (Eds.), *Proceedings of NECC 1981 National Educational Computing Conference.* Iowa City: University of Iowa, 1981, 297-301.
511. Judd, D.H. Sources for and evaluation of K-12 microcomputer software. In Sue G.K. Talley & Robert D. Nelson (Eds.), *AEDS-81 Convention Proceedings.* Washington: Association for Educational Data Systems, 1981, 150-156.
512. Judd, D.H. Microcomputers use in education: Curricular guidelines. In James R. Gerdes (Ed.), *Personal computer digest.* Chicago: AFIPS Press, 1981, 76-78.
513. Judd, D.H. The challenge of professional development: Potential microcomputer utilization. *Educational Computer Magazine*, May-June 1981, *1*, 6-7.
514. Judd, D.H. Exploring microcomputer applications in personnel training and development. In Sam Barone & Rao Tummala (Eds.), *Proceedings of 1981 Midwest AIDS Conference.* Atlanta: American Institute for Decision Sciences, 1981, 150-151.
515. Judd, D.H. Evaluation of instructional programs for microcomputers. *Educational Computer Magazine*, March-April 1982, *2*, 16-17.
516. Judd, D.H. Word processing in the classroom: Is it really practical? *Educational Computer Magazine*, May-June 1982, *2*, 18-19.
517. Judd, D.H. Microcomputer use in teaching adult reading. In David G. Gueulette (Ed.), *Microcomputers for adult learning: Potentials and perils.* Chicago: Follett, 1982.
518. LaFrenz, D. *The microcomputer—a new tool for reading instruction.* Paper presented at the 27th Annual Convention of the International Reading Association, Chicago, April 1982.
519. Manzo, Anthony V. *Accessing computers in education: One byte at a time.* Keynote address, Old Dominion University Reading Conference, November 1981.
520. Mark, D.A. *Use of computers in teaching reading to the learning disabled students.* Paper presented at the 26th Annual Convention of the International Reading Association, New Orleans, April 1981.
521. Mason, G.E. *An introduction to computer based reading instruction.* Paper presented at the Conference on Computers in Education, University of Montana, March 1980.
522. Mason, G.E. *Computers in reading instruction.* Paper presented at the Sixth Southeastern Regional Conference of the International Reading Association, Norfolk, Virginia, November 1980.
523. Mason, G.E. Reaction: Innovative approach to comprehension at the freshman level. In G.H. McNinch (Ed.), *Comprehension: Process and product.* First yearbook of the American Reading Forum. Hattiesburg, Mississippi: The Forum, 1982.
524. Mason, G.E., & Blanchard, J.S. Computerized reading: A review. *Proceedings of the annual conference of the association for educational data systems.* Washington, D.C.: The Association, 1978, 181-186.
525. Olson, A.J., & Matcgynski, B.A. *Using computers to teach basic reading skills to adults.* Paper presented at the 26th Annual Convention of the International Reading Association, New Orleans, April 1981.

Chapter 7

COMPUTERS IN READING RESEARCH

While many of the computer based programs have been subject to field testing with the pupils for whom they were designed, a limited number of investigations have carefully compared the reading achievement of well-defined groups of subjects whose instruction was computer assisted or computer managed. Most of the investigations listed in this chapter are one of a kind, however. Consequently, all from the original version are presented in three major sections: pupil attitudes and achievement, components of oral and printed language, and models of the reading process. The reference lists for each of these sections are in two parts: those from the original version (labeled 1978 references) and those from the revised version (labeled 1982 references).

In addition, a fourth section had to be created for 1982 references and is called "miscellaneous." The additional references are listed at the end of the chapter.

Pupil Attitudes and Achievement

Included in this section is research on the effectiveness of computer managed instruction and feedback of reading progress information to teachers. Also included is research using the computer to analyze eye movements in reading, to diagnose children's reading needs before prescribing remedial reading instruction, and to classify children as normal or dyslexic. Other investigations annotated in this section involve the assessment of student attitudes toward CAI; the prediction of science achievement from CAI word learning rate; the improvement of vocabulary, comprehension, and/or study skills; and the identification of problems in integrating CAI into the school curriculum.

1978 Annotated References

526. Aaron, R.L., & Muench, S. The effects of a computer managed, individualized treatment program on the achievement of behaviorally disordered, delinquent adolescents. *Reading Research Quarterly*, 1974-1975, *10* (2), 228-243.

When delinquents in a Georgia Youth Development Center were randomly assigned to experimental or control groups, the experimental groups (N = 36) earned significantly greater scores in reading and comprehension. This experimental group was taught with PLAN, a computer managed reading and mathematics program developed for the Westinghouse Learning Corporation.

527. Adams, D.P. *Effect of comprehensive achievement monitoring on student teaching.* Paper presented at the annual meeting of the American Education Research Association, Washington, D.C., March 1975.

Found no significant differences in reading achievement for students taught with the Comprehensive Achievement Monitoring (CAM) system and a control group. This finding was true for both standardized and criterion referenced measures.

528. Anelli, C.M. *Optimum length of computer assisted instruction for urban third and fourth grade reading programs.* Unpublished doctoral dissertation, Rutgers University, 1977.

Third grade girls made more gains than third grade boys when all received CAI (a drill and practice program) in reading as a supplement to their classroom instruction. Boys made better gains with 40 minute sessions than 20 minute sessions. Girls gained more than boys with both session lengths. Students receiving three to four hours of CAI in a three month period made the greatest progress per unit of time spent. CAI enthusiasm, while of considerable magnitude, decreased after seven or eight hours of machine instruction.

529. Caldwell, R.M. *A comparison of a programed text and a computer based display unit to teach reading skills to semiliterate adults.* Unpublished doctoral dissertation, Pennsylvania State University, 1973.

Young adults spent more time at the computer terminal than a comparable group spent at programed reading texts. The attitudes toward reading of the CAI taught group were more positive than those of the group taught with programed texts. However, there were no significant differences in reading achievement between the two groups.

530. Fey, T.F. *A comparision of computer and teacher prepared individualized reading prescriptions.* Unpublished doctoral dissertation, University of Florida, 1974.

After fifth graders had been administered the Gilmore Oral Reading Test, selected items from the Prescriptive Reading Inventory (McGraw-Hill), and an interest inventory, a group of classroom teachers and a group of reading teachers picked books and remedial materials which should be prescribed for each pupil tested. A computer program also prescribed from these same data. The computer generated prescriptions more closely paralleled prescriptions determined by a panel of experts than did the prescriptions written by either group of teachers.

531. Green, D.R., Henderson, R.L., & Richards, H.C. *Learning to recognize words and letters on a CAI terminal.* Paper presented to the annual conference of the International Reading Association, Boston, April, 1968.

Three experiments with four-year-old deprived children are reported. Using an IBM 1050 AV computer system, words were projected on a screen. The subjects were to hit a key upon which the word was printed. When they did so, they were told they were correct and were shown a picture of the word. After ten minutes daily for seven days, boys matched words better than girls. In a later experiment with a similar population, the authors found no difference in numbers of matches between a group taught to match letters and a group taught to match words. In a third experiment, the authors found that young middle class children learned through CAI to match letters faster than disadvantaged children.

532. Hansen, D.N. *Application of computers to research on instruction.* Paper presented at a meeting of the National Society of College Teachers of Education, Chicago, February 1966.

Reports three studies. The first found a trend toward correct modeling after twelve second graders had received eleven CAI lessons in remedial reading. The second dealt with solving the problem of integrating CAI (spelling) with the existing curricula in a school. The third described results of teaching spelling of part of a list of words as opposed to teaching the whole list.

533. Hendon, C.A. *A comparision of reading and vocabulary achievement of elementary students taught with two reading teaching methods.* Unpublished doctoral dissertation, University of Kansas, 1976.

Compared test results of basal reader instruction to forty classes with results of same instruction supplemented with computer managed teacher support system to forty classes the following year. Results favored the basal reader instruction without computer managed support.

534. Martin, J.G., & Meltzer, R.H. Visual rhythms: Report on a method for facilitating the teaching of reading. *Journal of Reading Behavior*, 1976, *8*, 153-160.

Reports an experiment with video presentation of printed syllables on the CRT screen simultaneously with the oral pronunciation of that syllable so that sentences appear syllable-by-syllable from left-to-right on the screen. The authors think it would help the deaf.

535. Mathis, A., Smith, T., & Hansen, D.N. College students' attitudes toward computer assisted instruction. *Journal of Educational Psychology*, 1970, *61*, 46-51.

College students were pretested on attitudes toward CAI, then assigned either outside reading or 45 minutes of computer assisted instruction. Students were found to have positive attitudes which became more positive after CAI instruction, especially if they made few errors during instruction.

536. Okey, J.R., & Majer, K. Individual and small group learning with computer assisted instruction. *AV Communication Review*, 1976, *24*, 79-86.

Undergraduate students studied Bloom's mastery learning strategy at the PLATO IV terminal. Some studied alone and some studied in pairs, trios, or groups of four. Groups selected one of their number to respond by using the keyboard. There were no differences in achievement, but pairs took more computer time than single students or groups of three or four. This time seemed to have been used for discussion of concepts presented.

537. Rankin, E.F., & Bryant, P.G. Use of prediction equations and computer simulation for identifying preferred sensory modality for training in reading. In G.H. McNinch, and W.D. Miller (Eds.), *Reading, Convention and Inquiry. 24th Yearbook of the National Reading Conference.* Clemson, South Carolina: National Reading Conference, 1975.

Computer simulations helped identify low achieving children whose modality preference might indicate one or another method of instruction.

538. Redfield, D.D., Donlon, B.A., & Teates, T.G. *CAI word rate: Student ability as predictors of achievement.* Technical Report Number 2, Intermediate Science Curriculum Study. Tallahassee, Florida: Florida State University, 1971.

Two measures of reading, word reading rate and word rate stability, were the best predictors of science achievement by seventh grade students bring taught science by CAI.

539. Robbins, W.E., & Tharp, A.L. A natural language computerized instruction system for elementary education. *Educational Technology*, 1976, *13* (3), 32-35.

This was an experiment to determine if a computer without teacher supervision or intervention could accept student input and satisfy student questions. The students could ask the computer questions about local geography and history. The approach enabled the students to gain local history and geography faces (including reading practice) through computer tutoring.

540. Sklar, B. *A computer classification of normal and dyslexic children using spectral estimates of their electroencephalograms.* Unpublished doctoral dissertation, University of California at Los Angeles, 1971.

Using the computer, twelve dyslexic children were differentiated from thirteen normal age and sex-matched children based on spectral estimates of their EEG readings. The greatest differences were in the parieto-occipital region during rest with eyes closed.

541. Strang, H.R. The automated instruction of practical reading skills to disadvantaged sixth grade children. *Improving Human Performance,* 1975, *4*, 43-52.

Sixth graders were pretested on such reading skills as using a telephone directory and locating topics in an encyclopedia. Then nineteen students were given CAI in some twenty-four of the skills. Posttests favored experimental subjects who learned not only the twenty-four skills taught but also several that were not taught.

542. Thompson, M.D., Jr. *The effects of spelling pattern training on the spelling behavior of primary elementary students: An evaluative study.* Unpublished doctoral dissertation, University of Pittsburgh, 1976.

Ten experimental second grade subjects were given CAI sound-letter correspondence training for twenty-four to thirty-five minutes, three times weekly for a school year. The on-line CAI work was supplemented with workbook pages. Experimental subjects outperformed control subjects on all posttests, one of which was a test of ability to read whole words. The author suggested that CAI in sound-letter correspondence might be an excellent supplement to the reading program.

543. Wadham, R. *Monitoring reading instruction through the use of a microcomputer.* Paper presented at the Rocky Mountain Regional Conference of the International Reading Association, Salt Lake City, October 1977.

Described preliminary research done in connection with the development of TICOR (Timed Interval Categorical Observation Recorder), a small suitcase-sized device which records classroom interaction during instruction on digital tape. Both the order and the duration of instructional events are recorded for computer analysis.

544. Wadham, R.A., et al. *An elementary education project for the evaluation of teacher effectiveness.* Provo, Utah: Department of Elementary Education, Brigham Young University, 1977.

Proposal submitted to the Research Division and BYU Research Support Program for funded support in extending and expanding the area of research activity related to the senior author's current TICOR research.

1982 Annotated References

545. Assessing CAI. In P.B. Mann (Ed.), *R & D: Research and development at ETS.* Princeton, New Jersey: Educational Testing Service, 1981.

Reports team of evaluators are completing a four year study of supplementary CAI reading and mathematics for disadvantaged children in grades 1-6.

546. Ballas, M.S. Computer drill and practice make the grade. *Developments*, 1982, *28*(1), 5-8.

Reports four year longtitudinal study of CAI in reading and math in Los Angeles. CAI programs were leased from Computer Curriculum Corporation. The math results were excellent. However, reading gains seemed to be earned only in the first year of program use.

547. Bath Elementary School *Results of computer assisted instruction at Bath Elementary School* (ED 195 245), 1979.

In a pilot project excellent gains in reading seemed to be a result of 20 minutes spent daily at the computer by 100 sixth graders. The displays appeared one letter at a time, seeming to speed-up the slower readers.

548. Blohm, P.J. *Effects of computer aided glossing on prose recall.* Paper presented at the second annual American Reading Forum, Sarasota,

Florida, December 1981.

Describes research in which researcher written glosses were activated by students as they desired during reading. The computed logged number of glosses requested. Results indicated no relation between number accessed and comprehension score.

549. Bozeman, W.C. *An investigation of psychological typology as an intervening variable in the implementation of a computer managed instruction system.* Technical Report No. 454. Doctoral dissertation, May 1978.

Investigated the relationships between psychological types of users and factors associated with WIS-SIM: Apprehension of human-machine systems, confidence in WIS-SIM, and perception of usefulness of WIS-SIM. A strong correlation was found between introversion and apprehension of human-machine systems and respondents, who preferred using feeling (as opposed to thinking) as a mode of judgment, displayed greater apprehension of human-machine systems. An association was found between extraversion and confidence in the system and between a thinking preference and confidence. A high correlation between extraversion and perceived usefulness of WIS-SIM was noted.

550. Caldwell, R.M., & Rizza, P. A computer based system of reading instruction for adult nonreaders. *AEDS Journal*, 1979, *12*(4), 155-162.

Says that "initial performance data from eight demonstration projects in adult basic education centers indicated that learners gained on the average one entire year in reading after less than 12 hours of instruction" (p. 155). Dropout rates of only 5 percent.

551. Carver, Ronald P., & Hoffman, James V. The effect of practice through repeated reading on gain in reading ability using a computer based instructional system. *Reading Research Quarterly*, 1981, *16*(3), 375-390.

Programmed prose, a computer program for the PLATO IV terminal connected to ERL (University of Illinois) by phone line, generated Bormuth's passages for repeated reading and various cloze (N = 5) nth deletions. Tested by two-choice maze in boxes which were timed. Results were favorable for fluency, but not for overall gain.

552. Diem, R.A., & Fairweather, P.G. An evaluation of a computer assisted education system in an untraditional academic setting—a county jail. *AEDS Journal*, 1980, *13*(3), 204-213.

Describes use of CDC PLATO Basic Skills Reading Program in Bexar County, Texas, Adult Detention Center. Made gains in math, but not in reading. Suggested that reading materials were not adult enough and that tutors should work at terminals with tutees (to provide voice, for one thing).

553. Geoffrion, L.D. Reading and the nonvocal child. *Reading Teacher*, 1982, *35*(6), 662-668.

Included in this research review is a section on CBELS (Computer Based Exploratory Learning Systems) including his own work (CARIS), work with LOGO, and computer mail (with deaf students).

554. Grabe, M., & Mann, S. *A technique for the assessment and training of comprehension monitoring skill.* Unpublished paper (available from the authors, University of North Dakota).

Found differences between good and poor fifth grade readers on a CAI task of finding one inconsistent sentence among four others in a "detective game." Found no benefits to result from practice on-line (although only six games were developed and two served as pretest and posttest).

555. Dennenberg, S.A. *An alternative curriculum for computer literacy development.* Unpublished doctoral dissertation, University of Massachusetts, 1977.

ACCOLADE allows learners to chose their own paths toward computer literacy using a "map," a CMI system, and a "communications file." Uses PLATO CDC IV system and TUTOR language. Used AUTHOR lessons.

556. Districtwide use of CBE lab. *T.H.E. Journal,* 1978, *5*(5), 23.

Beginning in August 1977, Red Wing, Minnesota schools have a Title IV sponsored CBE lab. Ten educational terminals hooked to either TIES or MECC. Two PLATO terminals (at the high school) hooked to CDC. Also has Hewlett-Packard delivered CCC program.

557. Feldman, S.; Alne, D.; & Seltzer, J. Use of a simulation program for teaching diagnostic skills. (ED 196 428)

Positive cognitive and affective gains were reported to have resulted from a computer simulation for reading diagnosis.

558. Guthrie, J.T. One computer literacy skill (RESEARCH section), *Journal of Reading,* 1981, *24*(5), 458-460.

Cites Xerox research center research (on users of word processing terminals) which found users to be consistent with themselves, but not with other users.

559. Howe, J.A.M.; Beattie, A.; Cassels, F.; Johnson, J.; & Anderson, A. *Teaching handicapped children to read.* D.A.I. research report No. 57. Edinburgh: Department of Artificial Intelligence, University of Edinburgh, 1978.

The reading section of the final report to the Leverhulme Trust Fund, 1978. Taught reading to young nonreaders using rear projected slides (against a touch screen).

560. Jelden, D.L. The microcomputer as a multiuser interactive instructional system. *AEDS Journal,* 1981, *14*(4), 208-217.

Feedback from 201 college students indicate best CAI lesson length was 30 to 45 minutes. Twenty-one percent indicated that "after 30 minutes the eye strain was a factor" (p. 211). Personalization of programs by use of student nicknames was rated as important by 85 percent. The author generated seventeen rules for software construction from this feedback.

561. Kahn, S. RSVP and reading. *RSVP Newsletter,* 1980, *2,* 2.

Describes research with junior college students in CAI reading. Those who preferred unstructured learning conditions achieved better scores when assigned to individually prescribed instruction. Those who preferred structured learning achieved better scores when assigned to

CMI reading. Positive attitudes also resulted from group assignments congruent with student preferences.

562. Kleiman, G.; Humphrey, M.; & Lindsey, P.H. Microcomputers and hyperactive children. *Creative Computing*, 1981, *7*(3), 93-94.
Eighteen hyperactive children (ages 6-14) worked arithmetic problems on the PET CRT no faster and no more accurately than they did paper and pencil problems—but they chose to do more of them.

563. Leslie, R.C., & Kamil, M.L. *Microcomputers: A possible answer for needed research facilities for information processing research in reading.* Paper presented at the annual meeting of the National Reading Conference, St. Petersburg, December 1978.
Outlines reading research tasks for which the microcomputer is (sometimes ideally) suited.

564. Lindsay, E. Jay. A discussion on the effectiveness of STRIDE, using *STRIDE Reading* as an example. Report No. 1, *TSC Current Research Topics.* Hanover, New Hampshire: Time Share Corporation, 1981.
Compares 95 STRIDE-using kids (grades 4-8) with matched pairs in two rural schools. Users did 15 minutes daily. In comprehension STRIDE group outgained controls 1.2 years (October-May) as opposed to .8, but in Word Recognition, controls won 1.5 to 1.3.

565. Lindsay, E. Jay. *STRIDE increases learning in language arts by three times.* Current Research Topics Report No. 2. Hanover, New Hampshire: Time Share Corporation, 1981.
Three months of STRIDE L.A., 15 minutes daily, led to greater gains by experiment than control groups on SRA usage subtest. Seventy-six percent on STRIDE made gains. Forty-three percent not on STRIDE made gains. Mechanics and spelling scores not much different.

566. Lutz, John E., & Taylor, Patricia A. A computerized home based curriculum for high risk preschoolers. *AEDS Journal*, 1981, *15*(1), 1-9.
Computerized instruction to tutors (CMI) gave higher scores on Boehm test and better maternal interaction with children at lower management cost that noncomputerized with human clerical work.

567. Moore, M.V.; Nawrocki, L.H.; & Simutis, Z.M. The instructional effectiveness of three levels of graphics displays for computer assisted instruction (ED 178 057), 1979.
A report to the Army Research Institute on research with CRT reading of text supplemented with one of three levels of graphics. Low level graphics (such as line drawings or boxes around text) was as helpful as medium or high level graphics support for enlisted personnel reading a passage on the psychophysiology of audition.

568. Mullinix, P.M.; Rizza, P.J., Jr.; & Heimer, R.T. *The PLATO basic skills learning system: Good news for functionally illiterate adults.* Paper presented at the annual conference of the Association for the Development of Computer Based Instructional Systems. San Diego, California, February 1979.
Reports pre/post testing of a one-group set of 24 adult subjects whose reading achievement gains using the PLATO system were greater than those predicted for a similar amount of time in classroom instruction.

569. Rizza, P.J., Jr., & Walker-Hunter, P. The basic skills learning system: An evaluation report on field tests conducted from January 1, 1978 to July 1, 1978. Summary Report. Minneapolis, Minnesota: Control Data Corporation, 1978.

570. Rubenstein, R., & Rollins, A. Demonstration of the use of computer assisted instruction with handicapped children. Cambridge, Massachusetts: Bolt, Beranek, & Newman, 1978.

Describes use of computer mail system in a school for the deaf. Forty hearing-impaired children generated more than 1,500 letters in eight months.

571. Saracho, O.N. The effects of a computer assisted instruction program on basic skills achievement and attitudes toward instruction of Spanish speaking migrant children. *American Educational Research Journal*, 1982, *19*(2), 201-219.

One hundred twenty-eight children received supplementary CAI in reading and mathematics, using programs from the Computer Curriculum Corporation. At the conclusion, the CAI group had higher achievement test scores, but the non-CAI group had more positive attitudes toward CAI.

572. Siegel, M.A., & Simutis, Z.M. *CAI for adult basic skills training: Two applications.* Paper presented at the 24th Annual Convention of the International Reading Association. Atlanta, Georgia, May 1979.

Study 1: Compared achievement of (N = 32) soldiers taught CAI GED classes with those (N = 32) taught a traditional curriculum in language arts. Described early problems with "dedicated" phone lines and the very favorable attitude of the soldier-students.

Study 2: Use of PLATO in GED-type classes at Menard Prison in Illinois led to higher percent passing than non-CAI instruction in another nearby prison. A nonrigorous, but valuable field study.

573. Thompson, B.J. Computers in reading: A review of applications and implications. *Educational Technology*, 1980, *20*(8), 38-41.

Reviews computers in reading, modes of CAI: drill-and-practice, tutorial, problem-solving, games, and simulations. Describes several CAI systems and computer based resource units and includes a brief review of research in computer effectiveness.

574. Wisher, R.A. *Using a minicomputer with voice synthesis to teach English vocbulary to nonnative speakers.* Paper presented at the University of Montana Computers in Education Conference, Missoula, Montana, March 1980.

CAI versus classroom-instructed subjects (N = 5 per group) of Navy personnel were compared. Five hours of CAI yielded more Navy manual words learned than did 12 hours of classroom instruction. The CAI efficiency was three times greater. Retention was also better.

575. Wisher, R.A. *Developing job related databases for computer assisted reading instruction.* Paper presented at the 23rd Annual Convention of the Military Testing Association, Alexandria, Virginia, October 1981.

Describes development of string-oriented software for generating comprehension development materials (using a PDP-11/34 minicomputer). After paragraphs from Navy training manuals were typed in, the program generated its sentences, each with a word randomly deleted. Students selected from a set of distractor words. The program also generated a three-by-three matrix of words and phrases. By interacting, the student created a previously read sentence. The third type of exercise called for students to order randomly arranged sentences to create a meaningful paragraph.

576. Wisher, Robert A., & O'Hara, John W. *Computer based approach to the Navy's academic remedial training, project PREST: A cost effectiveness evaluation.* NPRDC Special Report 81-18. San Diego, California: Navy Personnel Research and Development Center, May 1981.

Describes comparison of PREST (CAI consisting of 94 of CDC's 111 reading modules in their Adult Basic Skills program and six study skills modules developed for PREST, and augmented by off-line worktext drills) with ART (Academic Remedial Training) carried on by Navy instructors. Forty-four subjects (recruits) scoring between 4.0-6.0 on Gates-MacGinitie compared with similar control group. Twenty-four PLATO terminals involved (terminal [with 2K rom] downloads modules from CDC into its 16K RAM, then becomes 16K ROM-microtutor) ANOVA used.

Components of Oral and Printed Language

In this second section is research which sought to find elements of spoken and/or written language which, when listed or categorized, would facilitate teaching reading. Included are studies in which computers generate wordlists for instruction, studies in which computers count phoneme-grapheme correspondences or evaluate variations in initial consonants on these correspondences, and studies attempting to generate more readable written text or to edit existing text.

1978 Annotated References

577. Carver, R.P. *New techniques and improving reading comprehension.* Technical Report Number 1. Silver Spring, Maryland: American Institute for Research in Behavioral Sciences, 1973.

Details a computerized method for converting prose training materials into different form which forces trainees to read at some specified minimum level of comprehension.

578. Cronnell, B. *Designing a reading program based on research findings in orthography.* Report Number PP-14. Inglewood, California: Southwest Regional Educational Laboratory, 1972.

A lexicon of primary grade words of one and two syllables were computer processed, determining 166 spelling-to-sound correspondences requisite for beginning reading. Six thousand words were coded by their spelling-to-sound correspondences and then arranged in a sequence for instruction.

579. Durr, W.K. *A computer study of high frequency words in popular trade juveniles.* Paper read at the annual conference of the International Reading Association, Anaheim, May 1970.

A computer analysis of 105,280 words printed in 80 primary texts selected by teachers and librarians found 3,220 different words. Ten words accounted for one-fourth of the running words, 25 accounted for one-third, and 188 accounted for 70 percent.

580. Schallert, D.L. *Empirical investigations of the effects of differences between oral and written language on comprehension.* Paper presented at the annual meeting of the National Reading Conference, New Orleans, December 1977.

Describes effects of differing segmentations on children's abilities to comprehend and follow directions delivered by a PLATO terminal.

581. Pennock, C.D. Quick word lists for Canadian readers. *Alberta Journal of Educational Research*, 1974, *20*, 8-14.

Described computer processed word lists and derivatives which might supplement or replace older lists such as the Dolch Sight Word Vocabulary List.

582. Seigel, A.I., & Wolf, J.J. Computer analysis of textual comprehensibility. In O. Lecarme and R. Lewis (Eds.), *Computers in Education.* Amsterdam: North Holland Publishing Company, 1975.

Describes mechanization via computer of text analysis to determine comprehensibility measures. Names groups involved in developing computer response mechanisms for questions phrased in "Natural Language" (English). At the time of writing, eleven measures of comprehensibility were possible: 1) Guilford's "Cognitive of Semantic Units," 2) evaluation of symbolic implications, 3) cognition of figural units, 4) convergent production of semantic systems, 5) cognition of semantic relations, 6) convergent production of semantic implications, 7) divergent production of semantic units, 8) transformational complexity, 9) Yngve depth, 10) morpheme depth, and 11) self-embeddedness.

1982 Annotated References

583. A componential approach to reading and correcting reading disabilities. (Harvard University/Weaver), NR 154-440. Research in progress. Described in *Psychological sciences division 1980 programs.* Arlington, Virginia: Office of Naval Research, November 1980.

Includes a microcomputer simulation PAR-SYL. In PAR-SYL, input arrays are parsed and syllabified using simple heuristic rules. A specific vocabulary is drawn upon and the efficiency of the syllabifying words drawn from several dictionaries including a Navy Technical Vocabulary. Then an experiment with good and poor readers processing gives set of units.

584. A componential approach to locating and correcting reading disabilities of young adults. (Bolt, Beranek & Newman/Frederiksen), NR 154-448. Research in progress. Described in *Psychological sciences division 1980 programs.* Arlington, Virginia: Office of Naval Research, November 1980.

Several gaming formats are being implemented on a microcomputer to test the trainability of individual components of reading, and to allow a test of the spread of training effects to other components that are thought to interact with components related to decoding efficiency and the utilization of context. Four to six weeks of training to be tested.

585. McCaslin, E. *Using CAI to teach vocabulary concepts.* Paper presented at the 23rd Annual Convention of the International Reading Association, Houston, Texas, May 1978.

Described research (with Karen Block) in progress, using the PDP-15 computer to teach 154 word concepts to college students. After ten unknown words have been found by pretesting, they are taught to mastery in two sessions (one per day). Simulated DEC screen displays for three of seven possible teaching routines are provided.

Models of the Reading Process

This third section includes research in which computers are used to evaluate models of the reading process or to assess components of the process of comprehension.

1978 Annotated References

586. Aaronson, D., & Scarborough, H. Performance theories for sentence coding: Some quantitative evidence. *Journal of Experimental Psychology: Human Perception and Performance*, 1976, *2*, 56-70.

Computer recordings of word-by-word reading times showed prolonged pauses at phrase boundaries for subjects reading for later recall, but not for subjects reading for immediate comprehension.

587. Collins, A.M., & Quillian, M.R. Experiments on semantic memory and language comprehension. In L.W. Gregg (Ed.), *Cognition in learning and memory.* New York: John Wiley and Sons, 1972.

Describes a computer program which comprehends printed text by comparing it to a memory bank of stored factual semantic information.

588. Goltz, R.T. *Comparison of the eye movements of skilled and less skilled readers.* Unpublished doctoral dissertation, Washington University, 1975.

Good readers made longer fixation pauses when reading to generalize than when reading for detail. Poor readers did not.

589. Hawley, I.I.; Stern, J.A.; & Chen, S.C. Computer analysis of eye movements during reading. *Reading World*, 1974, *13*, 307-317.

Describes computer analysis of electrically recorded eye movements during reading. Five were identified as qualitatively and quantitatively different from the usual saccadic movements.

590. Herndon, M.A., & Bowden, D. *Evaluation of two pattern recognition algorithms for computer models of reading behavior.* Paper presented at the National Reading Conference, St. Petersburg, Florida, December 1975.

As part of any computer model of reading behavior, one must develop pattern recognition (identifying strings of letters and words as matches to similar patterns stored in memory). The authors tried two algorithms, deciding that the first was more sensitive and that the second was more economical.

591. Just, M.A., & Carpenter, P.A. Eye fixations and cognitive processes. *Cognitive Psychology*, 1976, *8*, 441-480.

Using computer controlled pictures and print, the authors found that print conflicting with the pictures it related to took longer to read.

592. Leton, D.A. *Computer program to convert word orthography to phoneme equivalents.* Final report. Honolulu: Hawaii University Educational Research and Development Center, 1970. (ED 038 266)

This report describes computer simulation of reading skill acquisition. The research aim was to convert orthography of English words to phoneme equivalents for computer programing. The conversion was done at the preprimer and primer levels of the Lippincott basal series. The results are included.

593. Leton, D.A. *Computer simulation of reading.* Paper presented at the annual meeting of the American Educational Research Association, Chicago, April 1972.

Computer simulation allows a detailed and complete study of the acquisition of reading skills. The program, called SIMUREAD, converts English orthography to segmented phonemes, which in turn are simulated by numerals.

594. Leton, D.A. Computer simulation of reading: A progress report. *Journal of Reading Behavior*, 1974, *6*(2), 131-141.

The article describes SIMUREAD, a computer program designed to aid in reading instruction and clarify its research applications.

595. McConkie, G.W., & Rayner, K. Asymmetry of the perceptual span in reading. *Bulletin of the Psychonomic Society*, 1976, *8*(5), 365-368.

Using computer controlled text displays, the authors found visual information to be derived from no more than four letter positions to the left of fixations during reading by three high school students, but all three derived information from letter positions farther than four to the right of the fixation point.

596. McKenna, M.C. *Computer simulation of cloze performance.* Paper presented at the National Reading Conference, New Orleans, December 1977.

Using PL/1, a language with good verbal capacity, a computer memory was programed to search wordlists for words appropriate for one, two, or three constraints. The computer search time was parallel to human response time to cloze responses with one to three constraints per word.

597. O'Regan, J.K. *Structural and contextual constraints on eye movements in reading.* Unpublished doctoral dissertation, University of Cambridge, 1975.

The author replaced letters in the visual periphery with Xs and found that little information is gained from peripheral vision.

598. Rayner, K. Parafoveal identification during a fixation in reading. *Acta Psychologica*, 1975, *39*, 271-282.

Readers seldom fixated between sentences. Computer controlled irregularities displayed on the screen to the right of the subjects' fixations (in the subjects, verb, or objects) within the sentences being read were not recognized differentially.

599. Rayner, K. Visual attention in reading: Eye movements reflect cognitive processes. *Memory and Cogntion*, 1977, *5*(4), 443-448.

Using computer controlled displays and computer data gathering, the author found main verbs to be fixated longer than other words in sentences.

600. Reder, S. On-line monitoring of eye-position signals in contingent and noncontingent paradigms. *Behavioral Research Methods and Instrumentation*, 1973, *5*(2), 218-228.

Describes use of computer controlled displays in which a region of text around a fixation point is displayed clearly and the remaining text is a bunch of letter-like rectangles arranged to simulate printed words.

601. Rumbaugh, D.M.; von Glaserfeld, E.; Warner, H.; Pisani, P.; Gill, T.; Brown, J.; & Bell, C. A computer controlled language training system for investigating the language skills of young apes. *Behavioral Research Methods and Instrumentation*, 1973, *5*(5), 385-392.

Describes the 46 classes in the YERKISH computer language and the electromechanical system devised for Lana (the chimp) to learn and use.

602. Rumbaugh, D.M.; Gill, T.V.; & von Glaserfeld, E. Reading and sentence completion by a chimpanzee. *Science*, 1973, *182*, 731-733.

A report of the linguistic skills acquired by Lana in communicating with the computer language YERKISH, named for the Yerkes Primate Laboratories.

603. *Visual search activity: A tool for the evaluation and development of computer assisted reading instructional programs.* Annual report, Behavior Research Laboratory. St. Louis: Washington University, 1975. (ED 112 362)

Eye movements of readers reading from the plasma panel of a PLATO terminal were analyzed by computer. Competent readers made fewer saccadic movements per line and had shorter fixation times. When reading for detail, competent readers changed only by increasing their fixation times. Less competent readers made more fixations when reading for detail. The authors suggest that the long lines of print make readers less efficient in reading the PLATO display than in reading books.

604. Wisher, R.A. *Linguistic expectations and memory limitations in reading.* Paper presented at the Annual Convention of the International Reading Association, Miami Beach, May 1977.

Subjects pressed buttons to cause a computer terminal to display each phrase they were to read. Average phrase reading time was computed in milliseconds. Fast college level readers appeared to prefer using semantic clues when syntactic features are known before reading.

Average readers seemed to prefer to use both semantic and syntactic clues to meaning.

605. Wisher, R.A., & Aiken, E. *Information overload during reading.* Paper presented at the National Reading Conference, New Orleans, December 1977.

Computer timed tones were sounded at certain points during fixations by Navy trainees reading from a college reading improvement text. By analyzing 12,000 eye movements interrupted by tones, authors determined that information learned during a fixation (while reading) is transient up through 100 milliseconds.

606. Wisher, R.A. *Improving language skills by computer.* Paper presented at the annual conference of the Association for the Development of Computer Based Instructional Systems, February 1978.

Reviews and illustrates what the computer offers in the field of language arts and highlights several programs under development at the Navy Personnel Research Development Center in San Diego.

1982 Annotated References

607. DenBuurman, R.; Roersma, T.; & Gerrissen, J.F. Eye movements and the perceptual span in reading. *Reading Research Quarterly*, 1981, *16*, 227-233.

Computer controlled text displays helped identify the text area from which information is drawn during reading. The spans found consisted of 12 to 15 letters to the right and/or left of the center of fixation (4 to 5 degrees of visual angle).

608. Kliegl, R. Automated and interactive analysis of eye fixation data in reading. *Behavior Research Methods & Instrumentation*, 1981, *13*(2), 115-120.

Describes five FORTRAN computer programs for analyzing reading eye fixation data. OLDEYE identifies six types of fixations and gives descriptive statistics on each. CONVRT changes text into a database which can be related to the data in OLDEYE. PLTFIX matches fixations with letters. MODDAT marks areas of poor measurement and MATCH calculates 11 measures for every word read.

609. Mandel, T.S. Eye movement research on the propositional structure of short texts. *Behavior Research Methods and Instrumentation*, 1979, *11*(2), 180-187.

Describes research to determine if more difficult propositions in text are associated with more fixations and with fixations of shorter duration.

610. McConkie, George W., & Rayner, Keith. An on-line computer technique for studying reading: Identifying the perceptual span. In Phil L. Nacke (Ed.), *Diversity in mature reading.* Twenty-Second Yearbook of the National Reading Conference. Boone, North Carolina: National Reading Conference, 1973, 119-130.

Used X-test with "moving window" of real text "opened" by eye movement to show phrase being read. Tried to find effect of distance from focal point. Good readers used letter and word shape information only 11-characters to the right of fixation point. But spaces in X-text showed an influence as far as 13-characters to right. Consequently, word length may affect fixations. Small window slowed rate. No effect on comprehension.

Experiment 2: Changes in words about 4 characters to left were not detected, but changes in first or last letters and word shape were noted 10-12 to right.

611. McConkie, G.W., & Rayner, K. The span of the effective stimulus during a fixation in reading. *Perception & Psychophysics*, 1975, *17*(6), 578-586.

Subjects found to acquire word length information (on a CRTO display of text) at least 12 to 15 character positions to the right of the fixation point. This seemed to influence saccade length. Specific letter and word perception was accurate no more than ten spaces to the right of the fixation point.

612. McConkie, G.W.; Zola, D.; Wolverton, G.S.; & Burns, D.D. Eye movement contingent display control in studying reading. *Behavior Research Methods & Instrumentation*, 1978, *10*(2), 154-166.

Describes system which permits control of CRT displays contingent upon viewers' eye movements.

613. Rayner, K. Foveal and parafoveal cues in reading. In J. Requin (Ed.), *Attention and performance VII.* Hillsdale, New Jersey: Erlbaum, 1978.

Using computer displayed text and computer monitoring of eye movements, the author found that fixations after a saccade of 1 to 3 degrees detected changes in target words that occurred during saccades. However, after saccades of 5 degrees or more, few changes made during saccades were detected.

614. Rayner, K. Eye movements and cognitive psychology: On-line computer approaches to studying visual information processing. *Behavioral Research Methods & Instrumentation*, 1979, *11*(2), 164-171.

Describes research in reading and picture observation using on-line eye movement recording procedures. Includes difficulties and advantages.

615. Rayner, K.; Inhoff, A.W.; Morrison, R.E.; Slowiaczek, M.L.; & Bertera, J.H. Masking of foveal and parafoveal vision during eye fixations in reading. *Journal of Experimental Psychology: Human Perceptions and Performance*, 1981, 7(1), 167-179.

Using computer controlled text display, the authors found that most of the visual information required for reading is acquired during the first 50 milliseconds of a fixation and that any parafoveal information is acquired after the foveal information (center of fixation) is extracted.

616. Reynolds, Ralph E.; Standiford, Sally N.; & Anderson, Richard C. Distribution of reading time when questions are asked about a restricted category of text information. *Journal of Educational Psychology*, 1979, *71*(2), 183-190.

Divided text into "48 PLATO-length" pages (each about three quarters of a normal typed page). Following every four of these pages there was a set of 6 questions.

617. Russo, J.E. A software system for the collection of retrospective protocols prompted by eye fixations. *Behavioral Research Methods and Instrumentation*, 1979, *11*(2), 177-179.

Discusses research in which subjects received numbered indicators of the locations of their fixations during reading. These indicators served as prompts for retrospective verbal protocols.

618. Stern, J.A. Eye movements, reading, and cognition. In J. Sanders, D. Fisher, & R. Monty (Eds.), *Eye movements and the higher psychological functions*. Hillsdale, New Jersey: Erlbaum, 1978.

Reports research on eye movements during reading and computer programs for abstracting data gathered and printing it out in useable formats. Also reported was a computer program to record and evaluate head movements during reading, movements which complicate measurement of eye movements. Using this program, line length of displays can be reduced until head movements fall below acceptable levels.

619. Sturges, P.T. Delay of informative feedback in computer assisted testing. *Journal of Educational Psychology*, 1978, *70*, 378-387.

Studied effect of delayed feedback on retention in computer assisted reading. 112 college students took a 30-minute multiple-choice computer assisted test and received the correct answers either 1) immediately after each item, 2) right after the entire test, 3) 24-hours later, or 4) not at all. A retention test containing the same 30 items and 17 others was given 1-3 weeks later. Retention was significantly better for delayed feedback than for immediate feedback and students with delayed feedback were more confident of their answers.

620. Taylor, G.A.; Klitze, D.; & Massaro, D. A visual display system for reading and visual perception research. *Behavior Research Methods & Instrumentation*, 1978, *10*(2), 148-153.

Discusses selection of a computer visual display system suitable for word recognition and reading research at the University of Wisconsin, where the laboratory is dedicated to such students.

Miscellaneous Research Involving Computer Applications in Reading

Included in this section are case studies, pilot studies of reading-client simulations for training diagnosticians, evaluations of the CRT (screen) display's effect on reading performance, studies using the computer to evaluate grouping and teacher performance in reading, and one comparison of computerized and traditional testing.

1982 Annotated References

621. Epstein, Kathy. The road to literacy: Teaching a 16 year old to read. *Journal of Reading*, 1981, *24*(6), 497-502.

A case study in which the clinician used "Speak 'N' Spell" to teach remedial reading.

622. Andolina, M. Reading tests: Traditional vs. computerized. *Classroom Computer News*, 1982, *2*(5), 39-40.
Found that test results comparable to paper and pencil results can be obtained through on-line testing.

623. Bader, L.A. *Clinical problem-solving behavior in reading diagnosis.* Paper presented at the annual conference of the American Educational Reserch Associates, April 1977.
Describes pilot studies with SIMCASE, a computer simulated reading clinic client. Observations of student diagnosticians were useful in refining the simulations.

624. Bishop, R.H.; Wadham, R.A.; Rencher, A.C.; Young, J.R.; Gale, L.; & Wilcox, R. Report of observation and data collection utilizing the TICOR microcomputer system to assess instruction in selected bilingual education project schools in three local education agencies in Utah. Provo, Utah: Eyring Research Institute, 1979.
A report to H.E.W., describing the system and its findings in three school districts where bilingual classes were operating. Included are descriptions of INSTAT (strategies used in interacting with pupils), EQUAT (equity of teacher attention to pupils) and MOBAT (teacher mobility and attention). Examples of reports based on use of these programs are provided.

625. Block, K.K., & McCaslin, E.S. *Efficiency in teaching vocabulary concepts: Attainable or not?* Pittsburgh: Learning Research and Development Center, University of Pittsburgh, 1979.
Describes work in progress on seven modules for testing a theory about vocabulary learning (word understanding, as opposed to word recognition). On-line pretests guarantee words to be learned in experiments are not already known. CAI then is used to teach words in one of seven ways, each of which is presented as a module. Two are described: 1) Classify and 2) Define. Instructional events within the modules include 1) Rule, 2) Example, 3) Practice, and 4) Test.

626. Geoffrion, L.D., & Goldenberg, E.P. Computer based exploratory learning systems for communication handicapped children. *Journal of Special Education*, 1981, *15*, 325-332.
Computer help for severely handicapped students is described.

627. Hoover, T. Empirical study of reading and comprehension as a function of CRT display (ED 161 002), 1977.
118 college students read and answered questions about four passages displayed on the CRT. Two passages were presented with text on every line ("paced," caps 3/16″ high with 1/16″ leading) and two were presented with text on every other line. No differences in rate or comprehension were found, although rates were *not* high ($\bar{x}$s = 181-226 wpm) and comprehension scores were *very* low ($\bar{x}$s = 41-60%).

628. Lassen, N.A.; Ingvar, D.H.; & Skinhoj, E. Brain function and blood flow. *Scientific American*, 1978, *239*(4), 62-71.
Using computer displayed graphic representations of blood flow (which shows active regions) in the brain, the researchers found that reading silently activates the visual association area, the frontal eye

field, the supplementary motor area, and Broca's speech center in the brain. Oral reading activated these four and also the mouth area and the auditory cortex.

629. Lesgold, A. *The computer and research in reading.* Paper presented at the NCRE sponsored session of the annual conference of the American Educational Research Association. New York City, March 1982.
Strongly recommended microcomputer based gaming strategies for teaching reading skills requiring speed and repetition.

630. Levine, J.M., & Stein, H. GROUPCOM: A computer program for investigating social processes in small groups. *Behavior Research Methods & Instrumentation,* 1978, *10*(2), 191-195.
Describes program for social research using groups in which each individual sits at a terminal and communicates with real or fictional "others." Cites several similar communication investigations involving computer use.

631. Wadham, R.A.; Rencher, A.C.; Teerlink, C.N.; & Pinegar, J.C. An outline for researching the effective teacher profile using a specialized microcomputer system. Provo, Utah: Brigham Young University and the Eyring Research Institute, 1979.
Describes hardware and software components of TICOR-DAC.

1982 Additional References

632. Henney, M., & Boysan, V.A. Effect of computer simulation training on ability to administer an informal reading inventory. *Journal of Educational Research,* 1979, *72,* 265-270.

633. Kieras, D.E. Doing it the vendor's way: Running multiple subjects in reading experiments using Data General's Diskette Operating System. *Behavior Research Methods and Instrumentation,* 1979, *11*(2), 221-224.

Chapter 8

BACKGROUND INFORMATION ABOUT COMPUTERS IN EDUCATION

In the past it has been difficult for those not familiar with computers to develop a clear perspective on the theme of computer delivered and/or managed reading instruction. During the past two decades (1960s and 1970s) plodding movement by mainframe and minicomputer users toward the potential of computer based reading instruction was mirrored by an equally plodding chronicling of the events. The shape and importance of the events were not easily definable by those unfamiliar with the computer. However, the heralded growth of the microcomputer has led to a plethora of reference resources which make it possible for everyone to acquire basic computer literacy. These resources now abound in books, journals, articles, and newsletters.

The reference resources annotated and listed in this chapter will allow those unfamiliar with the computer's potential to gain a clearer perspective and will provide those with previous computer experience some resources they may be unfamiliar with. The chapter includes references of a general nature on computer applications in education, a list of data-based bibliographic resources, and a list of book titles.

Annotated References

634. Barrett, B., & Hannafin, M. Computers in educational management: Merging accountability with technology. *Educational Technology*, 1982, *22*(3), 9-12.

The authors discuss eight factors that relate to CMI program accountability: curriculum continuity, systemization of content, individualization of instruction, neutralization of the clamoring public, withstanding the test of staff mobility, management of instruction, data-based instruction, and textbook and instructional material selection.

635. Bejar, I. Videodiscs in education. *BYTE*, 1982 *7*(6), 78-104.

Discusses state of the art developments in videodisc applications for education. Topics include: 1) choice of computers, 2) choice of videodisc player, 3) integrating computer and videodisc, 4) software issues, 5) courseware considerations, and 6) a list of vendors supplying interactive videodisc equipment.

636. Braun, L. Computer aided learning and the microcomputer revolution. *Programmed Learning and Educational Technology*, 1981, *18*(4), 223-228.

A review of microcomputer activities, including those in education.

637. Bylinsky, G., & Lane, Z. Wizard of Silicon Valley. *Omni*, 1979, *1*(11), 54-59.

Discusses the beginning of "Silicon Valley" (the home of semiconductors and microelectronics) and provides interviews with many of those involved in its development. Of historical importance to those interested in the beginnings of microcomputers.

638. Chambers, J.A., & Bork, A. Computer assisted learning in U.S. secondary/elementary schools, 1980. (ED 202 461)

Includes an introduction to computer assisted instruction as it has evolved in the public schools. The authors prepared a survey about computer assisted instruction and sent it to 974 school districts. Among the wealth of information gathered through the survey, it was found that 16 percent of CAI time was devoted to English, reading, or language arts and that most of these programs were drill and practice (50 percent). An interesting sidelight to the survey appears when the authors describe a conversation with Swinton (July 1980) of the Educational Testing Service who reports that PLATO showed positive math gains but just the opposite effect for reading achievement. A bibliography is included to support the authors' discussion.

639. Computer age in education: A special section. *Phi Delta Kappan*, 1982, *63*(5), 303-322.

Provides a special section in volume 63, number 5, on computers in education. The section forms an umbrella, covering many diverse points of view and activities concerning what has occurred, what is occurring, and what appears possible to occur in computers and education. A few of the titles include: The Silicon Age and Education; Bring the Microcomputer into the Junior High: A Success Story from Florida; and Instructional Computing in 2001: A Scenario. Few titles specifically relate to reading.

640. *Computers and the learning society.* Hearings before the Subcommittees on Domestic and International Scientific Planning, Analysis, and Cooperation of the Committee on Science and Technology, Report No. 47, 1978. (ED 162 643)

Noted authorities on computer applications gave testimonials on the efficacy of computers in society. Excellent reading for those interested in the history of computer applications in education.

641. Computers in the schools. *Educational Technology*, 1981, *21*(10), entire issue.

Selected articles include: "Education and the New Technology: A force of History," "Computer Managed Instruction System Implementation on a Microcomputer," and "The Intelligent Videodisc: An Instructional Tool for the Classroom."

642. Dickerson, L., & Pritchard, W. Microcomputers and education: Planning for the coming revolution in the classroom. *Educational Technology*, 1981, *21*(1), 7-12.

Warns of the need for computer literacy by teachers. Discusses the need for teacher training in computer literacy. The authors maintain "certain gaps" exist that must be filled before computer literacy training can be successful; namely, gaps between users and non-users and gaps between actual instructional uses and other uses.

643. Douglas, S., & Neights, G. Microcomputer reference: A guide to microcomputers. Microcomputers in Education Series, 1980. (ED 205 203)

Those interested in purchasing microcomputers for educational uses will find Microcomputers Reference of some help. Includes topics on: cost, flexibility, mainframe interface, keyboard layout, additional ports, execution time, loading speed, and memory capacity. Provides a glossary of terms as well as a list of computer organizations and periodicals.

644. Franz, F. Guide to microcomputers. Association for Educational Communications and Technology, Washington, D.C., 1980. (ED 192 818)

The Association for Educational Communication and Technology (AECT) provides a guide to microcomputer usage in education. The material, although dated, nonetheless provides the reader with background knowledge. The guide is lengthy (159 pages) and contains sections on: An Inside Look at Microcomputers; Computer Languages for Microcomputers; Disk Operating Systems and What They Can Do for You; What's in a Microcomputer System?; Special Accessories: State of the Art; Service and Maintenance; CAI Languages; CMI Systems; Graphics and Futureworld: CAI; Timesharing and Resource Sharing on Microcomputers; Potential Instructional and Media Center Application; Microcomputers in Education; Special Applications: Electronic Mail Networks and Videodiscs; Resources and Journals and Magazines; Resources: Languages, Disk Operating Systems, Editor/Assemblers and Utilities; and Resources: Books, Available Program Guides and Sources of Educational Programs.

645. Geoffrion, L.D. Holistic approaches to language remediation. *World yearbook of education, 1982: Computers in education.* (Leo D. Geoffrion, Department of Reading, State University of New York, Albany, New York 12222.)

Explores computer based language development, including reading development, with handicapped students. The Edison Responsive Environment, (ARIS, LOGO, Process Approach to Writing [with a word processor]), DAVID based caption programs, and communication networks are topics of discussion.

646. Gleason, G. Microcomputers in education: The state of the art. *Edu-*

cational Technology, 1981, *21*(3), 7-18.
The article reviews the extent of CAI involvement in education up to January 1981. The information provides historical background.

647. Gold, J. New technology partners: Video and computers. *Personal Computing*, 1982, *6*(4), 64-70.
Video and computers appear to offer much for education. The article discusses the future of a partnership between video and computers with specific applications in education.

648. Hall, K. Computer based education. *The best of ERIC, June 1976-August 1980*. (ED 195 288)
The 96-page ERIC document reviews most computer based programs of 1976 including both those in reading and those related to reading.

649. Hinton, J. Individualized learning using microcomputer CAI. 1980. (ED 196 409)
Focuses on a review of microcomputer uses in individualized instruction. No specific reading applications are included. An extensive bibliography on individualized learning and computers is provided.

650. Luehrmann, A. Planning for computer education—problems and opportunities for administrators. *NASSP Bulletin*, 1981, *64*(444), 62-69.
Discusses practical issues of starting a laboratory course in computing. (Who will teach the course? What department does the course belong in? What other courses should give way to make room for this one? Is there a ready-made curriculum for the computer course?) Also discusses such questions as: What is computer education? What goes on in a course in computing? Added cost versus added value.

651. Mathews, J. Microcomputer vs. minicomputer for educational computing. *Educational Technology*, 1978, *18*(11), 19-22.
Although somewhat dated, this still-important article explains differences between the instructional uses of microcomputers and minicomputers.

652. Miller, G. *Automated dictionaries, reading and writing.* Chairperson's report of a conference on educational uses of word processors with dictionaries, 1979. (ED 189 624)
Represents a summary of a conference on word processing (WP) and automated dictionaries (AD) held by the National Institute of Education. Discusses goals for WP/AD investigations, technical implementations, scientific bases and recommendations in an educational setting featuring reading and writing: A hand-held computer could serve as an AD using the commands DEFINE for the most common definition, and EXPAND for more definitions. Taken a step further in size, a videodisc could supply illustrations and other graphics that support many word meanings. Recommends more research on ways to develop and implement WP and AD projects in writing and reading. Also discusses ways to avoid the classic problems of introducing technology into the public schools: 1) devices promoted before educational need; 2) too complicated or expensive;

3) similar to other technologies tried, that have failed; and 4) technical difficulties.

653. Orlansky, J., & String, J. *Cost-effectiveness of computer based instruction in military training.* IDA paper P-1375. Arlington, Virginia: Institute for Defense Analysis, 1979.
Reviews 30 studies covering 18 years of CAI use in military training. Concludes that CAI saved time, caused no greater attrition and produced no learning differences.

654. Roberts, L.G. Overcoming barriers: Schools enter the computer age. *Proceedings of the fourth international learning technology conference and exposition, volume II: Videodisc, microcomputer, and system technologies in education and training.* Warrenton, Virginia: Society for Advanced Learning Technology, 1982.
Describes computer entry into schools as a grassroots phenomenon. Says May 1982 survey showed doubling of number of microcomputers in schools in 12 months. Provides seven "snapshots" of school programs using computers. Maintains implementation will be determined by expertise, imagination, vision, and common sense of educators.

655. Smith, L. Microcomputers in education. *AEDS Monitor*, 1979, *18*(4, 5, 6), 18-20.
Author provides an in-depth presentation on the history of microcomputer development, including discussions on the early leaders in the field.

656. Van Dusseldorp, R., & Spuck, D. (Eds.). Microcomputers: The selection and application in education. *AEDS Journal*, 1979, *13*(1), entire issue.
Contains eleven articles arranged around four sections: microcomputers in education, selecting a microcomputer, software development, and microcomputer applications.

657. Walker, R.J. An update on computers in the classroom, 1980. (ED 203 849)
A general overview on the development of computers in education, stressing the need for computer literacy amongst all students. Devotes special attention to mainframe and microcomputer applications with visually and hearing impaired students. Some of the special education computer programs described are: Gallaudet College, Washington, D.C.; Bernard M. Baruch College; City University of New York; Learning Center for Deaf Children, Farmington, Massachusetts; School for the Deaf, Randolph, Massachusetts; Clark School for the Deaf, Boston, Massachusetts; and California School for the Deaf, Berkeley, California. Includes lengthy bibliography.

Additional References

658. Grady, D. A hard look at the world of educational computing. *Personal Computing*, 1982, *6*(8), 40-44.

659. Leiblum, M. Computer managed instruction: An explanation and overview. *AEDS Journal*, 1982, *15*(3), 126-142.

660. Micro market booming in Florida. *Electronic Education*, 1981, *1*(2), 15.

661. Nation's schools going computers. *Electronic Education*, 1981, *1*(2), 28.
662. *Student use of computers in schools.* Washington, D.C.: National Center for Educational Statistics, 1981.

Sources on Computers in Education

Annotated References

663. *Resources in Computer Education* (RICE)
Available from the Northwest Regional Educational Laboratory through MicroSift. Five data bases (categories) of information are available: producers of computer based software, software packages, computer literacy, hardware applications, and research. Abstracts and bibliographic information are included.

664. *Microcomputer Index* (File 233)
Available from Dialog Information Services. Articles about microcomputers (from 21 computer sources) are abstracted and bibliographic information provided.

665. *Man-Computer Interaction*
Available from the University of Sheffield, Biomedical Information Service, University Arts Tower, Sheffield S10 2TN, England. Covers international references on topics related to man-computer interactions. Abstracts and bibliographic information are included.

Books

666. Baker, F. *Computer managed instruction: Theory and practice.* Englewood Cliffs, New Jersey: Educational Technology Publications, 1978.
667. Belzer, J.; Holzman, A.; & Kent, A. (Eds.). *Encyclopedia of computer science & technology.* New York: Marcel Dekker, 1975.
668. Billings, K., & Moursund, D. *Are you computer literate?* Beaverton, Oregon: Dilithium, 1979.
669. Bork, A. *Learning with computers.* Bedford, Massachusetts: Digital Press, 1981.
670. Burke, R. *CAI Sourcebook.* Englewood Cliffs, New Jersey: Prentice Hall, 1982.
671. Burton, P. *A dictionary of microcomputing.* New York: Barland, 1976.
672. Doer, C. *Microcomputers and the 3Rs.* Rochelle Park, New Jersey: Hayden, 1979.
673. Ellis, A. *The use and misuse of computers in education.* New York: McGraw-Hill, 1974.
674. Evans, C. *The micro millenium.* New York: Viking, 1979.
675. Evans, C. *The making of the micro: A history of the computer.* New York: Van Nostrand Reinhold, 1980.
676. Griffin, H. *A byte of computer literacy* (teacher's manual). Ocala, Florida: Marion County School Board, 1980. (mimeo, ringbound)
677. Horn, C., & Poirot, J. *Computer literacy problem solving with computers.* Austin, Texas: Sterling Swift, 1981.

678. Howe, J., & Ross, P. *Microcomputers in secondary education: Issues and techniques.* New York: Nichols Publishing, 1981.
679. Joiner, L.; Vensel, G.; Ross, J.; & Silverstein, B. *Microcomputers in education.* Holmes Beach, Florida: Learning Publications, 1981.
680. McCabe, D. (Ed.). *PCC's reference book of personal and home computing.* Menlo Park, California: People's Computing Company, 1977.
681. Northwest Regional Educational Laboratory. *Computer applications in instruction.* Hanover, New Hampshire: Time Share, 1978.
682. O'Neil, H. (Ed.). *Issues in instructional systems development.* New York: Academic Press, 1979.
683. Papert, S. *Mindstorms: Children, computers, and powerful ideas.* New York: Basic Books, 1980.
684. Ralston, A., & Meek, C. (Eds.). *Encyclopedia of computer science.* New York: Petrocelli/Charter, 1976.
685. Schneiderman, B. *Software psychology: Human factors in computer information systems.* Cambridge, Massachusetts: Winthrop, 1980.
686. Seidel, R. (Ed.). *Computer literacy.* New York: Academic Press, 1981.
687. Shelly, G., & Cashman, T. *Introduction to computers and data processing.* Fullerton, California: Anaheim Publishing, 1981.
688. Taylor, R. (Ed.). *The computer in the school: Tutor, tool, tutee.* New York: Teachers College Press, 1980.
689. Thomas, J. (Ed.). *Microcomputers in the schools.* Phoenix, Arizona: Oryx Press, 1981.
690. Weinberg, G. *The psychology of computer programming.* New York: Van Nostrand Reinhold, 1971.
691. Wilson, H., & Atkinson, R. *Computer assisted instruction—A book of readings.* New York: Academic Press, 1969.
692. Winston, P., & Brown, R. (Eds.). *Artificial intelligence: An MIT perspective*, vols. I, II. Cambridge, Massachusetts: MIT Press, 1982.

Chapter 9

SOFTWARE

Part One: INSTRUCTIONAL SOFTWARE

There has been an explosive growth in the quantity of instructional microcomputer software for reading. From a few programs in the late seventies, there are now over a hundred different computer programs designed for reading instruction. One would assume from such growth that a corresponding growth in the quality of reading software had occurred. Such an assumption, however, would be exceedingly optimistic, given the current state of reading software. Despite an enormous increase in the number of programs in the marketplace, the vast majority of language arts computer programs are still of the drill and practice variety, designed only to teach basic vocabulary and spelling. There have been some advances, particularly in the use of graphics and animation. Also, there is a trend toward making programs more reliable and easy to use. Nonetheless, few truly innovative instructional programs for reading have been developed since 1978.

The overemphasis on drill and practice modes of programing can be traced to a number of practical problems in developing microcomputer software. One limitation has been memory. Programs which are tutorial in nature use a great deal of instructional branching. This generally tends to require a lot of memory. This does not mean that such programs are impossible to design with microcomputers (some social studies programs are excellent examples of branched tutorial instruction), but these types of programs require great expertise in order to make them operate within the memory limitations of most microcomputers. Hardware limitations, though, are only a small part of the problem. The plethora of dull, noninnovative programs is primarily attributable to the fact that tutorial, simulation, and problem solving programs are usually more complex and thus tend to take much longer to design, program, and test. Even those publishers already established in educational publishing have been reluctant to risk the kind of capital and manpower required to develop expensive programs in a risky market that only recently has come into being.

Bleak though the existing picture may be, the horizon appears to be a great deal brighter. As more and more microcomputers take their places in schools and homes, there will be a compelling economic incentive for software publishers to design programs for them. Those major educational publishing firms that have already taken the plunge into this new market have learned first hand the pitfalls and profits of the software industry. There is every reason to believe that both they and their consumers will profit from their experiences. Finally, recent developments in microcomputer hardware, such as the creation of the low cost 16 bit microcomputer and the intelligible speech synthesizer, may lead the way to better instructional applications for reading.

Below is the most up-to-date listing of software we could acquire. By the time of publication it will already be somewhat outdated. Such are the rapidly changing times in which we live. For more current information you may wish to consult the software directories discussed in the next section. The majority of the programs listed will work with only one brand of microcomputer. However, this is rapidly changing as well. Many publishers are now taking the approach of designing software for a variety of computers. Therefore, a program which right now may exist only for the Apple, soon may be converted to run on an Atari, Pet, TRS-80, Sinclair, or other micro. If one is already limited to one type of hardware, call the publisher for up-to-date information about which hardware their software will run on.

INSTRUCTIONAL SOFTWARE PUBLISHERS

Adventure International
Box 3435
Longwood, FL 32750
- DRAGON OF HONG KONG
- LOCAL CALL FOR DEATH

American Educational Computer, Inc.
525 University Avenue
Suite 1400
Palo Alto, CA 94303
(415) 324-2811
- READING PROGRAM

Apple
10260 Bandley Dr.
Cuppentino, CA 95014
(408) 966-1010
- ELEMENTARY MY DEAR APPLE
- SPEED READER

ATARI
1265 Borregas Avenue
Sunnyvale, CA 94086
- TALK AND TEACH SERIES
  - GREAT CLASSICS
- KINGDOM
- HANGMAN

BLS
2501 Silverside Road, Suite One
Wilmington, Delaware 19810
(302) 478-2451
READING COMPREHENSION COURSE: 3-4
READING COMPREHENSION COURSE: 5-6

Borg-Warner Educational Systems
600 West University Drive
Arlington Heights, IL 60004
(312) 394-1010
CRITICAL READING
WORD STRUCTURE
COLLEGE ENTRANCE EXAMINATION PREPARATION
Part 1: The Verbal Series
Part 2: The Verbal Strategies/Mathematics Series
MICRO SYSTEM 80: SENTENCE STRUCTURE

Brain Box
601 West 26 Street
New York, NY 10001
(212) 989-3573
READING SKILLS
FOUR BASIC READING SKILLS
WORD ELEMENTS: SERIES 1-6

Computer Courseware Services
Div. of EMC Publishing
330 York Ave.
St. Paul, MN 55101
(800) 328-1452
BASIC SKILLS PRACTICE A-D
READING IS REWARDING

Computer Curriculum Corporation
P.O. Box 10080
Palo Alto, CA 94303
(800) 227-8324
AUDIO READING
BASIC READING
BASIC SENTENCES
CRITICAL READING SKILLS
READING
READING FOR COMPREHENSION

Computer Station
12 Crossroads Plaza
Granite City, IL 62040
(618) 452-1860
WORD FUN-THE DEFINITION GAME

Creative Computing Software
P.O. Box 789-M
Morristown, NJ 07960
SENSATIONAL SIMULATIONS
READING COMPREHENSION

Creative Curriculum, Inc.
Computer Courseware Division
15632 Producer Lane
Huntington Beach, CA 92649
(800) 854-2443
STEPS TO ADVANCED READING: SPEED READING COURSEWARE

Data Command
670 W. Broadway
Bradley, IL 60915
BIG DOOR DEAL
TANK TACTICS
RIDDLE ME THIS
TENNIS ANYONE
ALPINE SKIER
PIK-PEK-PUT

Dorsett Educational Systems
Box 1226
Norman, OK 73070
AB
CD
READING BY PHONICS
READING COMPREHENSION
GREAT CLASSICS
T, U, V, W, X, Y, Z

Dr. Daley
425 Grove Avenue
Berrien Springs, MI 49103
(616) 471-5514
DR. DALEY'S BEST SOFTWARE

Dynacomp
425 Rippingale Road
Pittsford, N.Y. 14534
TEACHERS PET I

Educational Activities
Microcomputer Department
P.O. Box 392
Freeport, NY 11520

DIASCRIPTIVE READING

Educational Activities, Inc.
1937 Grand Avenue
Baldwin, NY 11510
(516) 223-4666

CRITICAL READING PROGRAM: READING WITH CRITICAL UNDERSTANDING
ENGLISH BASICS—CONCEPTS IN LANGUAGE ARTS
HOW TO READ IN THE CONTENT AREAS
LITERAL COMPREHENSION PROGRAM: READING WITH UNDERSTANDING
OUR WEIRD AND WACKY WORLD
READ AND SOLVE PROBLEMS
SCRAMBLED LETTERS
CRYPTO

Edutek Corporation
415 Cambridge #14
Palo Alto, CA 94306
(415) 325-9965

SYLLABICATION
BASIC READING SKILLS
MAIN IDEA
PICNIC

EDU-Ware Services, Inc.
22222 Sherman Way, Suite 102
Conoga Park, CA 91303
(213) 346-6783

PERCEPTION
COMPU-READ
PSAT AND SAT WORD ATTACK SKILLS

Eisi
2225 Grant Road
Los Altos, CA 94022

READING COMPREHENSION

George Earl
1302 S. General McMullen
San Antonio, TX 78237

ALICIA—A BILINGUAL READER
MOTHER GOOSE RHYMES
READINGS IN LITERATURE

Harcourt Brace Jovanovich, School Dept.
757 Third Avenue
New York, NY 10017
(212) 888-4433

HBJ BOOKMARK READING PROGRAM: EAGLE EDITION

Hartley Courseware, Inc.
P.O. Box 431
Dimondale, Michigan 48821
(616) 942-8987

VOWELS
CONSONANTS
VOCABULARY—ELEMENTARY
VOCABULARY—DOLCH
LETTER RECOGNITION
MULTIPLE SKILLS
OPPOSITES
WORD FAMILIES
ROOTS/AFFIXES
HOMONYMS
ANTONYMS/SYNONYMS
WHO, WHAT, WHERE, WHEN, WHY
WORD FAMILIES

Instant Software
Peterborough, NH 03458
(603) 924-7296

VIDEO SPEED READING TRAINER
WORDWATCH

Instructional/Communication Technology, Inc.
10 Stepar Place
Huntington Station, NY 11746

COMPREHENSION POWER PROGRAM

Instructional Development Systems (IDS)
2927 Virginia Beach Boulevard
Virginia Beach, VA 23452
(804) 340-1977

ASSISTED INSTRUCTIONAL DEVELOPMENT SYSTEMS (AIDS)

International Software Marketing
120 E. Washington Street
Suite 421, University Building
Syracuse, NY 13202
(315) 474-3400
PRISM

Krell Software
21 Milbrook Drive
Stony Brook, NY 11790
WORD RELATIONSHIPS

Learning Well
200 South Service Road
Roslyn Heights, NY 11577
(516) 621-1540
CAUSE AND EFFECT COMPUTER GAME
DRAWING CONCLUSIONS COMPUTER GAME
FACT OR OPINION COMPUTER GAME
GETTING THE MAIN IDEA COMPUTER GAME
INFERENCE COMPUTER GAME
READING FOR DETAIL
SEQUENCE COMPUTER GAME

Little Bee Educational Programs
P.O Box 262
Massillon, OH 44648
(216) 832-4097
LONG/SHORT VOWEL SPACE SHIPS

Micro-ed
P.O Box 24156
Minneapolis, MN 55424
CAPITALIZATION SERIES
HAIKU
WORD DEMONS
VOCABULARY
READING
REFERENCE SKILLS

Micro Learningware
P.O. Box 2134
North Mankato, MN 56001
WORD SCRAMBLE
SPEED READER
HANGMAN
NAME THAT LETTER
WORD PUZZLE

Micro Power & Light Co.
12820 Hillcrest Road, Suite 224
Dallas, TX 75230
(214) 239-6620
WORD PREP

Microcomputer Workshops Corporation
103 Puritan Drive
Port Chester, NY 10573
(914) 937-5440
CONSONANT-VOWEL-CONSONANT

Microcomputers Corporation
P.O. Box 8
34 Maple Avenue
Armonk, NY 10504
(914) 273-6480
CONSONANT BLEND BULL'S-EYE
PHONICS
FINAL CONSONANT AND WORD FAMILY BINGO
TIC-TAC-TOE (VOWELS)

Micrograms Inc.
P.O. Box 2146
Loves Park, IL 61130
(815) 965-2464
MR. READWELL
SEQUENCING SAM
VOCABULARY
VOCABULARY CROSSWORDS

Micromatics, Inc.
181 N. 200 West
Suite 5
Bountiful, UT 84010
MICRO-EDUCATIONAL TEACHING SYSTEM

Microphys Programs
2048 Ford Street
Brooklyn, NY 11229
VOCABULARY PROGRAMS
SENIOR AND JUNIOR HIGH VOCABULARY DISKETTE

Milliken Publishing Co.
1100 Research Blvd.
St. Louis, Missouri 63132
(314) 991-4220
- MILLIKEN LANGUAGE ARTS
- READING COMPREHENSION

Milton Bradley Company
443 Shaker Road
East Long Meadow, MA 01101
(413) 525-6411
- VOCABULARY SKILLS: CONTEXT CLUES
- VOCABULARY SKILLS: PREFIXES, SUFFIXES, ROOT WORDS

Minnesota Educational Computing Consortium (MECC)
2520 Broadway Drive
St. Paul, MN 55113
(612) 376-1118
- ELEMENTARY—VOLUMES 2, 5, 7, 11, & 12
- SPECIAL NEEDS—VOLUMES 1 & 2
- SCHOOL UTILITIES—VOLUME 2
- TEACHER UTILITIES—VOLUME 1

Orange Cherry Media
7 Delano Drive
Bedford Hills, NY 10507
(914) 666-8434
- ACTIVE READER—WORLD OF NATURE SERIES
- THE CLOZE TECHNIQUE FOR DEVELOPING COMPREHENSION
- ADVENTURES AROUND THE WORLD
- STRANGE ENCOUNTERS: YOU DECIDE
- WORD FACTORY
- WORKING WITH THE ALPHABET
- VOCABULARY BUILDERS

Powersoft, Inc.
P.O Box 157
Pitman, NJ 08701
(609) 589-5500
- PERQUACKY

Program Design, Inc.
11 Idar Court
Greenwich, CT 06830
(203) 661-8799
- ANALOGIES
- ASTRO QUOTES
- MINICROSSWORD
- READING COMPREHENSION: WHAT'S DIFFERENT
- STORY BUILDER
- SPELLING BUILDER
- VOCABULARY BUILDER 1: BEGINNING
- VOCABULARY BUILDER 2: ADVANCED
- TIME BOMB
- WORD SKILLS 1: PREFIXES

Psychological Corporation
757 Third Avenue
New York, NY 10017
(203) 355-3452
- READING 1 AND 2

Radio Shack
1300 One Tandy Center
Fort Worth, TX 76102
- HIGH MOTIVATION READING SERIES
- ALPHAKEY
- PHILADELPHIA C.A.R.D. READING PROGRAM
- SHOW AND SPELL
- VOCABULARY TUTOR

Random House School Division
Department 985, Suite 201
2970 Brandywine Road
Atlanta, Georgia 30341
(800) 241-6402
- ALPHABET, SEQUENCE, AND ALPHABETIZING
- CUSTOMIZED ALPHABET DRILL
- HOMONYMS IN CONTEXT
- TUTORIAL PHONICS AND WORD ATTACK
- TUTORPROGRAM: FOLLOWING DIRECTIONS
- TUTORPROGRAM: INFERENCES
- TUTORPROGRAM: READING INTERPRETATIONS 1
- WORD BLASTER
- STORY BUILDER
- STORY STARTER

Readers Digest Services, Inc.
Educational Division
Pleasantville, NY 10570
(914) 769-9000

- THE CHAMBERS OF VOCAB
- KEY LINGO
- TRICKSTER COYOTE

Right On Programs
Computeam, Inc.
P.O. Box 977
Huntington, NY 11743
(516) 271-3177

- A BATCH OF ENDINGS
- ANTONYMS
- DEFINITIONS
- THE END OF ENDINGS
- EYTMOLOGY
- GLOSSARY OF USAGE
- HEARING THE HOMONYMS
- SEQUENCE AND LOGIC IN STORYTELLING
- SYNONYMS
- WORD CATEGORIES
- WORD RELATIONSHIPS

Scholastic
904 Sylvan Avenue
Englewood Cliffs, NJ 07132

- VOCABULARY BUILDER I, II
- SENTENCE COMPLETION
- ALPHABET/GUESS THE NUMBER/ REVERSE
- SCRAMBLE
- COMPU-READ
- STORY BUILDER/WORD MASTER
- WORD FAMILIES
- LETTER RECOGNITION
- LONG/SHORT VOWEL SPACESHIPS
- WORD SCRAMBLE
- MISSING LETTER
- POETRY WRITING
- READING COMPREHENSION: WHAT'S DIFFERENT
- EARLY LEARNING FUN
- UPPER/LOWER CASE MATCHING
- VOCABULARY 12th GRADE
- ANTONYMS
- THE HOMONYM MACHINE
- BLASTOFF
- ALPHABETIZING
- BOOKSHELF

Science Research Associates (SRA)
155 N. Wacker Drive
Chicago, IL 60606
(800) 621-0644

- CROSS CLUES
- PHONICS
- WORDSKILL FOR THE MICROCOMPUTER

Scott, Foresman and Company
1900 East Lake Avenue
Glenview, IL 60025

- SPEAK & READ MODULES

Sliwa Enterprises
P.O.Box 400
Big Flats, NY 14814
(607) 562-3287

- VOCABULARY BUILDER
- WORD ANALOGY
- VERBAL SKILLS PAK

Softogon
P.O. Box 774
Morristown, NJ 07960
(210) 539-3770

- MY ABC'S
- NOW I CAN RHYME

Softswap
333 Main Street
Redwood City, CA 94063

- CINQUAIN
- SPEED READ
- HANGMAN
- WORD LADDER
- PET, PIT, PUT, POT
- COMPUTER POETRY
- BART
- CRUSHMAN
- SCRAMBLED WORD
- TACHISTOSCOPE
- WORD HUNT

Special Delivery Software
Apple Computer, Inc.
20525 Mariani Avenue
Cupertino, CA 95014
(408) 996-1010
- MAGIC SPELLS
- SPEED READER

Sunburst Communications
39 Washington Avenue
Pleasantville, NY 10570
(800) 431-1934
- MICRO SKILLBUILDER SET II:
  - HI/LO NEWBERY
- NEWBERY WINNERS

Teaching Tools
P.O. Box 50065
Palo Alto, CA 94303
- MATCHING GAME
- LETTERS AND NUMBERS

Texas Instruments
P.O. Box 10508
Lubbock, TX 79408
- EARLY LEARNING FUN
- BEGINNING GRAMMAR

T.H.E.S.I.S.
P.O. Box 147
Garden City, MI 48135
(313) 595-4722
- FISHING FOR HOMONYMS
- WORD SCRAMBLE
- WORDMATE

Total Information Educational Systems (TIES)
1925 W. County Road B2
Roseville, MN 55113
(612) 633-9110
- ELECTRIC ENGLISH
  - PARTS OF SPEECH
  - PHRASES, CLAUSES AND SENTENCES
  - PUNCTUATION
- QUESTION/ANSWER AND VOCABULARY FACILTIES
- WORD WISE
  - BASAL SERIES 1
  - BASAL SERIES 2
  - BASAL SERIES 3

TSE (The Software Exchange)
Box 68
Midford, NH 03055
- CHALLENGE
- HIS MAJESTY'S SHIP IMPETUOUS
- TWO HEADS OF THE COIN
- SIX MICRO STORIES
- NINE GAMES FOR PRESCHOOLERS

Tycom Associates
68 Velma Avenue
Pittsfield, MA 01201
- VOCAB

UNICOM
297 Elmwood Avenue
Providence, RI 02907
(401) 467-5600
- LANGUAGE/READING DEVELOPMENT PROGRAM

Universal Systems for Education, Inc.
2120-E Academy Circle
Colorado Springs, CO 80909
(303) 574-4575
- PAL PLACEMENT TEST
- PAL READING CURRICULUM SERIES

Part Two: THE INSTRUCTIONAL USE OF NONINSTRUCTIONAL SOFTWARE

It seems somewhat absurd at first, but it may well be that some of the best instructional software for reading is software that was not designed for the purpose of instruction at all. If you consider that the primary activity in the operation of nearly any computer program is reading (reading instructions, reading data, reading output), then the possibilities may be a little more apparent. Consider also that the microcomputer may be the greatest tool ever devised for the manipulation and generation of words. The processing of words (*word processing*) has become the primary motivating force behind the implementation of computers in modern society. With computers one can take any piece of text completely apart, restructure sentences, search for key words, and phrase and rephrase thoughts ad infinitum, all with relative ease. Surely, in the hands of a reading specialist such a tool could be used for the purpose of instruction.

Though modern word processing software is a tremendously powerful tool for reading instruction, to date there has been only a minimal attempt to apply such software to the task of reading instruction. This is not to say that such an application is not possible. Think for instance of the frequently used beginning reading method usually referred to as the *language experience approach.* One of the primary weaknesses in this method is the inordinate amount of time required for a teacher to type and edit individual or class compositions. With word processing software, this time could be more than cut in half. Moreover, the ease with which one can edit text using a word processor would make the rewriting and updating of diaries and class stories simple and unintimidating.

Other types of software may prove equally useful to the reading instructor. For example, discoveries of the past decade in the area of cognitive psychology such as schema theory, have shown us the importance of such skills as categorizing and sequencing. What better way to practice these skills than with simple data base software. The entire purpose of such software is to organize and categorize information. In the hands of a knowledgeable teacher such software could provide a new and exciting avenue for approaching the teaching of these skills.

The point to be made here is that it is the teacher, not the software that is the primary determiner of the success of most computer programs. Programs that were never intended for reading instruction can, with the aid of a talented instructor, be adapted to fill a variety of educational needs. Word processing software and data base software are but two examples of this. Surely others exist.

Listed below are several of the most popular word processing and data base programs for microcomputers. Many others can be found in the software directories previously listed. This particular type of software, because it was designed for business, tends to be some of the finest quality software currently available. It will prove invaluable to any instructor when used for its intended purpose. (Try typing your next letter to a parent on a word processor and see the difference it makes.) It can also prove exceedingly valuable when used for another worthy purpose, reading instruction.

SOME NONINSTRUCTIONAL SOFTWARE THAT CAN BE USED FOR INSTRUCTION

Word Processing Software

APPLE PIE 2.0
Hayden/Programma
50 Essex Street
Rochelle Park, NJ 07662
(800) 631-0856

APPLE WRITER
Apple Computer Co.
10260 Brandley Drive
Cupertino, CA 95014
(800) 538-8400

EASYWRITER VERSION 2
Captain Software
P.O. Box 575
San Francisco, CA
(415) 841-6500

EXECUTIVE SECRETARY
Personal Business Systems
4306 Upton Avenue South
Minneapolis, MN 55410
(612) 770-6161

MAGIC WAND
Retail Sciences, Inc.
Suite 700 Corporate Square
Atlanta, GA 30329
(800) 241-3649

MAGIC WINDOW
Softape
10432 Burbank Blvd.
North Hollywood, CA 91601
(213) 985-5763

SUPERSCRIBE
On-Line Systems
36575 Mudge Ranch Road
Coarsegold, CA 93614
(209) 683-6858

SUPER-TEXT VERSION 2
The Muse Company
330 N. Charles Street
Baltimore, MD 21201
(301) 659-7212

WORD POWER
Systems Design Lab
2612 Artesia Blvd.
Redondo Beach, CA 90278
(213) 374-4471

WORDSTAR
MicroPro International Corp.
1299 4th Street
San Rafael, CA 94901
(415) 457-8990

WRITE ON!
Datamost
19273 Kenya Street
Northridge, CA 91326
(213) 366-7160

Data Base Systems

DATADEX
Information Unlimited Software
281 Arlington Avenue
Berkeley, CA 94707
(415) 525-9452

DATA FACTORY
Micro Lab
2310 Skokie Valley Road
Highland Park, IL 60035
(312) 433-7550

DB MASTER
Stoneware
50 Belvedere Street
San Rafael, CA 94901
(415) 454-6500

INFORMATION MASTER
High Technology, Inc.
P.O. Box B-14665
8001 N. Classen Blvd.
Oklahoma City, OK 73106
(405) 840-9900

THE MODIFIABLE DATABASE
Synergistic Software
5221 120th Avenue, S.E.
Bellevue, WA 98006
(206) 226-3216

PFS: PERSONAL FILING SYSTEM
Software Publishing Company
2021 E. Landings Drive
Mountain View, CA 94043
(415) 962-8911

VISIDEX
VISIFILE
Personal Software
1330 Bordeaux Drive
Sunnyvale, CA 94086
(408) 745-7841

Part Three: SOFTWARE DIRECTORIES

One of the best tools the teacher has in winding the path through the maze of computer software that is now available is a new type of book called a software directory. Software directorics are essentially large catalogs describing software from a variety of companies and often providing information on the price of the software as well as the name and address of the publisher. Early software directories, such as *Skarbek's* covered software of all kinds, not just educational software, for most of the major microcomputers. More recent directories, such as the *Sterling Swift Educational Software Directory*, are devoted specifically to educational software, sometimes for only one brand of computer. The more complete directories break down computer programs according to educational subject area and level such as Elementary Language Arts. By using the indexes in these directories it is possible to reduce the time required to locate and evaluate software to a fraction of what it would be without the directory.

As with anything else involving software, directories must be approached with a note of caution. Even those which attempt to update their listings annually can quickly become outdated, especially for information on price. Also, in a few cases, the evaluations or descriptions are taken directly from the publisher's promotional literature. Finally, a number of publishers have been known to list software which in reality is still in the development stage. The teacher may request the material only to find it has not been released yet. Most of these shortcomings can be avoided by consulting more than one directory when investigating software. Overall, the directories are the best starting point for the teacher who wants to find out what software is available.

SOME CURRENT SOFTWARE DIRECTORIES

THE APPLE II BLUE BOOK
THE APPLE SOFTWARE DIRECTORY: EDUCATION
Visual Materials, Inc.
P.O. Box 504
Gurnee, IL 60031

APPLESEED
Software Publications
6 South St.
Milford, NH 03055

THE BOOK OF APPLE COMPUTER SOFTWARE 1982
The Book Co.
16720 Hawthorne Blvd.
Lawndale, CA 90260
(213) 371-4012

EDUCATIONAL SOFTWARE DIRECTORY
Sterling Swift Publishing Company
1600 Fortview Road
Austin, TX 78704
(Apple software only)

EDUCATOR'S HANDBOOK AND SOFTWARE DIRECTORY
Vital Information, Inc.
350 Union Station
Kansas City, MO 64108
(Apple software only)

THE ELECTRONIC LEARNING SOFTWARE DIRECTORY
Electronic Learning
1982, 1(5), 1a-10a

HUNTINGTON COMPUTING CATALOG
P.O. Box 787
Corcoran, CA 93212

INSTRUCTOR COMPUTER DIRECTORY FOR SCHOOLS
INSTRUCTOR Publications, Inc.
757 Third Avenue
New York, NY 10017

INTERNATIONAL MICROCOMPUTER SOFTWARE DIRECTORY
Imprint Software
420 South Howes St.
Fort Collins, CO 80521

MICROCOMPUTERS CORPORATION CATALOG
P.O. Box 191
Rye, NY 10580

QUEUE
5 Chapel Hill Drive
Fairfield, CT 06432

SCHOOL MICROWARE DIRECTORY
Dresden Associates
Dept. CCN
P.O. Box 246
Dresden, ME 04342

SKARBEK'S SOFTWARE DIRECTORY
11990 Dorsett Road
St. Louis, MO 63043

TRS-80 SOFTWARE DIRECTORY
Radio Shack
1600 One Tandy Center
Fort Worth, TX 76102

VANLOVE'S, 1982 APPLE II/III SOFTWARE DIRECTORY
Vital Information, Inc.
350 Union Station
Kansas City, MO 64108

Part Four: AUTHORING SYSTEMS and AUTHORING LANGUAGES

One of the reasons the use of computers in reading instruction has not yet been as productive as might be expected is that it has been difficult for teachers to make instructional computing an inherent part of the reading curriculum. Few publishers of traditional educational materials (such as basal readers) have made CAI materials an integral component in their instructional offerings. Even with the advent of microcomputers, the predominant use of computer technology has been in building management systems rather than in creating instructional courseware. At the same time, most of the software created by the smaller software firms has been rather limited in scope and has not been designed to meet instructional objectives consistent with basal reader systems. Consequently, teachers have often felt obligated to make or modify software to fit their needs.

Making and modifying software, however, is a far from simple task. A teacher might attempt to program the instruction from scratch, but high quality instructional computer programs take a great deal of time, effort, and skill to develop. A program that may provide only a few minutes of instruction may take literally months to develop, even by a skilled programer. The reality is that teachers have been trained to teach, not to design computer programs. Few have the necessary resources in terms of time, equipment, or training to take on major programing projects. It may seem that it would be easier to simply modify existing programs to meet the needs of particular students but this, too, is difficult. Most commercial software is electronically protected so that it can be altered or copied only with great difficulty. Furthermore, to do so would probably violate the software vendor's copyright. There are, however, certain types of programs which are designed so they CAN be modified. These programs provide an excellent alternative for the teacher who wishes to make the courseware fit the course being taught. These special types of programs are called authoring systems.

An *authoring system* is a type of computer program which is designed to allow the user to add or modify part of the content of the program, without actually having to do any computer programing. Educational authoring systems vary greatly in the amount of content which the teacher can add to the system and in the simplicity with which the input can be made. Many authoring systems are drill and practice vocabulary programs in which the teacher can enter in both word lists and instructions. The words then can be used by the computer for a game type drill such as "hangman" or "scramble," or simply be presented tachistiscopically. The teacher utility disks from MECC are an example of this type of system. Other authoring systems are a bit more sophisticated and allow the teacher to create more complete lessons by inserting graphics as well as text. The BLOCKS authoring system by Ted Perry and the Word Wise authoring system by TIES are examples of this type of authoring system. By using word lists and graphics which match the content of traditional reading materials such as basal readers or storybooks, these programs can be made to correspond precisely with the student's regular classroom materials. This makes it much easier for the teacher of reading to integrate the software into the reading curriculum.

Authoring systems offer a number of benefits to the teacher who may wish to fit more software into the curriculum, but who lacks knowledge of computer programing. Most of the well-designed authoring systems are relatively simple to use and can be mastered within a few hours. However, in order to gain simplicity, the systems quite intentionally sacrifice flexibility. If the teacher wishes to create simple drill and practice vocabulary lessons, even the simplest authoring system will do. However, if a teacher wishes to create something more complex, such as a customized tutorial lesson on the use of antonyms, most authoring systems would be unable to handle the job. This does not mean that the teacher must immediately abandon hope or break out the BASIC manual. There is one option left: an authoring language.

An *authoring language* is a computer language like BASIC or FORTRAN. However, it is a language which has been specifically designed for use by novices such as teachers or students who are unfamiliar with traditional programing. Authoring languages actually might be thought of as being on the easy end of programing language continuum. They are much simpler than assembly programing, a little simpler than BASIC, and some (such as LOGO) are so simple that a child can use them. Authoring languages, like authoring systems, vary greatly in terms of price and sophistication. One of the most popular authoring languages, PILOT, often can be obtained for under $100. Others, such as Bell & Howell's sophisticated PASS authoring language, may cost as much as $15,000.

Whether using an authoring system or an authoring language, one must keep in mind that either option involves considerably more time and effort than do traditional computer programs. It may be that one's educational objectives make such customizing of software essential. Nonetheless, it should probably be considered only if one has concluded that there is no traditional software that meets that particular need.

SOME AUTHORING SYSTEMS AND AUTHORING LANGUAGES

Apple Computer, Inc.
10260 Bandley Drive
Cupertino, CA 95014
(408) 996-1010
SHELL GAMES
APPLE PILOT
SUPERPILOT
SUPERPILOT LOG
APPLE LOGO

Atari, Inc.
1265 Borregas Avenue
P.O. Box 9027
Sunnyvale, CA 94086
ATARI PILOT

Automated Simulations, Inc.
P.O. Box 4247
Moutain View, CA 94040
(415) 964-8021
JABBERTALKY

Avant-Garde Creations
P.O. Box 30161
Eugune, OR 97403
(503) 345-3043
ZENITH EDUCATION SYSTEMS (Z.E.S.)

Bell & Howell
7100 McCormick Road
Chicago, IL 60645
(312) 673-3300
GENIS I (authoring system)
PASS (authoring language)

Minnesota Educational Computing Consortium (MECC)
2520 Broadway Drive
St. Paul, MN 55113
(612) 376-1118
TEACHER UTILITIES—VOLUMES 2, 3, & 4

Hartley Courseware, Inc.
P.O. Box 431
Dimondale, Michigan 48821
(616) 942-8987
CREATE YOUR OWN SERIES

Micro Lab
811 Stonegate Drive
Highland Park, IL 60035
THE LEARNING SYSTEM

MicroGnome, Fireside Computing, Inc.
5843 Montgomery Road
Elkridge, MD 21227
CAIWARE

Orange Cherry Media
7 Delano Drive
Bedford Hills, NY 10507
(914) 666-8434
BASIC LANGUAGE SKILLS

Micro Lab
811 Stonegate Drive
Highland Park, IL 60035
THE LEARNING SYSTEM

Roklan Corporation
10600 W. Higgins Road
Suite 200-i
Rosemont, IL 60018
EDUGRAMMAR

San Juan Unified School District
3738 Walnut Avenue
Carmichael, CA 95608
(916) 484-2011
BLOCKS II AUTHORING SYSTEM
THE GRAPHICS LIBRARY

Teck Associates
P.O. Box 8732
White Bear Lake, MN 55110
(612) 429-5570
E-Z PILOT

TIES
1925 W. County Road, B2
St. Paul, MN 55113
(612) 633-9110
QUESTION/ANSWER AND VOCABULARY FACILITIES
WORD WISE AUTHORING SYSTEM
BASAL READERS 1
BASAL READERS 2
BASAL READERS 3

Whitney Education Services
2701 Tenth Avenue
San Francisco, CA 94116
C.A.T.I. (Computer Assisted Television Instruction)

Annotated References

693. Eyster, R.H. Seymour Papert and the LOGO universe. *Creative Computing*, 1981, *7*(12), 70-74.
The author describes his impressions of a two week workshop held by Seymour Papert on the use of the LOGO computer language.

694. Gagne, R.M.; Wage, W.; & Rojas, A. Planning and authoring computer assisted instruction lessons. *Educational Technology*, 1981, *21*(9), 7-26.
Suggests that the guidelines provided for the users of computerized authoring systems will be more effective if they are based around the "nine different events of instruction": 1) gaining attention, 2) informing learner of lesson objective, 3) stimulating recall of prior learning, 4) presenting stimuli with distinctive features, 5) guiding learning, 6) eliciting performance, 7) providing informative feedback, 8) assessing performance, 9) enhancing retention and learning transfer. Provides a set of CAI guidelines based on these learning "events."

695. Kahn, T. *The advantage of PILOT as a design language for computer assisted instruction programs with microcomputers.* Paper presented at the University of Montana Computers in Education Conference, Missoula, Montana, March 1980.

Discusses the use of PILOT in early learning programs in Montessori schools.

696. Merrill, D. Doing it with authoring systems. *Educational Technology*, 1982, *22*(5), 36-38.

The author discusses the hierarchy of computer languages from machine code to the authoring language PILOT. He then compares this hierarchy to a hierarchy of educational and psychological theory. He concludes that both authoring languages and specific "instructional templates" are required for the development of true "authoring systems."

697. Scandura, J.M. Microcomputer systems for authoring, diagnosis, and instruction in rule based subject matter. *Educational Technology*, 1981, *21*(1), 13-19.

Author describes a system of task analysis which he calls "structural learning theory." He then relates this theory to his attempts to develop microcomputer based authoring systems. Scandura was one of those responsible for the development of the Borg Warner reading software.

698. Wagner, W.J. Author languages: Instruction without programing. *Classroom Computer News*, 1981, *1*(6), 42-43.

Defines what an authoring language is and provides brief descriptions of eight different authoring languages currently available.

699. Wise, W.S. Improving user/machine interaction. *AEDS Journal*, 1981, *15*(1), 23-30.

A discussion of educational concepts bearing on the ease of interaction between users and their computer programs. Concepts reviewed are "typographical cuing," "advanced organizers," "paced output," "contextual clues," and "conceptual hierarchies."

Additional References

700. Jelden, D.L. A CAI "coursewriter" system for the microcomputer. *AEDS Journal*, 1981, *44*(3), 17-26.

701. Spitler, C.D., & Corgan, V.E. Rules for authoring computer assisted instruction programs. *Educational Technology*, 1979, *19*(11), 12-20.

Part Five: SOFTWARE EVALUATION

Making judgments as to the quality of educational materials always has been difficult. In some ways, modern computerized materials may be even more difficult to evaluate because an adequate job of evaluating educational software (courseware) requires the evaluator or evaluation team to have classroom teaching experience, some expertise in curriculum design, and some knowledge of the technical aspects of computer programing. Such a combination of talents is rare. Consequently, few of the early evaluations of educational courseware succeeded in sufficiently analyzing all aspects of the materials. If a programer was given the task of evaluation, the software was often judged on the basis of its technical merits even if its educational value was suspect. Reviews performed by classroom teachers, while often educationally sound, frequently failed to take note of any technical breakthroughs or deficiencies present in the program.

The problem of evaluating software has been further hampered by the lack of standards common in any emerging field. Some standards from other areas could be applied, but only in a limited fashion. Many of the standards for evaluating textbooks often did not apply to the nonlinear programed materials or to the display environment of a cathode ray tube. In addition CAI materials contained a number of unique features, such as animation, for which no evaluation standards existed. Neither were standards for designing computer programs totally adequate. In instructional computer programs, factors such as sort time or calculation accuracy were often relatively unimportant, while factors such as formatting, readability, and error trapping could be much more critical than in other types of computer programs. Only recently have standards begun to emerge which allow for thorough evaluation of instructional software.

One of the major sources of these emerging standards has been the MicroSIFT Project. The MicroSIFT Project was started in 1978 through the Northwest Regional Educational Laboratory to deal with the task of developing and implementing a set of standards for evaluating educational software. The MicroSIFT staff has spent several years in developing and piloting a system for software evaluation at a national level. Two sets of evaluations have been released from MicroSIFT. The evaluations are based on a combination of observations by students, subject area classroom teachers, and software experts. They are some of the most thorough evaluations of educational software done to date.

A number of other educational agencies involved in developing software, such as MECC and CONDUIT, have developed evaluation forms of their own. In addition, software evaluations can be found in many of the new technologically oriented magazines such as Classroom Computer News, Creative Computing, Educational Technology, and Educational Computer. It would be wise to keep in mind when reading magazine software reviews, that some of the magazine's funds come directly from advertisements paid for by software publishers. This does not mean that they will give good reviews to poor software, though this has occurred. It does mean that commercial magazines may tend to avoid printing harsh reviews of software (even when justified) and may print only those reviews which are somewhat positive.

Annotated References

702. Anderson, R.E. Courseware deserves evaluation, including peer review. *AEDS Monitor*, 1982, *20*(10), 10.
Author presents a brief outline for reviewing software and suggests that the use of field observation and outside expert analysis are necessary if commercial software vendors are to avoid the development of unmarketable software.

703. Bardige, A. Hodge podge. *Classroom Computer News*, 1982, *2*(4), 45.
Generally favorable review of an educational, nonreading program for preschoolers.

704. Bejar, I.I. Show and spell from Radio Shack, *Creative Computing*, 1981, *7*(3), 22, 24.
Explains and criticizes this program.

705. Bingham, M. Software evaluation: A coordinated effort needed. *AEDS Monitor*, 1982, *20*(10), 11.
Another vote in favor of a national level unified system for software evaluation.

706. Brent, F. Ed tech product reviews: CAIWARE-2D. *Educational Technology*, 1982, *22*(4), 50-51.
A review of an educational authoring system by MicroGnome for the TRS-80. The author found the system to be powerful, but far too complex for most teachers to learn to use quickly. Publisher's response included.

707. Caputo, P. MicroSIFT: National network to evaluate software. *Classroom Computer News*, 1981, *1*(3), 3.
Short description of the objectives of the MicroSIFT Project.

708. Dawson, J., & Palmer, P. Milliken Power Program earns high marks. *Electronic Education*, 1982, *1*(6), 18-19.
A comprehensive CAI reading program designed to build comprehension in grades 4-12 is reviewed. Twenty-five skills are addressed by exercises consisting of stories followed by questions. There is also a management system.

709. Dean, Jay W. What's holding up the show? *Today's Education*, 1981, *71*(2), 22-25.
Claims the reason for lack of sound educational software is the lack of an easy-to-learn, easy-to-use computer language for teachers so that teachers can create software. Briefly discusses BASIC, PILOT, PASCAL, and LOGO.

710. Forman, D. Courseware evaluation for curriculum integration. *AEDS Monitor*, 1982, *20*(10), 7-9.
An excellent discussion of software evaluation from the broader perspective of integration within a designated curriculum and educational setting. Seven questions are discussed which help to

outline the nature of the classroom setting, the needs of the users, the instructional objectives, and the content of the software itself.

711. Garson, J.W. The case against multiple choice. *Computing Teacher*, 1980, *7*(4), 29-34.

Excellent discussion of weaknesses and strengths of drill and practice computer programs. The author suggests programs carry built-in systems to enable students to help authors in revising. Also suggests new forms of evaluation "at the terminal."

712. Goldberg, L. Ed tech product reviews: Comprehension Power Program. *Educational Technology*, 1982, *22*(5), 53-54.

A description and evaluation of the Comprehension Power Program by Instructional/Communications Technology. The courseware was rated good; the documentation, excellent.

713. Hilgenfeld, R. Checking out software. *Computing Teacher*, 1981, *8*(3), 24-27.

Explains and includes a software evaluation form used by Sweetwater County ISD in Wyoming.

714. Huntington, J.F. Ed tech product reviews: Big door deal. *Educational Technology*, 1981, *21*(11), 52-53.

A review of a game style reading package for the TRS-80. Author felt the graphics were well done but would grow redundant over time.

715. Jelden, D.L. The microcomputer as a multi-user interactive instructional system. AEDS *Journal*, 1981, *14*(4), 208-217.

Pages 212 and 213 give 17 guidelines for software development.

1. Content specified both in course objectives and terminal performance objectives.
2. Pace controlled by student.
3. Individual differences taken into account.
4. Extensive feedback made use of.
5. Branching and looping available.
6. Student evaluation built-in.
7. Student given knowledge of results.
8. Correct answers should be required before more complex instruction given.
9. Recyling should be possible.
10. 85 percent probable success.
11. Instructor assistance available.
12. Practical (hands-on) as much as possible.
13. Verbal integrated with practical.
14. Major portion should be CAI, only if it is more economical than other ways.
15. Liberal use of graphics.
16. Vocabulary controlled (FOG gr 10 or below).
17. No more than three frames before call for response.

716. Jostad, K. Search for software. *AEDS Monitor*, 1982, *20*(10), 25-27.

Jostad discusses different options available for obtaining and evaluating software prior to making a purchase decision. Includes a brief list of magazines which publish reviews, software directories, and addresses for about 50 vendors. This issue of AEDS also includes a complete copy of both the MECC and MicroSIFT evaluation forms.

717. Kansky, B.; Heck, W.; and Johnson, J. Getting hard-nosed about software: Guidelines for evaluating computerized instructionaal materials. *Mathematics Teacher*, 1981, *74*(8), 600-604.

Points out problems in software selection and lists guidelines for deciding whether to buy.

718. Kimmel, S. How to write a software review. *Creative Computing*, 1982, *8*(8), 242-244.

Just what the title says—with examples of how to and how not to evaluate software, and what software to review and what not to review.

719. Kleiman, G.; Humphrey, M.; & Buskirk, T. Evaluating educational software. *Creative Computing*, 1981, *7*(10), 84-90.

Discusses several questions which should be asked when evaluating computer software. Provides some specific examples of poor design features.

720. Kosel, M. Software review: Critical reading. *AEDS Monitor*, 1981, *19*(8), 30.

Another review of the Borg Warner program. On the plus side: good use of upper-lowercase, ease of use. On the minus side: poor screen formatting and generally uninteresting content.

721. Lathrop, A. Microcomputer software for instructional use: Where are the critical reviews? *Computing Teacher*, 1982, *9*(6), 22-26.

Lathrop says less than 5 percent of educational computer programs have been critically reviewed in print. Lists 10 computer journals, 4 educational journals, 2 newsletters, 7 educational computing journals, and 6 review journals; tells the type of reviews printed, names the reviewers; and gives the number of reviews per issue and average length of each review.

722. Lubar, D. Educational software. *Creative Computing*, 1981, *7*(3), 20-21.

Includes a review of the "Word Relationships" package from Krell Software and the "Word Families" program from Hartley Software.

723. Lubar, D. Educational software. *Creative Computing*, 1980, *6*(9), 64, 66, 68, 70, 72.

Describes and reacts (favorably) to the Edu-Pak I software package from Edu-ware. The package includes "Compu-read" (a tachistoscopic type program), "Perception" (line length judging and matching), and "Statistics." Lubar also describes and reacts to a number of other packages some of which relate to reading. These include "Flash Spelling" and "Scrambled Letters" from Educational Activities; the "Talk and Teach" programs from Atari; and Readability Index from Educational Associates.

724. Mason, G.E. *Purchasing computerized reading instruction*. Paper presented at the Second National Basic Skills Conference, Nashville, Tennessee, November 1979.

Describes the first three successful uses of the computer in teaching reading. Lists the drawbacks of using computers to instruct reading, and concludes that these drawbacks do not outweigh the positive effects of the computer on instruction. Gives detailed description of reading programs which use computers at the elementary, secondary, and college levels.

725. Meyer, R. Computer buffs: Questionnaire for evaluation of computer programs. *Collage*, 1981, *6*(6), 4.
Lists 21 questions to answer before buying a program.

726. A levelheaded guide to software evaluation. *Classroom Computer News*, 1981, *1*(6), 22-23.
Provides some suggestions for classroom teachers on how to evaluate instructional software and gives a sample evaluation form.

727. Nilson, J. A critical look at critical reading programs. *Classroom Computer News*, 1982, *2*(5), 61-65.
One of the harsher reviews of Borg Warner's reading program. The program is criticized primarily as being simply an automated page turner. A response by the publisher is included.

728. Novick, H. Software legal forum. *Creative Computing*, 1982, *8*(7), 224-226.
Discussion of new guidelines of the Patent and Trademark Office (PTO). New section 2110 (Patentable Subject Matter-Mathematical Algorithms or Computer Programs) of the *Manual of patent examining procedure* includes: "claims seeking coverage for a computer program would be nonstatutory...only if, when considered as a whole, they merely recite a mathematical algorithm or a method of calculation" (p. 224).

729. Olds, H.F. Always friendliest, evermore frumious. *Classroom Computer News*, 1982, *2*(5), 66-69.
A review of an unusual type of word combining program in which the user can create what the author calls "minilanguages." The program is given high grades for originality and educational value but low grades for programing and execution. Response by publisher included.

730. Peters, H.J., & Hepler, M.H. Reflections on ten years of experience. *AEDS Monitor*, 1982, *20*(10), 12-15.
A thorough description of the software review process used by CONDUIT, an educational agency in Iowa that evaluates and distributes secondary level software. The evaluation system was originally created for time-share materials and later adapted for microcomputer software. Was one of the forms upon which the MicroSIFT form was based.

731. Potts, M. Smart programs, dumb programs. *Creative Computing*, 1980, *6*(9), 100-102.
Discusses the author's most and least favorite programs, giving specific examples of good and bad instructional programing techniques.

732. Potts, M. Wombats: A program to generate word problems. *Creative Computing*, 1981, *7*(10), 216-222.
Contains a description and listing of a TRS-80 program designed to generate word problems.

733. Price, R.V. Selecting free and inexpensive computer software. *Educational Computer Magazine*, 1982, *2*(3), 24-26.
Lists and discusses five sources of low cost software: 1) computing

journals, 2) books, 3) computer clubs, 4) educational agencies, and 5) software exchanges. Presents a checklist for evaluating free software. Includes a number of useful names and addresses.

734. Randall, L.G., & Alluisi, J.C. Ed tech product reviews: Critical reading. *Educational Technology*, 1981, *21*(9), 51-53.
A thorough and very favorable review of the Borg Warner software package, "Critical Reading."

735. Rauch, M., & Samojeden, E. Computer assisted instruction: One aid for teachers of reading (ED 204 702), 1981.
Lists advantages of CAI for reading instruction and offers suggestions for designing programs and for choosing and evaluating software.

736. Roblyer, M.D. Developing computer courseware must be easier than some things. *Educational Technology*, 1982, *22*(1), 33-35.
A brief but very well written discussion of three major types of problems involved in developing good quality software, one of which is formative evaluation. Roblyer uses several examples to show that developing and evaluating microcomputer courseware is in many ways a far more difficult task than developing and evaluating other instructional materials.

737. Roblyer, M.D. Ed tech product reviews: The learning system. *Educational Technology*, 1981, *21*(11), 53-54.
Finds this authoring system to be well designed, easy to use, and well documented.

738. Roblyer, M.D. Ed tech product reviews: Z.E.S. *Educational Technology*, 1982, *22*(1), 53-54.
Reports this software to be very flexible but very difficult to use. System not recommended for inexperienced users.

739. Roblyer, M.D. When is it "good" courseware? Problems in developing standards for microcomputer courseware. *Educational Technology*, 1981, *21*(10), 1981.
Discusses problems in trying to apply evaluation standards developed for mainframe software to microcomputer software. Suggests that evaluation systems be flexible enough to discern good quality regardless of the particular instructional model used in designing the material. Divides software criteria into three categories: essential characteristics for instruction of any type, aesthetic characteristics, and characteristics which are dependent upon the learner and the objectives being taught. Argues that a review team rather than one individual should perform software evaluation.

740. Wager, W. The software evaluation dilemma. *AEDS Monitor*, 1982, *20*(10), 5-6.
Argues that instructional effectiveness, ease of use, and user acceptance should be considered in evaluating software.

Additional References

741. Allee, J.G., Jr., & Williams, R.L. A challenge for the language arts CAI developer. *Creative Computing*, 1980, *6*(9), 120-125.

742. Developments in learning psychology—implications for instructional design, and effects of computer technology on instructional design and

development: An interview with Robert M. Gagne. *Educational Technology*, 1982, *22*(6), 11-15.
743. Kehrberg, K.T. Microcomputer software development: New strategies for a new technology. *AEDS Journal*, Fall 1979, 103-110.
744. Kingman, J.C. Designing good educational software. *Creative Computing*, 1981, *7*(10), 72-81.
745. Kurshan, B. Computer technology and instruction: Implications for instructional designers. *Educational Technology*, 1981, *21*(8), 28-30.
746. Olds, H.F. The making of software. *Classroom Computer News*, 1981, *1*(6), 20-21.
747. Roblyer, M.D. Instructional design versus authoring of courseware: Some crucial differences. *AEDS Journal*, Summer 1981, 173-181.

Part Six: REFERENCES TO SOFTWARE AND ITS DEVELOPMENT

Although instructional and noninstructional software should be run in order to be understood, much can be learned by reading what knowledgeable authors write. Many articles about software include listings of programs which can be copied by typing them into an available computer and then saving them on diskettes or tape. The articles included here deal with software for microcomputers, minicomputers, and large mainframes.

Annotated References

748. Ahl, D. Computer poetry: Not so new. *Creative Computing*, 1982, *8*(7), 172.
Lists and gives sample runs of two poetry programs, POET and BARD, which date back to the 60s and 70s.
749. Allen, R.J.; Wyatt, S.Y.; & Blohm, P.J. *Using the COMPUGLOSS system: An operator's manual.* Technical report No. 105. Lafayette, Lousiana: University of Southwestern Louisiana, 1981.
Describes program to make "glosses" (easier sentences) available to on-line readers.
750. Athey, M.K. *Individualizing the education of handicapped children with microcomputer programing.* Unpublished doctoral dissertation, University of Georgia, 1980.
Describes and lists a CMI program useful for reading and other subjects.
751. Beck, I.A. Personal communication, July 1, 1982.
Describes ongoing project developing game like microcomputer programs for improving word recognition through matching initial consonants with ending phonograms (BUILD-A-WORD) and through identifying medial vowel letter-phoneme correspondence (HINT-AND-

HUNT). Programs presently use a touch screen; one employs digital speech.

752. Bell, S.D., & Wells, B.J. A new approach to teaching reading: Using cloze and computer assisted instruction. *Educational Technology*, 1980, *20*(3), 49-51.

Describes the Computer Assisted Instruction Project directed by the All Indian Pueblo Council. This project helped elementary Pueblo students to develop better reading skills through culturally relevant reading materials and the cloze procedure. A HP200F computer was used to provide lesson materials employing a modified cloze procedure. The article describes how the program worked and gives a sample lesson.

753. Berenbon, Howard. The word board. *Creative Computing*, 1981, *6*(4), 64, 66, 68.

Lists and describes two uses of technique in which keys are covered with "word tags" and the process is similar to having a card with one English word on one side and a French translation of that word on the other. Suggests use by speech impaired person.

754. Blachowicz, C.L., & Fairweather, P.G. A computer assisted preservice program in reading. *Reading Horizons*, Fall 1978, *19*, 71-74.

In 1975, the National Right to Read effort funded an experimental project at Northwestern University involving the application of computer facilities to the operation of a preservice program for teacher preparation in reading. Utilizing a competency based model, the computer component of the program managed the student's entry into and progress through a series of on-line, interactive tutorials by assessing their initial behaviors, assigning lesson plans, guiding use of a bibliographical data base, and monitoring progress.

755. Brandt, R. On reading, writing, and computers: A conversation with John Henry Martin. *Educational Leadership*, 1981, *39*(1), 60-64.

With a simplified alphabet and interactive computer programing, John Henry Martin has developed a system by which children can learn to read and write. Martin discusses the aspects of his program which is used in an elementary school in Stuart, Florida. He describes how the success of the program is measured and the results that have been found in the areas of reading and writing with these children.

756. Brown, B. Automated tests and quiz production. *Classroom Computer News*, 1982, *2*(4), 33, 35.

Describes development and use of a large data bank of items on a 74 megabyte Winchester disk run by an Ohio Scientific C3-B. The central processor serves individual school microcomputers acting as terminals.

757. Bruce, B., & Collins, A. *Microcomputer based writing activities.* Paper presented at the NCRE sponsored session of the annual meeting of the American Educational Research Association, New York City, March 1982.

Describes work of Bolt, Baranek, and Newman, Inc. in developing Storymaker, etc. for children in grades 3-6.

758. Cicciarella, C. Test writer. *Classroom Computer News*, 1982, *2*(4), 36-37.
Explains and lists a simple program for creating multiple choice tests and answer keys from a question pool entered and maintained by the user. Program is in Applesoft Basic for the Apple II plus microcomputer with 32K of memory.

759. Clark, D.B.; Wilkins, C.T.; & Tuma, D.T. Computer aided sight reading. *Creative Computing*, 1980, *6*(6), 84-88.
Describes and provides a listing of a fixed-do sight-reading program for teaching music reading. An interactive program with immediate feedback, it operates on the TRS-80, Level II, 16K. When article was written, program was successfully in use.

760. Collier, Bernard. How to read super fast. *Parade*, December 23, 1979, 9-11.
Stephen J. Andriole developed URR (Ultra Rapid Reading). He is director of the Cybernetic Technology Office of the Defense Advanced Research Project Agency (DARPA) to solve crises; they need instant information. RSVP (Rapid Serial Visual Presentation) displays one word at a time at a very fast rate within a 2 inch wide space in the center of the screen. "Reader's eyes remain fixed and don't move at all" (p. 9).

761. Cummins, R.P. *University of Montana computer simulated reading fluency project.* Unpublished paper, University of Montana, 1979.
Describes development of a computer program which presents printed material in arrays based upon the eye-movement patterns of readers having various levels of reading skill development. This makes the computer an improved version of a controlled reading device.

762. Daniel, D. *Microcomputers as an environment for reading.* Paper presented at the 27th Annual Convention of the International Reading Association, Chicago, April 1982.
Describes four ways to obtain software and recommends a few programs. Explains why programs for obtaining hard copy have been difficult to obtain.

763. Davison, N.H. Verse weaving: A challenge for all ages. *Creative Computing*, 1982, *8*(7), 166, 168, 170, 172.
An Atari program for generating poetry from data lines typed in by the "poet." It gives ten variations, each in 17 lines.

764. Earle, W.H. Eyetracker. *Technology Illustrated*, December/January 1982, *9*.
Child who can control only her eyes has a "voice" and a "writing capability" with computer controlled device developed by research engineer Mark Firedman and students at Carnegie-Mellon.

765. *Examples of RSVP applications in basic skills.* Miami, Florida: Computer Based Instructional Development and Research, Miami-Dade Community College, 1980.
A series of reports giving examples of RSVP applications to management of instruction in various areas, including reading. The

CMI program in reading includes two criterion-referenced tests for each of 28 objectives. Report shows computer punchcards, sample printouts, etc.

766. Fortier, G. *The microcomputer: A magic aide for teachers of reading?* Paper presented at the Seventh Annual Conference of the Georgia Council of the International Reading Association, Atlanta, Georgia, March 1982.

Describes development of a cloze generating program and demonstrates prototype (with a compucolor microcomputer).

767. Frederiksen, J.; Warren, B.; Gillote, H.; & Weaver, P. The name of the game is literacy. *Classroom Computer News*, 1982, *2*(5), 23-27.

Discussion of rationale for using computer arcade games to teach reading and a description of experimental games now being field-tested in a high school. These include:

Speed—rapid recognition of letter clusters within words (*ler* in "couplers" or "filter").

Racer—say displayed words fast, then recognize oral version from tape.

Ski Jump—context + slower and slower tachistoscopic word presentation.

Games are in C Basic on the "Sorcerer."

768. Fry, M.A., & Harris, J.D. *Management system: Microcomputer version HBJ bookmark program.* New York: Harcourt Brace Jovanovich, 1981.

Using a Chatsworth Mark 500 card reader to input test-answer cards, the program runs on either an Apple II, a TRS-80 Model I or a TRS-80 Model III. Teachers choose from menus of five options: 1) class set up, 2) score tests cards, 3) print a report, 4) change records, and 5) back up the class records.

769. Glowinski, D. *CADPP 1981: Computer assisted diagnostic prescriptive program in reading and mathematics.* Dillwyn, Virginia: Buckingham County Public Schools, 1981.

A description, complete with costs, of a computer managed "shell" program which prescribes reading materials entered by the teacher using the program.

770. Goodnow, Judy. Talking to the computer. *Electronic Learning*, 1982, *1*(3), 64.

Discusses and lists 3 programs, Talk 1, Talk 2, and Story. All are very short and are written in BASIC for the H-P2000. Good for introducing students in grades 4-6 to the computer.

771. Heuer, Randy. Reading comprehension for the SOL-20. *Creative Computing*, 1980, *6*(4), 36, 38-39.

Describes development of a reading comprehension program as a contract job for his company, Creative Computing Software.

772. Hines, T.C., & Warren, J. A computerized technique for producing cloze text material. *Educational Technology*, 1978, *18*, 56-58.

A cloze text generating program with options on length of blank and particular (every fifth word) deletions on random deletions of one in five words. Operates in batch mode from a mainframe computer and must be hand scored.

773. Howze, G. An interactive software system for computer assisted testing. *AEDS Journal*, 1978, *11*(2), 31-37.
Describes TICAT and EBUILD programs for the Hewlett-Packard 100-Access System. TICAT creates a file of test questions. EBUILD creates an actual test.

774. *IFC Staff.* More new NDN programs. *The IFC ETC, 1979, 5*(3), 4-6.
Lists CADPP (Computer assisted diagnostic prescriptive program in reading and mathematics) of Dillwyn, Virginia, as a newly validated project. "A computer assisted management system providing diagnosis of basic needs in reading, grades three to nine, and mathematics grades three to seven, and prescriptions to assist in teaching those needs" (p. 5).

775. Interactive fiction puts you in the plot, FAMILY and home section. *Mechanix Illustrated*, 1981, *1*(3), 44.
Describes some of six micro stories and four compu-novels.

776. Jelden, D.L. Computer generated testing. *AEDS Monitor*, 1982, *20*, 32-35.
Describes development of test generator program on hard disk IBM 370 system with line printer. Card input.

777. Joos, L.W. SING—A computer program for grouping students for instruction. *AEDS Journal*, 1980, *13*(3), 214-220.
Scheduling for Instructional Needs Groups used since 1973 in Oakland County, Michigan, uses optical scanning of pencil marked answer sheets to generate skill group clusters. "What is not obvious to many people is that a computer program can handle the logic of best grouping as well as might be done by teacher judgment" (p. 215).

778. Kimmel, Stephen. Programs for preschoolers: Starting out young. *Creative Computing*, 1981, *7*(10), 44, 46, 50-53.
Lists and describes the best and favorite programs of the author's preschooler (on his TRS-80), and a few poor and nonrequested programs.

779. Kosel, M. *Computers in reading.* Paper presented at the regional AEDS conference on computers in instruction, Washington, D.C., March 1980.
Gives an overview of programs available in Minnesota for the Apple computer or through time-sharing and provides several sample runs or displays.

780. Kosel, M. Computer bibliography. *Mathematics Teacher*, 1981, *74*(8), 646, 658-659.
A bibliography of student texts, resources, periodicals, and organizations. The texts were "currently being used in schools" (p. 658).

781. La Frenz, D. Scott, Foresman and education computing: Corporate viewpoints on computers in education. *Educational Technology*, 1982, *22*(3), 27-29.
Presents some reasons for Scott, Foresman involvement in microcomputer instructional materials. Also contains a description of the Scott,

Foresman Reading Series, Course Manager, and Speak and Read programs.

782. Leslie, R.C., & Peters, N.A. *Symbolic communication interface for the multi-handicapped.* Paper presented at the 29th annual meeting of the National Reading Conference. St. Petersburg, Florida, December 1978.
Describes LICOS (Language Interface Communication System), a picture dictionary type program which is commanded by the handicapped child in a number of ways, including phonetic typing and voice commands. The program responds to 11 different commands from the user and responds in either print-on-screen or in synthesized speech.

783. Liddil, Bob. Interactive fiction: Six micro stories. *Byte*, 1981, *6*(9), 436.
Reviews and criticizes 1) limited vocabulary, 2) small choice of outcomes.

784. Litman, G.H. CAI in Chicago. ERIC Document Reproduction Service (ED 087 423), 1973.
Although in 1973 the average gain for eight months of compensatory education was only 5.8 months of achievement, twenty-one Chicago elementary schools averaged nearly eight months, using CAI (from CCC) delivered by UNIVAC 418-III.

785. Lubar, David. Another look at educational software and books. *Creative Computing*, 1981, *7*(1), 36, 38.
Lists and criticizes materials of six developer-publishers: "Books are easy to deal with; they've been around a long time, and you pretty much know what to expect from them. Software is another matter. The computer can be used merely to replace a book, or to take some of the load off a teacher. Is this approach desirable? This question, and other related problems, will have to be answered sooner or later by both the software writers and the reviewers. With this unanswered problem peering over my shoulder, it's time to take a look at some educational materials" (p. 36).

786. Martin, M., & Trombino, J. What a wordweb we can weave, when we practice... "Spider"—an idea spinning program. *Classroom Computer News*, 1982, *2*(5), 45-47.
Describes and lists a program for stimulating and then editing and printing creative writing.

787. Mason, G.E. Reading instruction with computers. *North Carolina English Teacher, 39*(1), 11-16.
Describes types of programs for particular purposes and identifies one or more programs of each type.

788. McDowell, N.A., & Young, P. *Program READER.* Ashland, Oregon: Reading Center, Southern State College, 1982.
A report of the development of an on-line testing program developed at Southern Oregon State College. Consists of six passages, each in a different subject area, followed by four multiple-choice questions asking for higher order and factual information. Passage dependency was assured by giving the tests to people who hadn't read the passages. Timing is accomplished by the computer which records the hitting of

the RETURN key. Student feedback (time, rate [in WPM], and comprehension) is given after each reading.

789. Meyer, R. Computer buffs...know alphabetic sequence. *Collage*, 1980-1981, *6*(4), 10.
A listing of a simple computer (TRS-80) program for drill and practice in alphabetizing. The program can be used with whatever list of words is entered on the data lines.

790. Meyer, R. Computer buffs...programs you might try. *Collage*, 1981-1982, *6*(5), 10.
Lists three very simple Level II Basic programs for use as feedback or reinforcement loops in teachers' self-developed programs. Also lists a correction for an alphabet program listed in the previous issue.

791. Millman, J., & Outlaw, W.S. Testing by computer. *AEDS Journal*, 1978, *11*(3), 57-72.
Describes a program for the PDP-11/40. This program stores item programs, rather than items that will appear in the tests proper. The number of items which can be generated from a specified input is thereby increased.

792. *Minnesota Learning Disabilities Consortium.* St. Paul: Minnesota State Department of Education, 1979.
An explanation and partial demonstration of a CAI-CMI effort. Since it is a printout (ringbound) of a PLATO system curriculum, it can be accessed by typing Iddemo in the author mode. Phase I teaches keyboard use and word attack. Phase II is on reading comprehension with 240 short texts accompanied by approximately 2,000 questions. Students are assigned to these based on their Phase I performance. The basis of the Phase I curriculum is an approximately 5,000 word dictionary constructed after study "of numerous phonetically oriented reading curricula" (p. 18). These words are searched to find those for 500 behavioral objectives.

793. Nelson, Ted. Interactive literature. *Creative Computing*, 1981, *1*(3), 42.
Review of Bob Lafore's "Interactive Fiction." Says it's great. "Essentially, interactive fiction is a Dialogue Adventure, a combination of Adventure and Eliza—since the programs behind the stories must parse your replies and branch appropriately" (p. 42).

794. Newcomer, N.J. *CAI development in reading.* Paper presented at the 24th Annual Convention of the International Reading Association. Atlanta, Georgia, May 1979.
Outlines history of Computer Curriculum Corporation's involvement in CAI reading and describes five CAI reading programs marketed by the company.

795. Nicastro, A.R. Exam time: Reading and comprehension tests for language arts. *Creative Computing*, 1979, *5*(5), 62.
A program for the PDP-11-03. The teacher underlines phrases from the text to be entered and also creates questions. Clerks type in the passage (in phrases). Pupils read tachistoscopically-presented text and answer questions.

796. Piestrup, A.M. Preschool children use Apple II to test reading skills programs. ERIC Document Reproduction Service (ED 202 476), 1981.
Fifty-five 3 and 4 year old children learned terms (*above, below, left*, and *right*), learned to operate computer, and care for diskettes during a three week tryout at a nursery school on the Stanford University campus. Used as an activity center, the computer was accepted enthusiastically by children, teachers, and parents.
797. Potts, Michael. Wombats: A program to generate word problems. *Creative Computing*, 1981, *7*(10), 216, 218, 220, 222.
Describes and lists a program by which the teacher can generate word problems. Teacher uses menu to select 1) Max (hardest operation), 2) Default (number of variables), 3) Largest number, 4) Five objects (words to be used). Program scans for correct capitalization and nonsense of child entries (words must be under 16 characters, and vowels and consonants in balance).
798. Powers, David E. Perquackey. *Creative Computing*, 1981, *6*(4), 70, 72, 74, 76, 78.
Describes conversion of published word game (similar to Scrabble) to computerized version with time limits and computer scoring—for one to four players. TRS-DOS-32K minimum.
799. Racter. Soft ions. *Omni*, 1981, *4*(1), 96-98, 147-148.
A story (science fiction) written by a computer program (RACTER) developed by Bill Chamberlain of Greenwich Village on his Ohio Scientific (home) Computer.
800. Roberts, Ralph. A computerized identikit for alien beings. *Creative Computing*, 1980, *8*, 88-89.
Describes and lists a program to generate descriptions of aliens. Sort of a "story-starter" for young science fiction writers.
801. Rogers, John F. The first "R." *Creative Computing*, 1981, *6*(4), 62.
Describes and explains (to a programer) author's abbreviated program for teaching three Dolch words. User must add 217 more to data statement starting at line 30. TRS-80 Level II Basic is used with the Speech Synthesizer.
802. Ryder, J.R. A microcomputer software program for word recognition. *North Carolina English Teacher*, 1982, *39*(2), 21-26.
Describes phonics word recognition program run on Apple II (diskette) at the University of Wisconsin. Program uses analogues to help with pronunciations and tones to help reinforce.
803. Sampson, James P., Jr. CASSI: A computer assisted approach to improving study skills. *NASPA Journal*, Winter 1981, 42-47.
Describes development and use of system for assisting students in improving their academic performance.
804. Schreiner, R. *A computer program for teaching beginning reading skills to adults.* Paper presented at the 26th Annual Convention of the International Reading Association, New Orleans, April 1981.
805. Sharples, M. *Poetry from LOGO*, DAI Working Paper 30. Edinburgh: Department of Artificial Intelligence, University of Edinburgh, 1978.
Describes a project in which three junior high pupils learned language generalizations by using a computer program, LOGO, to generate poetry. The generated programs are called POEM (I, II, III).

806. Shostak, R. Computers and teaching English: Bits 'N' pieces. *Computing Teacher*, 1981, 35-39.

Relates information about the development of a teaching program involving sentence combining. This program is under development by the Southwest Regional Laboratory for Educational Research and Development in Los Angeles. Lists a program (for the TRS-80) designed to help students separate fact and opinion.

807. Smith, C.F., Jr. Applications of microcomputers to sentence combining. *North Carolina English Teacher*, 1982, *39*(2), 17-20.

Describes a program being designed by the author to teach sentence combining with the Apple II (Pascal language board inserted). Students actually order words rather than choosing from multiple-options.

808. Smith, Robert W. Speed reading with the personal computer. *Creative Computing*, 1981, *7*(10), 162, 164, 166.

Nine sets of 12 words and/or phrases are stored so that a random selection from each generates a sentence. Almost 2 million sentences can be created. Four options: 1) words; 2) phrases; 3) short sentences; and 4) longer, complex sentences. Users set their own speed for each option. The words, phrases, or sentences are flashed tachistoscopically.

809. Spring, C., & Perry, L. Computer assisted instruction in word decoding for educationally handicapped children (ED 201 075), 1980.

A field test of a drill-and-practice program in sounding out words led to "significant word decoding improvement" on the part of twelve educationally handicapped elementary school children.

810. Thompson, H.W.; Saha, H.; & Wang, H.C. *Computer assisted instruction: An innovative approach to the development of comprehension at the college freshman level.* Paper presented at the First Annual Conference of the American Reading Forum, Sarasota, December 1980.

A discussion of the need for CAI in the Alabama Agricultural and Mechanical University (AAMU) Reading Program. This was followed by a description of the procedure by which special materials were developed for this program. Students responded positively to the program and there was a net gain in students' ability to comprehend main ideas.

811. vonFeldt, J.R. A description of the DAVID interactive instructional television system and its application to post high school education of deaf. Rochester, New York: National Technical Institute for the Deaf, 1978 (mimeo).

DAVID (Digital And Video Interactive Device) is a WANG-based system for controlling interactive videotaped lessons. This paper details its development and initial field tests.

812. Wiggers, T. A computerized test question storage and examination preparation system. *Educational Computer Magazine*, 1980, *2*(2), 30-31.

Describes a multiple-choice test generating program for the Apple II (48K).

813. Wiggers, T. Utilization for the Apple microcomputer for the generation of matching-type examination questions. *Educational Computer Magazine*, 1982, *2*(4), 32-33.

Describes a program for making matching tests from a file of up to 50 items.

814. Williams, Robert L. Sentence construction with a computer. *Creative Computing*, 1981, *6*(4), 46, 48, 50-51.
A "conversational" type program started by menu calling for choices of verbs, subjects, tenses, etc. Students can "gossip" with the computer. Describes development of program listed (text) small screen BASIC.

815. Zacchei, D. The adventures and exploits of the dynamic Storymaker and Textman. *Classroom Computer News*, 1982, *2*(5), 28-30, 76.
Describes development of "Storymaker," "Prefab Storymaker," and "Storymaker Maker." Also describes "Textman" (Hangman, based on guessing which sentences go together to make a coherent paragraph). Article ends by stating software considerations guide their development.

Part Seven: HARDWARE EVALUATION

It is no accident that this section on hardware evaluation comes after, not before, the section on software evaluation. More and more frequently, those responsible for the selection of instructional computing materials are discovering that it is software, not hardware, that is the most crucial component in the implementation of effective computer assisted instruction. A reasonable analogy can be made between the computer as an instructional delivery system and other mediums such as film projectors. Most teachers pay little attention to what brand of movie projector their school buys as long as it is reliable. On the other hand, if you give them the best projector money can buy, but give them only one reel of old cartoons to use, you are likely to find yourself facing a very hostile group of teachers (not to mention some rather disappointed students). Similarly, the most sophisticated, most expensive computer system has very little value to most teachers if there aren't any good computer programs (software) to use with it.

This analogy is not intended to suggest that hardware is not an important consideration. It merely suggests that the hardware is probably best considered only after the teacher has determined the educational objectives and found software to meet those objectives. Once this is done, then hardware must be very carefully considered. This is because microcomputer programs are usually written in a specific dialect of the BASIC computer language, one that works with only one brand of computer hardware. If, for example, you decide to use the Scott, Foresman courseware called Early Reading, you would *have* to use it with a Texas Instrument 94/4A Microcomputer. Similarly, the Borg Warner Critical Reading program is designed for use only with the Apple computer. A number of computer vendors have designed software for use with more than one kind of computer, but this is more the exception than the rule at this time.

If the software you wish to use is not restricted to a particular brand of computers or, if you have a number of software options, then there are a number of instructional questions to be considered. Where are the computers going to be located in the building? Where are the electrical outlets? What will the ratio of students to computer be? How much inservice will be required to make the staff familiar with the computer? All of these may have a major effect upon the hardware that is chosen. In addition, there are always technical factors which need to be examined. How much memory is required? Will the computer be able to display graphics or generate sound? Will a color or black and white monitor be needed? Will a printer be needed and, if so, which type? Many of these questions can be answered by looking at the type of software you intend to use. Nonetheless, the sheer volume of factors to be considered may seem rather intimidating, especially to those with no experience working with computers.

Fortunately, articles appearing in most of the computing magazines can serve as guides to the process of evaluating hardware. Several of them provide checklists of evaluation criteria and means for weighting them. When software considerations alone are not sufficient for evaluation, such checklists may prove very useful. Many of the new computer magazines contain regular columns for evaluation of hardware as well as software. In addition, MECC and Houston's Region IV Education Service Center have both drawn up rather extensive guidelines for evaluating microcomputer hardware. These guidelines were used to help them in selecting the best computer in an extensive bidding process.

Annotated References

816. Blank, G. The quest for the perfect printer. *Creative Computing*, 1981, *7*(7), 130-137.

Compares a variety of printers on the market. Contains an excellent comparison chart on printers, and the July issue as a whole is devoted entirely to the topic of electronic printers for micros.

817. Braun, L. How do I choose a personal computer? *AEDS Journal*, 1979, *12*(1), 81-87.

Braun describes a weighted value analysis system for evaluating microcomputers that he developed under an NIE grant. His value assessment table is already outdated in terms of cost, but the hardware characteristics that he delineates may still be quite useful.

818. Brumbaugh, K. Microcomputers vs. timesharing. *Creative Computing*, 1981, *7*(3), 132.

Brumbaugh (currently director of the Minnesota Educational Computing Consortium [MECC]) argues that large timesharing systems should be maintained as potential backups in the event of repeated failures by microcomputers. His contention that "The cost of maintaining a standard microcomputer system for a machine that is two or three years old could be approaching 40 percent of the cost of the equipment" has been strongly disputed by both hardware vendors and many user groups. Most microcomputers have been found to operate well in excess of three years without any major failures, and most hardware repairs do not usually amount to anywhere near the 40 percent figure Brumbaugh gives.

819. Frederick, F.J. *Guide to microcomputers* (ED 192 818), 1980.

A comprehensive, simple guide deals with computer compatability, service and maintenance, systems operation, languages, and special applications such as videomail and networking. Contains a useful bibliography of references.

820. Matthews, J.I. Problems in selecting a microcomputer for educational applications. *AEDS Journal*, 1979, *12*(1), 69-79.

Takes a rather technical approach to hardware evaluation which is very much minicomputer oriented, even though the author perports to be discussing microcomputers. Describes an ideal microcomputer system containing so many advanced features (1/2 megabyte of internal memory, timesharing capability, and both high speed and daisy wheel print capability) that it probably would cost in excess of $10,000.

821. Ricketts, D., & Seay, J.A. Assessing inexpensive microcomputers for classroom use: A product-oriented course to promote instructional computing literacy. *AEDS Journal*, 1979, *12*(1), 89-99.

Describes an inservice program designed to provide teachers and administrators with sufficient background knowledge to evaluate microcomputers. The article contains a well organized and much needed checklist for evaluating documentation, an aspect of evaluation that is often neglected.

822. Shetler, P., & Stephen. Choosing the right computer: A general method. *On Computing*, Winter 1980, 67-71.

A weighted needs analysis for evaluating microcomputers is presented and discussed.

823. Staples, B. Van helps school select the right computer. *Creative Computing*, 1981, *7*(3), 106-112.

Description of an interesting approach used by the Pennsylvania Department of Education in which a van filled with a variety of microcomputers goes to visit districts considering purchases of computer materials. The equipment is then used as part of a literacy inservice program to assist educators in making decisions about both hardware and software. Article includes some of the forms used to aid in the evaluation. The form for evaluating projected uses is well worth noting.

824. Sturdivant, P., & Finkel, L. Selecting a microcomputer: It's more than the hardware. *Classroom Computer News*, 1981, *10*.
Both Sturdivant and Finkel argue essentially that factors such as software support, maintenance, and inservice training support, are far more important factors than cost when it comes to the selection of a microcomputer. Guidelines for writing bid specifications for these factors are provided and discussed.

825. Thomas, D.B., & McClain, D.H. Selecting microcomputers for the classroom. *AEDS Journal*, 1979, *12*(1), 55-68.
Provides a model for the evaluation of hardware that begins with an instructional needs analysis and then breaks down computer applications into eleven categories of usage (strategies): drill, tutorial, problem solving, programing, simulation, testing, computer managed instruction (CMI), data analysis, information retrieval, word processing, and computer literacy. Presents a number of tables which analyze each of these strategies in terms of its instructional requirements and the hardware capabilities of the different models of microcomputers.

Additional References

826. Jongejan, T., & Johnson, J. The selection of a computer system: A dilemma for educators. *Oregon Computing Teacher*, 1978, *6*(2).

827. Zinn, K.L. Considerations in buying a personal computer: What, which, when, how much? *Creative Computing*, 1978, *4*(5), 102.

Part Eight: COMPUTER MANAGED INSTRUCTION FOR READING

Not all useful reading applications for microcomputers are purely instructional. In fact, if there is any area where major progress has been made in reading software, it would be in the area of noninstructional programing. There are four types of programs that reading teachers may find useful in reducing time required to complete paperwork drudgery which is all too prevalent in most schools: 1) instructional management programs, 2) gradebook programs, 3) testing programs, and 4) readability analysis programs. These programs greatly add to the classroom teacher's ability to provide instruction—not because the programs themselves instruct, but because the less time teachers have to spend grading papers or recording scores, the more time teachers will have for performing their primary task, teaching.

Instructional management programs are a type of data base system: the data being manipulated is information on students. This can include information such as lessons completed, scores on lessons completed, words correctly or incorrectly identified, and response time on a particular identification task. Some management systems are designed to record and manipulate information on student performance on other educational software. For example, the Milliken instructional software contains a built in management system that the teacher can access to determine student progress on the instructional programs. This type of management system has proven useful to many teachers, largely because of the logistics of microcomputer use. Most schools have only a few microcomputers which are usually placed in a central location, such as the media center. The teacher often must send the students out of the classroom to complete lessons on the computer, making it very difficult for the teacher to monitor and observe student performance. By using a built in management system, however, the teacher can go back at the end of the day and see how each student did. If a printer is available, the teacher can print out on paper the current list of student scores for a more permanent record.

Management systems seem sensible—so sensible that one is led to wonder why all instructional programs do not make use of them. The reason is that there is a major drawback to their use, *memory space*. On larger mainframe and minicomputers there is usually much external storage. Consequently, most software designed for timesharing systems such as PLATO include extensive management systems. On a microcomputer, however, even a simple management system that keeps records on perhaps five classes of 30 students, could easily take more than one-half of a diskette. More complex systems may take up an entire diskette. This means either that the diskette will have room for only a few short lessons, or the teacher will have to resort to switching back and forth between a management system and a lesson diskette. Either option may be unsuitable for some teachers.

Not all managment systems are designed to manage instruction on computers. Some systems (such as the HBJ Bookmark Management System) are designed to manage student use of traditional basal reader instruction. Many of these systems also administer and record both pretests and posttests for each level within the basal series. Thus management and testing functions are combined. Compared to previous methods for handling the management of large basal programs, microcomputer managed systems are a vast improvement. They cut the time required to manage a large basal program down to a fraction of what it would be otherwise.

The electronic gradebook is another type of educational management tool that is extremely useful. These programs are designed solely for the purpose of recording, averaging, and totaling scores on lessons and tests, just as one would do by hand in a gradebook. Most gradebook programs are designed to work with a printer so the teacher can easily maintain permanent (hard copy) records. Like most software, the gradebook programs differ widely in complexity and ease of use, but even the weakest of them will simplify the chore of churning out grade reports. Since most gradebook programs sell for well under $100, this type of software must be considered a bargain.

In the early years of microcomputing, there was talk that some day in the distant future we would be able to do complete statistical readability analyses on personal size computers. That day has already arrived. There are now a number of commerically available programs designed to do readability analysis. The better quality programs will perform and compare the readability analyses using a variety of methods, including those requiring word lists, such as the Spache or Dale-Chall methods. Readability analyses now can be done so simply with these programs that there is little reason for teachers not to use them in evaluating and writing educational materials.

MANAGEMENT, GRADEBOOK, TESTING AND READABILITY SOFTWARE

Suppliers

Blue Lakes Computing
3420 University Avenue
Madison, WI 53705
(608) 233-6502
TEACHER'S GRADEBOOK

Charles Mann & Assoc.
7594 San Remo Trail
Yucca Valley, CA 92284
(714) 365-9718
ELECTRIC GRADEBOOK
GRADING SYSTEM PROGRAMS III

COMPress
P.O. Box 102
Wentworth, NH 03282
THE GRADER

Creative Computing
P.O. Box 789
Morristown, NJ 07960
(800) 631-8112
GRADEBOOK

Educational Activities, Inc.
1937 Grand Avenue
Baldwin, NY 11510
(516) 223-4666
O'BRIAN VOCABULARY PLACEMENT TEST
READABILITY INDEX AND GRADE AVERAGES

Ginn and Company
P.O. Box 2649
Columbus, OH 43216
(800) 848-9500
COMPUTER MANAGEMENT SYSTEM

Harcourt Brace Jovanovich
757 Third Avenue
New York, NY 10017
(212) 888-4444
HBJ BOOKMARK PERIODIC TESTS/MANAGEMENT SYSTEM

Instructional Development Systems (IDS)
2927 Virginia Beach Boulevard
Virginia Beach, VA 23452
(804) 340-1977
ASSISTED INSTRUCTIONAL DEVELOPMENT SYSTEMS (AIDS)

Micro Power & Light Co.
12820 Hillcrest Road, Suite 224
Dallas, TX 75230
(214) 239-6620
GRADE BOOK

Milliken Publishing Co.
1100 Research Blvd.
St. Louis, MO 63132
(314) 991-4220
MILLIKEN LANGUAGE ARTS
READING COMPREHENSION

Micromatics, Inc.
181 N. 200 West
Suite 5
Bountiful, UT 84010
MICROEDUCATIONAL TEACHING SYSTEM

Milton Bradley Company
443 Shaker Road
East Long Meadow, MA 01101
(413) 525-6411
VOCABULARY SKILLS

Progressive Software, Inc.
P.O. Box 273
Plymouth Meeting, PA 19462
(215) 279-4438
ROSTER

Random House School Division
Department 985, Suite 201
2970 Brandywine Road
Atlanta, GA 30341
(800) 241-6402
READABILITY ANALYSIS PROGRAM
CUSTOMIZED INSTRUCTIONAL MANAGEMENT SYSTEM

Scott, Foresman and Company
Electronic Publishing
1900 East Lake Avenue
Glenview, IL 60025
(312) 729-3000
SCHOOL MANAGEMENT APPLICATIONS

Serendipity Systems, Inc.
225 Elmira Road
Ithaca, NY 14850
(607) 277-4887
INSTRUCTOR GRADEBOOK

TIES
1925 W. County Road, B2
St. Paul, MN 55113
(612) 633-9110
READABILITY ANALYSIS

UNICOM
297 Elmwood Avenue
Providence, RI 02907
(401) 467-5600
GRADE REPORTING SYSTEM

Annotated References

828. Baker, F.B. *Computer-managed instruction: Theory and practice.* Englewood Cliffs, New Jersey: Educational Technology Publications, 1978.

One of the most substantive works on CMI, this book describes the history and development of computer managed instruction in the U.S. prior to 1978. The author defines CMI and contrasts it to other administrative computer functions, such as test construction or comprehensive achievement monitoring (CAM). Most chapters are directed at the educational components of CMI and require little technical knowledge. Chapters V and VII require a bit more background but are well worth reading. An excellent source of information on large-scale CMI.

829. Barnett, B.D. Grading made easy. *Creative Computing*, 1980, *6*(9), 146-149.

Contains a description and listing for a gradebook program written in the North Star version of BASIC.

830. Bozeman, W.C. Computer managed instruction: State of the art. *AEDS Journal*, 1979, *12*(3), 116-137.

Contains an excellent analysis of the literature. Designed to answer two questions: What CMI programs are available? What evidence exists concerning the effectiveness of CMI? Five major CMI projects are discussed: 1) Program for Learning in Accordance with Needs (PLAN), 2) Wisconsin System for Instructional Management (WIS-SIM), 3) Navy CMI System, 4) Managed Instruction with Computer Assistance (MICA) and 5) TRACER. Seventeen other CMI systems are briefly noted and evaluated. Author concludes that "CMI appears to have suffered from numerous reinventions of the same wheel by different agencies." Feels that this is due to inadequate information sharing between the many research and development groups. Concludes that research generally indicates that CMI is associated with high student achievement and a generally favorable attitude toward CMI. He notes, however, that existing research suffers from a lack of longitudinal studies. A complete bibliography is included.

831. Crouse, D.B. The computerized gradebook as a component of a computer managed curriculum. *Educational Technology*, 1981, *21*(5), 16-20.

Describes a gradebook and attendance program designed for use with a Cromemco microcomputer and an optical scanner.

832. Haugo, J.E. Management applications of the microcomputer: Promises and pitfalls. *AEDS Journal*, 1981, *14*(4), 182-187.

Examines the advantages and disadvantages of using microcomputers for financial, personnel, and student information systems as compared with large scale systems. It contains a comprehensive listing of potential school management applications for microcomputers.

833. Hazen, M. An argument in favor of multimethod research and evaluation in CAI and CMI instruction. *AEDS Journal*, 1980, *13*(4), 275-284.

Hazen performs a meta-analysis on the literature on the effectiveness of CAI and CMI instruction. She makes an impressive argument in favor of using a variety of measuring devices for determining the success of such programs.

834. Hedges, W.D. Lightening the load with computer managed instruction. *Classroom Computer News*, 1981, *1*(6), 34.

A brief description of CMI. Includes listing of some of the major producers of CMI packages.

835. McIsaac, D.N., & Baker, F.B. Computer managed instruction system implementation on a microcomputer. *Educational Technology*, 1981, *21*(10), 40-46.

Describes the evolution of the Wisconsin WIS-SIM CMI project which was handled by a large mainframe computer, to the current MICRO-CMI project which, as its name suggests, is handled by a microcomputer. The article contains an excellent history of the early project as well as a detailed accounting of the excessive costs which led to its lack of success. It lauds the new CMI project as delivering basically the same degree of course management at far less cost and with a greater degree of user control.

836. Rodel, L.J. Apple II helps teacher and students manage instruction. *AEDS Monitor*, 1982, *20*(10), 29-30.

A description of the CAM program for the Apple II which was developed by the Hopkins School District in Minnesota. The CAM system allows for the creation and monitoring of educational objectives using a microcomputer. It has been recently modified to work with the HEI card reader.

837. Roecks, A.L. The MICA project: A final look. *AEDS Journal*, 1979, *12*(3), 146-153.

Describes the development and subsequent evaluation of a Title III CMI project in Madison, Wisconsin. The project was designed to manage the math program at a districtwide level. The evaluation showed no significant difference between students managed with CMI over those managed by traditional methods. The evaluation also showed that there was very little parent support or understanding of the project. The project was discontinued in 1977.

838. Solntseff, N. What do we tell the administrators? *Creative Computing*, 1981, *7*(3), 100-102.

Author lists several ways in which computers assist in school administration.

839. Teoh, W. Grades: A class record updating system. *Creative Computing*, 1981, *7*(10), 166-168.

A description and listing of a program for the Apple II which a teacher could use for maintaining and updating grades for a course.

Additional Reference

840. Cavin, C.S. Microcomputer generation of interactive quizzes. *Educational Technology*, 1982, *22*(2), 31-32.

Part Nine: SOURCES OF COMPUTER SERVICES

COMPUTER USER GROUPS

One interesting social phenomenon that has emerged from the microcomputer revolution has been the widespread and nearly spontaneous development of computer user groups. The user groups (or computer clubs) were formed partly in response to the lack of support from both microcomputer hardware and software manufacturers. When microcomputers were first introduced in the late 70s there were few, if any, computer programs available. There was no place for a new microcomputer enthusiast to acquire information on programing or using micros. Therefore, the users turned to each other for help and are still doing so. There are now user groups for nearly every brand of microcomputer in production in almost every part of the United States. These groups together comprise what may be the most highly informed sources of information on microcomputing. Many of them produce newsletters and some of the larger groups produce comprehensive magazines. Most of the user groups have developed procedures for the sharing of software and for the bartering of hardware components, and many have developed special interest groups for those specifically interested in educational applications. All in all, user groups must be considered one of the best sources of help for teachers interested in microcomputing.

Below are listed addresses for some of the major user groups and computer organizations. Some limit themselves to one brand of microcomputer. Some focus specifically on educational applications, while others deal with any type of application. Often the latter proves to be the most beneficial since a great deal of software being used in other areas, such as business, can prove quite useful in the hands of an enthusiastic teacher. If you do not see a group listed for your particular area, check with businesses in your area that sell microcomputer hardware. Very often they are aware of local user groups.

USER GROUPS AND LOCAL PROFESSIONAL ORGANIZATIONS

ALASKA ASSOCIATION FOR COMPUTERS IN EDUCATION
Kathleen L. Castle
The Northern Institute
650 W. International Airport Road
Anchorage, AK 99502

APPLE FOR THE TEACHER
c/o Ted Perry
5848 Riddio Street
Citrus Heights, CA 95610

THE BOSTON COMPUTER SOCIETY
Educational Resource Exchange
Three Center Plaza
Boston, MA 02108
(617) 367-8080

COMPUTER EDUCATION SOCIETY OF IRELAND
Ann Brebner
Mt. Anville Secondary School, Goatstown
Dublin 14, Ireland

COMPUTER-USING EDUCATORS (CUE)
c/o W. Don McKell
Independence High School
1776 Educational Park Drive
San Jose, CA 95133

COMPUTER-USING EDUCATORS OF BRITISH COLUMBIA
3264 St. Georges Avenue
North Vancouver, B.C. V7N 1V3
Canada

EDUCATIONAL COMPUTING ORGANIZATION OF ONTARIO (ECOO)
Robert E. Drake
252 Bloor Street West
Toronto, Ontario M5S 1V6
Canada

EDUCOM
P.O. Box 364
Princeton, NJ 08540
(609) 734-1915

INDIANA COMPUTER EDUCATORS
David A. Flowers
Ft. Wayne Community Schools, Adm., Cwt.
1230 South Clinton Street
Ft. Wayne, IN 46802

MICHIGAN ASSOCIATION FOR COMPUTER USERS IN LEARNING (MACUL)
c/o Wayne County Intermediate School District
33500 Van Born Road
Wayne, MI 48184
(313) 326-9300

NEW HAMPSHIRE ASSOCIATION FOR COMPUTER EDUCATION STATEWIDE (NHACES)
Anne Knight
University of New Hampshire
Computer Services
Durham, NH 03824

NORTHWEST COUNCIL FOR COMPUTERS IN EDUCATION
Howard Bailey
Computer Center
Eastern Oregon State College
La Grande, OR 97850
(503) 963-2171

NORTHWEST COUNCIL FOR COMPUTERS IND EDUCATION
Howard Bailey
Computer Center
Eastern Oregon State College
La Grande, OR 97850
(503) 963-2171

SASKATCHEWAN ASSOCIATION FOR COMPUTERS IN EDUCATION
Duncan Campbell
Mt. Royal Collegiate
2220 Rusholme Road
Saskatoon, Saskatchewan S7L 4A4
Canada

TEXAS COMPUTER EDUCATION ASSOCIATION
Vicki S. Smith
7131 Midbury
Dallas, TX 75230
(214) 361-9472

THE UTAH COUNCIL FOR COMPUTERS IN EDUCATION
Larry C. Christensen
1295 North 1200 West
Mapleton, UT 84663

WEST AUSTRALIAN COMPUTER EDUCATORS
P.C. Farrell
12 Lilac Place, Dianella, 6062
Western Australia

NATIONAL PROFESSIONAL ORGANIZATIONS: VANGUARDS OF INNOVATION

Professional organizations have long been the vanguard of innovation in education. Nonetheless, until recently, most of the major educational professional organizations have largely ignored computer assisted instruction. Most articles on the subject have been directed either to educational research journals, such as the *American Educational Research Journal*, or to the journals of the computing industry, such as *ACM Communications*. In recent years, however, some educational organizations have shown a renewed interest in educational computing. The National Council of Teachers of Mathematics (NCTM) has led the way by taking the position of fully supporting computers in the classroom at all levels and has published one of the best guidelines to date for evaluating computer software. The International Reading Association now has formed a special interest group on microcomputers in education which is publishing a newsletter on computer applications in reading. This newsletter can be obtained by contacting Karen Foley, P.O. Box 166, New Almaden, CA 95042.

NATIONAL PROFESSIONAL ORGANIZATIONS INVOLVED IN EDUCATIONAL COMPUTING

ASSOCIATION FOR EDUCATIONAL DATA SYSTEMS (AEDS)
Publications: *AEDS Bulletin, AEDS Monitor, AEDS Journal*
1201 16 St., N.W.
Washington, D.C. 20036
(202) 833-4100

AEDS serves educators and those involved in educational data processing. Traditionally, AEDS has focused on administrative computing but now it is becoming more involved with educational microcomputing. Each year it devotes at least one issue of its magazines to microcomputer applications. AEDS has a number of chapters at the state level which also publish journals, and its national convention is one of the most informative events on instructional computing.

ASSOCIATION FOR COMPUTING MACHINERY (ACM)
Publications: *Communications, Computing Reviews, The ACM Guide to Computer Science and Computer Applications Literature*
1133 Avenue of the Americas
New York, NY 10036
(212) 265-6300

Like most computer organizations ACM was originally oriented toward mainframe computer professionals, but is now involving itself more and more with instructional applications and microcomputing. The special interest groups for small computing systems, personal computing, and computer use in education may very well be of special interest.

ASSOCIATION FOR THE DEVELOPMENT OF COMPUTER BASED INSTRUCTIONAL SYSTEMS (ADCIS)

Publications: *The Journal of Computer Based Instruction, ADCIS Newsletter*

Bond Hall
Western Washington University Computer Center
Bellingham, WA 98225
(206) 676-2860

The membership of ADCIS includes a variety of elementary, secondary, university, and governmental personnel all interested in the advancement of computer based instruction of any type. The journal is a good place to look for more research oriented articles on microcomputing.

ASSOCIATION FOR EDUCATIONAL COMMUNICATIONS AND TECHNOLOGY (AECT)

Publications: *Educational Communication and Technology Journal, Journal of Instructional Development, Instructional Innovator*

1126 16 St., N.W.
Washington, D.C. 20036
(202) 833-4180

AECT membership consists primarily of media specialists. Its 1982 convention focused on microcomputer applications and it supports a special task force on microcomputing.

INTERNATIONAL COUNCIL FOR COMPUTERS IN EDUCATION (ICCE)

Publication: *The Computing Teacher*

Department of Computer and Information Science
University of Oregon
Eugene, OR 97403
(503) 686-4408

The ICCE is one of the few organizations devoted specifically to instructional computer applications. The organization has undergone rapid growth in recent years under the direction of David Moursand. Its journal, *The Computing Teacher*, is one of the most popular and widely distributed of the professional magazines.

NATIONAL COUNCIL OF SOCIAL STUDIES (NCSS)

Publication: *Social Education*

3615 Wisconsin Avenue, N.W.
Washington, D.C. 20016
(202) 966-7840

The NCSS journal frequently carries articles on computers in education and has prepared a booklet entitled *Computers in the Social Studies Classroom.*

NATIONAL COUNCIL OF TEACHERS OF MATHEMATICS (NCTM)

Publications: *Arithmetic Teacher, Mathematics Teacher, Journal of Research in Mathematics Education, NCTM Newsletter*

1906 Association Drive
Reston, VA 22091
(703) 620-9840

NCTM fully supports educational computing and is a good source for general articles on computing applications. The *Mathematics Teacher* provides software reviews and the NCTM has published an excellent set of guidelines for the evaluation of software.

NATIONAL SCIENCE TEACHERS ASSOCIATION (NSTA)
Publications: *Science and Children, The Science Teacher, Journal of College Science Teaching*
1742 Connecticut Avenue, N.W.
Washington, D.C. 20009
(202) 328-5840

This organization primarily serves secondary school science educators. In addition to actively seeking articles on computer applications, NSTA has also become involved in the development of science software for microcomputers.

SOCIETY FOR APPLIED LEARNING TECHNOLOGY (SALT)
Publications: *Journal of Educational Technology Systems, SALT Newsletter*
50 Culpepper Street
Warrenton, VA 22186
(703) 347-0055

The members of SALT are mostly professional trainers from industry and government. Their journal is a good source for information on the latest in instructional computing hardware. It is also a good source for information on the use of computer controlled videodisk technology.

MAGAZINES ON COMPUTERS AND EDUCATIONAL TECHNOLOGY

ABACUS, an APPLE Newsletter
2850 Jennifer Drive
Castro Valley, CA 94546

AEDS Monitor
AEDS Bulletin
AEDS Journal
Association for Educational Data Systems
1201 Sixteenth St. N.W.
Washington, D.C. 20036

ANALOG 400/800 MAGAZINE
P.O. Box 615
Holmes, PA 19043

Apple Education News
10260 Brandley Drive
Cupertino, CA 95014

Apple Educators Newsletter
9525 Lucerne
Ventura, CA 93004

Apple Orchard
P.O. Box 1493
Beaverton, OR 97075

APPLESAUCE
12804 Magolia
Chino, CA 91710

The Atari Connection
ATARI
1265 Borregas Ave.
Sunnyvale, CA 94086

Audiovisual Instruction
(Instructional Innovator)
Educational Communication & Technology Journal
Association for Educational Communication & Technology
1126 16th St. N.W.
Washington, D.C. 20036

British Journal of Educational Psychology
Council for Educational Technology
3 Deconshire Street
London, WlNLBA England

BYTE
McGraw-Hill
70 Main Street
Peterborough, NH 03458

Call APPLE
8710 Salty Drive NW
Olympia, WA 98502

Centurion News
Centurion Industries
Menlo Park, CA 94025

Chromasette
P.O. Box 1087
Santa Barbara, CA 93102

Classroom Computer News
P.O. Box 266
Cambridge, MA 02138

Closing The Gap
Route 2, Box 39
Henderson, MN 56044

Communications of the ACM
Computing Reviews
Association of Computing Machinery
1133 Avenue of the Americas
New York, NY 10036

Compute
515 Abbot Drive
Broomall, PA 19008

Computer Age
4 Valentine Place
London, SE1
Great Britain

Computer Education
British Computer Society
National Computing Centre
Quay House, Quay Street
Manchester, M33HU England

Computers & Education
Pergamon Press, Journals Division
Maxwell House, Fairview Park
Elmsford, NY 10523

Computers and the Humanities
Queens College
City University of New York
Flushing, NY 11367

Computers, Reading & Language Arts
Gerald H. Block, Editor
P.O. Box 13039
Oakland, CA 94661
(*new journal)

Computer World
Computer World, Inc.
797 Washington Street
Newton, MA 02160

Computing Resources for the Professional
University of Washington
Computer Information Center HG-45
3737 Brooklyn Avenue N.E.
Seattle, Washington

Computing Teacher
Department of Computer & Information Science
University of Oregon
Eugene, OR 97403

Contact 6
APPLE Computer, Inc.
10260 Brandley Drive
Cupertino, CA 95014

Courseware
4919 N. Millbrook #222
Fresno, CA 93726

Creative Computing
51 Dumont Place
Box 789-m
Morristown, NJ 07960

CUE Newsletter
(Softswap Newsletter)
San Mateo County Office of Education
P.O. Box 18547
San Jose, CA 95158

Datamation
1801 South LaCienega Blvd.
Los Angeles, CA 90035

Dr. Dobb's Journal of Computer Calisthenics and Orthodontia
People's Computer Co.
Box E 1263 El Camino Real
Menlo Park, CA 94025

Educational Computer Magazine
P.O. Box 535
Cupertino, CA 95015

Educational Technology
140 Sylvan Avenue
Englewood Cliffs, NJ 07632

80 Microcomputing
Wayne Green, Inc.
80 Pine St.
Petersborough, NH 04358

Electronic Education
Suite 220
1311 Executive Center Dr.
Tallahassee, FL 32301

Electronic Learning
50 West 44th St.
New York, NY 10036

IBM's Personal Computer
and
Personal Computer Age
P.O. Box 70725
Pasadena, CA

Info World
530 Lytton
Palo Alto, CA 94301

Instructional Innovator
1126 Sixteenth St., N.W.
Washington, D.C. 20036

Interaction
Detroit Interact Group
15356 Prevost
Detroit, MI 48227

Interface Age
P.O.Box 1234
Cerritos, CA 90701

International Journal of Instructional Media
Baywood Publishing Co.
120 Marrie St. Box D
Farmington, NY 11735

Journal of Computer-Based Instruction
Association for the Development of Computer Based Instructional Systems (ADCIS)
Computer Center
Western Washington University
Bellingham, WA 98225

Kilobaud MICROCOMPUTING
Subscription Department
P101 Box 977
Farmingdale, NY 11737

MALA
P.O. Box 325
Milford, MI 48042

Man Computer Interaction
University of Sheffield
Biomedic Information Service
University Arts Tower
Sheffield S102TN, England

Media and Methods
1511 Walnut Street
Philadelphia, PA 19102

Microcomputers in Education
QUEUE
5 Chapel Hill Drive
Fairfield, CT 06432

Micro-Scope
JEM Research-Discovery Park
The University of Victoria
Box 1700
Victoria, B.C. V8W 2Y2
Canada

MicroSIFT News
Northwest Regional Laboratory
300 S.W. 6th Avenue
Portland, OR 97204

Nibble
P.O. Box 325
Lincoln, MA 01773

On Computing
Box 307
Martinsville, NJ 08836

Peelings II
945 Brook Circle
Las Cruces, NM 88001

Performance & Instruction
National Society for Performance & Instruction
Suite 315
1126 16th Street N.W.
Washington, D.C. 20036

Personal Computing
Hayden Publishing Co.
50 Essex Street
Rochelle Park, NJ 07662

Popular Computing
P.O. Box 307
Martinsville, NJ 08836

Pursor's Magazine
P.O. Box 466
El Dorado, CA 95623

Recreational Computing
People's Computing Co.
1263 El Camino Real, Box E
Menlo Park, CA 94025

School Courseware Journal
4919 N. Millbrook Ave.
Suite 222A
Fresno, CA 93726

School Microware Reviews
Dresden Associates
P.O. Box 246
Dresden, ME 04342

Small Computer Program Index
ALLM Books
21 Beechcroft Road
Bushey, WATFORD, Herts WD2 2JU
England

Softalk
Softalk Publishing Inc.
11160 McCormick Street
North Hollywood, CA 91601

Softside
Box 68
Milford, NH 03055

80 Software Critique
RWC Microcomputing Services
P.O. Box 134
El Dorado, CA 95623

Software News
666 Fifth Avenue
New York, NY 10103

Southeastern Software
7270 Culpepper Drive
New Orleans, LA 70126

SYM-PHYSIS
SYM-1 Users Group
Chico, CA

SYNC
39 E. Hanover Ave.
Morris Plains, NJ 07950

Technological Horizons in Education
Information Synergy-Reader Service Department
P.O. Box 992
Action, MA 01720

Timely TIES Topics
Instructional Services TIES
1925 W. County Road B2
Roseville, MN 55113

TRS-80 Weekly Newsletter
80 Newsletter
3001 Route 27
Franklin Park, NJ 08823

Users: The MTS Newsletter
MECC User Services
2520 Broadway Drive
St Paul, MN 55113

Chapter 10

THE FUTURE OF THE COMPUTER AS AN AID TO READING INSTRUCTION

This chapter has two sections. The first section is exactly as it was written in 1977 and 1978 for the first edition of this book. The second section predicts the future from the vantage point of Fall 1982.

Section 1: The Future As It Looked in 1977-78

In the preparation of this book, the authors read numerous reports, articles, books, and reviews. It was readily apparent that the vast majority of computer based education projects were in mathematics or applications of mathematics (economics, bookkeeping, and statistics) or in physics, chemistry, and the other sciences. Fewer were in the humanities, and comparatively few were in reading.

There seem to be several reasons for this inequality. One is that the original purpose of computers was computation, the natural realm of the mathematician. A second reason is that CAI requires instruction to be programed and many reading specialists are averse to programing instruction. A third reason is that the less costly CAI terminals (teletypes-TTSs) require the operator or student to be able to do some reading and writing in order to use the terminal. A fourth reason is that the equipment once thought necessary for teaching beginning reading (random access audio and light pencil and/or touch panel) is complex and very expensive and was not available until the early 1960s. When it became available, reading people were frequently not asked to involve themselves. In computer based education, reading specialists have been conspicuously absent.

Now, however, after a slow start, the projects and the interest are increasing. Most encouraging is the involvement of Pikulski and Pelosi

(University of Delaware), Hansen and Wadham (Brigham Young University), Geoffrion (University of New Hampshire), and Kamil and his associates (Purdue University) in computerizing remedial reading, college reading, beginning reading, and inservice reading education, respectively.

Their work, and the work of other reading specialists hoping to capitalize on the capabilities of computers, will probably lead to the development of some exciting new programs in the remaining years of this century. When coupled with the developments in computer manufacturing technology, their efforts may well lead to advances beyond our present dreams.

There is little doubt that most American homes will have microcomputers before 1990. They will be preprogramed to do such things as control the heat in the house; turn lights off and on; count calories and plan meals; store and display recipes, phone numbers, addresses, and income tax information; record favorite radio and TV shows for later viewing; play games using the TV set as a display panel; and provide academic drill and practice activities as well as do-it-yourself information.

Schools will also have microcomputers, perhaps with several terminals per classroom computer connected to a larger minicomputer which serves the entire school and which is, itself, connected to a CPU serving the school district network. The reading programs available on these computers will be as varied as the printed basal and supplementary programs available today.

When machines are put in classrooms, teachers do one of two things. They find ways to make use of the machine, or they leave the machinery to gather dust (perhaps hiding it in a closet). Just as some of today's reading teachers make use of tape recorders, slide and filmstrip projectors, and movies, so will some of tomorrow's reading teachers use computers to aid in their teaching of reading.

Some teachers will use computers to teach sight vocabulary. Children will match words and pictures on the display screen. Many teachers will use computers as diagnostic devices, allowing students to be tested on-line so that the teacher may receive an immediate estimate of instructional level and skills to be taught. Nearly all teachers will be required by their school district or system to record attendance, grades, and progress in reading on one of the terminals in their classrooms.

Books will *not* become obsolete and neither will teachers. The vacuum cleaner has not yet replaced the broom; the washer, dryer, and dishwasher have not replaced the housewife nor eliminated housework. The computer will not eliminate the need for teachers to teach. Instead, it will present much of the drill and take care of the extensive individual record keeping which is the bane of present day teachers who individualize instruction.

In the future, books frequently will be accompanied by a tape or a floppy disk upon which is printed a computer program providing testing, diagnosis and prescription, or drill and practice activities to accompany the book's content. The practice exercises may be assigned as homework to be done with the home microcomputer. Basal reading programs will offer as options, not only the trade books, workbooks, word cards, ditto masters, and criterion referenced tests they offer today but, also, computer programs for diagnosing and prescribing using those tests and materials, as well as drill and practice programs keyed to the skills and stories contained in the printed materials.

A long sought for intercorrelation of language arts instruction will be formed by the typewriter keyboard basic to most computer terminals. As a part of playing computer games, practicing reading exercises, and solving mathematics problems, pupils will learn to write and spell (within the contexts allowed by the programs to which they are exposed) the words and sentences appropriate to the games, exercises, and problems.

Some schools will provide children with personal computers. Perhaps microcomputers, similar to those already under development at the Xerox Research Center in Palo Alto, will store and present at the call of the student any information stored in their memory banks which will contain the equivalent of several thousand pages of information. With such personal computers, students will be able to access (call up) at will the equivalent of an encyclopedia of information—to create artistic creations or musical compositions impossible to produce by hand or check the spelling of words using computer stored picture dictionaries or glossaries. On personal computers, students in these schools will store their assignments and the completed work assigned. Forgetting to bring one's computer to school may become an excuse as common as "I forgot my homework," or "I left my book at Grandma's house."

In the future, the emerging interdependence of computers and instructional television may well form the basis for semiprogramed instruction viewed daily by most Americans as well as the stop action pictures required for reading print, diagrams, and schematics.

Adult basic education, consumer education, career retraining, and do-it-yourself activities will become available on videodisc which many schools will be equipped to use. Using videodisc, the memory power of the computer, with its feedback response capabilities, can be coupled with the motivational power of television. The videodisc—a shiny, silver-colored disc that looks much like an LP record—may well come into more common use by educators than the LP records of today.

The rapid growth in technology will, of course, require software in order to generate sales of computers and computer operated equipment. Well known educators will be asked to create programs (or to consult with computer companies) especially appropriate for computer interactive presentation. Successful printed and boxed reading instruction materials may be stored in minicomputers and made available to homebound students who dial into the school's computer so that their home computer or terminal can display the reading material and questions.

The programs stored in the memories of the various computers developed in the past twenty years of this century will be just as good and just as bad as those available in print today and educators will have to study well in order to choose wisely. One thing is sure: Educators will be bombarded by sales representatives and brochures of the type parodied in the third from the last reference for the first section of this chapter.

Section 2: The Future As It Appears in 1982

The uses of computers in reading instruction are still increasing and the rate of increase will undoubtedly accelerate in the 1980s. One reason for this acceleration is the improvement in hardware. Numerous computer-chip controlled teaching devices are reaching a market of teachers and parents eager to buy. Such specialized devices as Speak-N-Spell, Speak-N-Read, the Talking Picture Book, and Alphamaster will appear in classrooms in every school in developed nations (creating a need for dry cell batteries everywhere). Furthermore, such devices will probably be constructed for comprehension skills as well as for word recognition skills (to which they are limited at this moment). Battery powered reading devices may become more widely accepted than plug-in devices because the inadequate wiring facing today's technology promises to be a continuing problem for tomorrow's technology.

Some authors have indeed predicted the end of the book as we know it. Encyclopedias are already available (through networks) at your microcomputer terminal and computer-voice input and output are making great strides. Yet the CRT screen poses eyestrain problems for constant users and the schools of the future may well propose restrictions on computer screen viewing times. Such restrictions will, of course, promote continued use of paper, pencils, and ink.

Interactive videodisc systems seem to have great promise because they combine the great potential of the computer with the marvelous audiovisual facility of the television receiver. Such systems will become widely available in schools by 1990, occupying a place in the classroom which once was predicted for the movie projector.

Materials collection and disbursement are among the school record-keeping and management jobs which will be assigned to computers. Soon most librarians will use computers to replace or supplement card catalogs. Eventually most book checkouts and returns will be computer controlled. During the transition to such systems, librarians will be faced with monumental changeover tasks. When the change has been accomplished, more of the librarian's effort can be devoted to discussion with library clients, book replacement and repair, and assistance to those conducting literature searches. Of course, the collections will also change. Libraries will have whole sections devoted to software, just as many libraries now have sections for microfiche collections.

The content of children's books will also be affected by the evolution of the computer. Individualized stories in which children's names and other related information are printed out by computer will be widely sold to parents who may be able to use electronic mail to learn whether their children really have "no assignments tonight."

State education departments will probably inaugurate software adoption procedures similar in function to their present book adoption procedures. The adopted software then will sell better within the borders of an adopting state.

Because most of the present software for educational use is programed for computers which rely on the BASIC language, it will continue to be the most popular language used by educational computer users. However, LOGO will become the computer language for children, and primary grade teachers will probably be required to learn it. All teachers may well be expected to master PILOT, a language useful in creating lessons. Software will soon be interchangeable (with some effort or expense) from one computer to another and larger school districts will pride themselves on their systemwide software evaluation and distribution systems.

The software programs available to schools will become quite controversial. Already some authors are decrying the ubiquitous drill-

and-practice programs and recommending that, instead, children learn to create their own programs or interact with interactive fiction, simulations, poetry generators, or tutorial programs. Some authors recommend using computer games to teach and others recommend using computer games as rewards for academic performance. Yet, at the same time, many professional teachers view any kind of game (computer *or* paper and pencil) as counterproductive to achieving educational goals.

One breakthrough which may have a profound impact on reading instruction is the development of machines which, when attached to computerized speech synthesizers, can read printed text aloud. Such machines may eventually play a variety of roles in beginning and remedial reading instruction.

Reading educators who believe that writing instruction and practice is conducive to improved reading achievement will support teaching children with word processing equipment (computers that are specially programed for proofreading, editing, and printing one's own writing). It is possible that such programs will eliminate our need for spelling and eventually (but not in the 1980s) may replace the writing of stories using handwriting. However, before any sizeable vocabulary can be dictated to a computer, many breakthroughs must be made.

The changes which computer technology may make in school reading instruction will be limited by more than just the lack of adequate wiring in the school buildings. Inadequate school funding, teachers unschooled in computer use, lack of adequate software, and technological limitations in computer hardware will also slow the advance of computers as vehicles for reading curricula.

The first of these problems is one that reading educators and other school personnel are accustomed to, and it probably will remain. The second can be solved by large scale inservice programs as soon as educational leaders themselves master this new technology. For the solution to the third, we must wait for computer programers to learn the technology of reading instruction, for reading specialists to learn computer programing, or for representatives of the two groups to form productive working relationships.

The technological limitations in computer hardware include the extra cost of lowercase letters, the glare problems pupils face in constant reading from the CRT screen, the legibility problems caused by blurring of print near the edges of the CRT screen, and the limited transportability of today's school microcomputers. All of these problems can be solved, but few of the solutions will be immediate and many will be expensive. Computers will not totally replace books in this century.

Annotated References (Section 1)

841. Bennion, J., & Schneider, E.W. Interactive videodisc systems for education. *Journal of the Society of Motion Picture and Television Engineers*, 1975, *84* (12), 949-953.
Describes how videodisc enables programers to develop interactive educational TV instruction utlizing "freeze frames," electronic address, and fast random access. The relationship of videodisc instruction to the TICCIT program is described and cost estimates are graphed.

842. Blackwell, F.W. *The probable state of computer technology by 1980.* Santa Monica: Rand Corporation, 1971.
Suggests that improved communication links, such as cable TV, can bring equal computer opportunity to children in diverse kinds of schools and at home. Simple English is predicted as a common author language.

843. Curtis, A.R. Everyman's home computer is here. *Popular Mechanics*, 1977, *148* (4), 92-93, 192.
Introduces the novice to home microcomputers and their uses, memories, and display features.

844. Elementary school sets up own minicomputer data bank. *Educational Technology*, 1970, *10* (4), 89.
Describes 35-pound minicomputer at Juliette Low Elementary School in Elk Grove Village, Illinois. This is believed to be the first elementary school computer installation in the United States. The computer has an 8,192 word memory, disk pack data storage, and input/output terminals.

845. Hardin, B., & Carroll, R. On the reading horizon. *Teacher*, 1977, *93* (5), 53-56.
A discussion of trends and how they might effect the teaching of reading. Includes computerized reading programs.

846. Hawkins, W.J. What's new in electronics. *Popular Science*, 1977, *211* (3), 104.
Describes and shows pictures of a computer device for changing the home TV into a teaching device as well as a game board, for less than $150.

847. Heuston, D.H. *The promise and inevitability of the videodisc in education.* Paper submitted to the National Institute of Education, New York: WICAT, 1977.
Describes the promise of the videodisc and methods of program authoring, makes recommendations for NIE, discusses strengths and weaknesses of various educational systems, and estimates costs required for large scale educational development.

848. Hodges, D.A. Microelectronic memories. *Scientific American*, 1977, *237* (3), 130-131, 135-136, 138-140, 142, 144-145.
Describes recent improvements in computer memory using semiconductor technology which places thousands of circuits on a tiny

silicon chip. The storage possibilities of these circuits are now being increased with magnetic bubble and charge coupled devices.

849. Holton, W.C. The large scale integration of microelectronic circuits. *Scientific American*, 1977, *237* (3), 82-94.

Reports that today's $1,000 minicomputer can very nearly equal the capabilities of the $20 million dollar computers of fifteen years ago, describes computer binary arithmetic, and gives excellent simplified diagrams of how computer circuits work. Includes some history of computer development.

850. Kay, A.C. Microelectronics and the personal computer. *Scientific American*, 1977, *237* (3), 230-232, 234, 236-242, 244.

Describes development of a notebook sized personal computer at the Xerox Palo Alto Research Center, its language (SMALLTALK—a new type language dealing with parallel messages) developed to let children and nonexpert adults write sophisticated computer programs and its tryout by 250 children (aged six to fifteen) and 50 adults. Includes the prediction that the personal computer will not revolutionize education.

851. Levien, R.C.; Barro, S.M.; Blackwell, F.W.; Comstock, G.A.; Hawkins, M.L.; Hoffmayer, K.J.; Holland, W.B.; & Mossman, C. *The emerging technology: Instructional uses of the computer in higher education.* New York: McGraw-Hill, 1972.

A detailed report to the Carnegie Commission on Higher Education that gives a nontechnical introduction to computers and their potential for college instruction, estimates the extent of their use at the time, and examines the possibilities for the future.

852. Mossman, C. *Evaluating instructional computing: Measuring needs and resources for computing in higher education.* Educom Monograph Series Number 2. Princeton, New Jersey: Educom, 1977.

Reports a 1975-1976 NSF project funded to determine computing resources for assessing college students' proficiencies, capabilities, and needs. A large part is a report of a questionnaire study of opinions of faculty, students, and staff members at the University of California at Irvine.

853. Papert, S.A., & Minsky, M. *Condon Lectures.* Corvallis, Oregon: Oregon State System for Higher Education, 1974.

Explains the LOGO program for creative programing and problem solving by children. LOGO was developed at MIT and at Bolt, Beranek, and Newman, Inc. Children using it create programs which generate music, make a turtle image crawl around and draw lines on the display screen, and make a robot turtle perform the same acts on the floor.

854. Ryan, M.J. Finie's great teaching machine. *Phi Delta Kappan*, 1977, *59* (2), back cover.

A satirical presentation of an imaginary computerized audiovisual teaching device using play-on-words with the specialized vocabulary of CAI and videotronics.

855. Seidel, R.J., & Rubin, M.L. (Eds.) *Computers and communications: Implications for education.* New York Academic Press, 1977.

A 428-page set of reports, predictions, and discussions of a conference sponsored by the Human Resources Research Organization (HumRRO) to provide information on computer technology in language understandable to educational planners concerned with implications for 1985.

856. Wisher, R.A. *Innovations in computer assisted instruction for reading.* Paper presented at the annual conference of the International Reading Association, Houston, May 1978.
Reviews five CAI projects examining the feasibility of teaching reading skills to differing groups of people. Includes reasons why the reading teacher must become involved in CAI and a prediction for the future of CAI in reading classrooms.

Annotated References (Section 2)

857. Ahl, David H. International computer electronics show, January 8-11, 1981 (Las Vegas). *Creative Computing*, 1981, *7*(3), 52-54.
Describes Tiger's "K-2-8" talking learning computer which talks to its user with a 1500 word vocabulary.

858. Ahl, D.H. Scrabble goes electronic. *Creative Computing*, 1981, *7*(9), 264-266.
Describes LEXOR, a Scrabble-type hand-held computer game. Also describes SENSOR, a MASTERMIND-type word game; and READER'S DIGEST Q & A, sort of "It pays to enrich your word power" electronic game.

859. Associated Press. Machine can read printed material aloud to the blind. *Atlanta Constitution*, February 25, 1979.
Kurzweil Computer Products of Cambridge, Massachusetts, developed the Kurzweil Reading Machine and has a $2 million contract with HEW to put 64 of them in schools, colleges, libraries, and rehabilitation centers. Prototypes (at $50,000 each) have been in use since 1976. The new versions cost $19,400 each. The machine will *spell* the word also, if the proper key is hit.

860. Atkinson, R.C.; Attala, E.E.; Bitzer, D.L.; Bunderson, C.V.; Charp, S.; & Hirschbuhl, J.J. Futures: Where will computer assisted instruction (CAI) be in 1990? *Educational Technology*, 1978, *17*(4), 60-63.
Six prominent specialists in educational computing predict the future. Predictions include continued miniaturization, "intelligent videodisc books," better educational software, transferable programs, terminals in homes, increased computer literacy, major preschool use of CAI, and continued use of time-sharing along with microcomputers in schools.

861. Bingham, M. Pinging the way to success the North Carolina way. *Electronic Education*, 1981, *1*(2), 22-24.
Describes statewide contract (1980-1981) awarded to Apple, TRS-80, and (in 1981-1982) those two plus TI 99/4A. Schools get discounts of from 10 to 26 percent. This was established by the NC Instructional Computing Project. The project has three other objectives: 1) to provide coordination and leadership, 2) establish a centralized courseware library, and 3) assist with and conduct inservice programs.

862. Braun, L. A national tragedy is taking shape. *Classroom Computer News*, 1981, *2*(2), 3.

Points out budget cuts in NSF's science education budget will render us unable to train our students in electronic technology because our teachers will not be trained.

863. Carter, R. Schooldays 1991. *Classroom Computer News*, 1982, 17-19, 27.

Describes schooldays in 1991 using 1) "dynabook," a personalized hand-carried computer which can generate music; 2) a message center on the terminal to the mainframe; 3) computerized library search; and 4) saving work in file for teacher to check. At the end, the author points out that the technology is available today—it's the appropriate use that lags.

864. Cavin, C.S., & Cavin, E.D. A case study of an intercomputer transfer of CAI programs. *AEDS Monitor*, 1979, *17*(13, 14, 15), 14-15.

Although there is no way to eliminate the difficulty in transferring programs from one type of computer to another, minimizing the difficulty can be accomplished by programing *for* transfer.

865. Christoffersson, J. MARVEL update. *Interface*, 1978, *5*(10), 1978.

Explains barcode system for labelling books for computer access.

866. Cole, P. Learning by computer and scheduling living away. *Education Week*, 1982, *1*(26), 19.

Describes experiment starting in Fall 1982. Districts #2 and #3 in Manhattan and #9 in the Bronx will have groups starting kindergarten with computers and learning all subjects with a combination of computerized and traditional teaching through sixth grade.

867. Colligan, D. The gamesman. *Technology Illustrated*, 1982 (Dec./Jan.), 72-73, 75-76, 78.

Includes an interview with Hans Berliner, an AI researcher at Carnegie Mellon who designed a computer backgammon program that beat the 1979 world's champion backgammon player. "In his own work Berliner has already seen the effects of a simple form of computer dependence. Accustomed to having desired information flashed onto his terminal screen in seconds, he points out that, by comparison, reading a book seems like a clumsy way to retrieve information" (p. 78).

868. Daiute, C. Word processing: Can it make even good writers better? *Electronic Learning*, 1982, *1*(4), 29-31.

Lists 18 word processing programs (for five different microcomputers) and predicts that, in the future, voice typewriters will enable writers to receive hard copy to edit without ever spelling, typing, or writing. "It remains to be seen, though, whether writers prefer producing written words from a silent inner voice or a spoken one" (p. 31).

869. Davis, S., & Zacharias, J. Testing in the service of education. *Classroom Computer News*, 1982, *2*(4), 28-29.

Proposes the development of a publicly available national test item bank. The feasibility of such a bank comes from the widespread availability of computer networks.

870. Evans, C. An invitation to the (near) future. *Today's Education*, 1982, *71*(2), 14-17.

Predicts portable, personal, pocket-sized computers to be available soon and available at low cost. Chips with over one hundred kilobytes are *now* in production and, "By the mid-eighties, complete dictionaries will easily be packed into calculator-sized devices.... Pocket computer translators and vocabulary teachers will soon be found in the briefcases of traveling businessmen and, as production soars and prices plummet, in the pockets of school teachers and school children as well" (p. 14).

Predicts typed-in responses rather than multiple-choice. Need issues in the "hows" of teaching to be resolved in order to know how to program computers. Predicts a possible computer elite as a sort of "eagles" group with nonliterate as "crows."

871. Eye tracker. *Technology Illustrated*, 1982 (Dec./Jan.), *9*.
Eye movements to a particular quarter of the screen can serve a handicapped child as a menu selection response.

872. Garris, B. Summer computer programs. *Creative Computing*, *8*(5), 91.
A listing of computer camps for children and adults.

873. Goodman, D. Electronic learning aids. *Creative Computing*, 1981, *7*(9), 272, 274.
Describes 9 hand-held electronic learning aids, gives cost, producer, learning activities, number of program modules, and age group (targeted).

874. Grady, D. A hard look at the world of educational computing. *Personal Computing*, 1982, *6*(8), 40-44.
Predictions of Talmis, an Oak Park, Illinois consulting firm. Talmis maintains that "demand for educational microcomputer software will outstrip supply two to one...for the next five years." The author suggests that availability of hardware will be more of a problem than availability of software.

875. Hereford, N.J. Let's forget about drill and practice...computers are objects to think with: An *Instructor* interview with Seymour Papert. *Instructor*, 1982, *91*(7), 86-87, 89.
Papert reiterates belief that children should not be drilled by computers but, rather, should learn to program and control the computer.

876. Herriott, J. CAI: A philosophy of education and a system to match. *Creative Computing*, *8*(4), 80, 82, 84, 86.
Points out "there is a strong possibility that before the end of this century, students will be receiving all of their instruction from computers, with no contact with live teachers whatsoever. It can be done, and very well."

877. Humphrey, M.M. All the scientists in the world smushed into one: What kids think about computers. *Creative Computing*, 1982, *8*(4), 96-98.
Results of interviews with 74 children (who were familiar with computers), aged 7-12 in regular, special education, and gifted classes. Kids were asked "What happens when you load a computer?" "What would you like to be able to do with a computer?" "How would you design a computer for yourself?" "What's inside a computer?"

878. Project Best: Basic education skills through technology. Henry T. Ingle, Project Director, Association for Educational Communications and Technology, 1126 Sixteenth Street, N.W., Washington, D.C. 20036.
Project Best is an attempt through the use of Federal funds, to strengthen the capacity of State Education Agencies (SEA's) to support technological advances in teaching basic skills. The project is funded through June 1983.

879. Jabs, C. Game-playing allowed. *Electronic Learning*, 1981, *1*(2), 62-65.
Cites Denise Korngold, a third grade teacher in Boston, who uses several electronic games to "reinforce what I teach." Also cites Dolores Shanahan who uses games to camouflage drill in her school's computer learning center. Margie Mason of MASS (ILL.) gives criteria including a warning about overuse of graphics.

880. Lesgold, A.M. Cognitive simulation modeling on the VAX-11. *Behavior Research Methods and Instrumentation*, 1981, *13*(2), 192-194.
Discusses capabilities of VAX-11 for cognitive simulation. Includes discussion of LISP, EUNICE, NIL, and other versions of LISP as languages to use in such simulations. Predicts that in the future we will have intelligent theory based simulations in a variety of interactions with experimental subjects.

881. Levinson, S.E., & Liberman, M.Y. Speech recognition by computer. *Scientific American*, 1981, *244*(4), 64-76.
States that after forty years of research, the automatic recognition of speech by computers remains a Utopian goal. Current devices have small vocabularies and little ability to deal with fluent sequences of words. Explains Bell Laboratories' prototype system involving word decoding, decision making about which word (within sentence syntax context), and decision making about which sentence within a semantic context called "word concept." Concludes by predicting continued progress.

882. Lawler, R. LOGO ideas. *Creative Computing*, *8*(5), 83.
Describes how to make your own LOGO commands and explains and lists two useful commands (not primitives).

883. MacLeod, I.D.G. A simple touch panel digitizer. *Proceedings of the Seventh Australian Computer Conference*, 1976, *2*, 938-945.
Teaches basic handwriting to severely handicapped children by having them trace along a touch screen.

884. McConkie, G.W. *Studying the reader's perceptual processes by computer.* Reading Education Report No. 34. Urbana, Illinois: Center for the Study of Reading, University of Illinois, 1982.
Suggests that computer controlled text manipulation with simultaneous recording of eye movements may enable reading diagnosticians to determine whether specific reading skills are developing normally and (if not) what deviations may need remediation.

885. Merrill, P.F., & Bunderson, V.C. *Guidelines for employing graphics in a videodisc training delivery system. ISD for videodisc training systems.* First Annual Report, Vol. 3. Orem, Utah: WICAT, Inc., 1979. (ED 196 413).

A report to the Army Research Institute. Gives guidelines for use of color, line, motion, and pictures (as opposed to text) and presents questions for research.

886. Molnar, A. *The next great circle in American education: Computer literacy*. Washington, D.C.: National Service Foundation, 1978. (ED 191 733)
Predicts the future based on 1977 events. A bibliography is provided for those interested in earlier applications (1972-1977) of computers.

887. Moursund, D. Artificial mind (editor's message). *Computing Teacher*, 1982, *9*(9), 3-4.
Predicts the development of hundreds of "expert systems" which can perform as well or better than humans working in the same area. The challenge to educators is determining which jobs to do for themselves and which jobs to have "expert systems" do for them.

888. Nolen, P.A. Electronic aids in spelling. *Language Arts*, 1980, *57*(2), 178-179.
Poem questioning and extolling "Speak and Spell" computer.

889. Nolen, P. Sound reasoning in spelling. *Reading Teacher*, 1980, *33*(5), 538-542.
Discusses the advent of affordable computer assisted means in practicing spelling. However, there is a danger in using these spelling computers for teaching spelling. Describes these potential dangers and the new demands spelling computers make on diagnosis and teaching as a search for language patterns.

890. Onosko, T. Vision of the future. *Creative Computing*, 1982, *8*(1), 84, 86, 91-92, 94.
Predictions for interactive videodisc, including "whodunits" in which you frequently respond to multiple choice options, movie maps (to learn about cities), a tour of the National Art Gallery, "Discover" (which includes a tour of American colleges), and eventually home videodisc recording.

891. Papert, S. Computers and computer cultures. *Creative Computing*, 1981, *7*(3), 82, 84, 86-88, 90, 92.
Since computers will be increasingly privately owned, there will be less conforming and more control of education by the learner who will buy "programs" in the open market. Better for the child to be a programer than to be programed.

892. Sesame Place game centers.... AEDS *Bulletin*, 1979, *5*(1), 5.
The first of these "theme parks" opened in Oxford Valley, Pennsylvania, in 1980. It features participatory displays, exhibits, and computers for children aged 3-11. The fifty-plus computers run from three to ten games and/or simulations. Major participants include Creative Computing, CTW, Busch Gardens, Lawrence Hall of Science, Marin Computer Center, ATARI, and architect Eric McMillan.

893. Skoman, L. Organizing a microcomputer software collection. *Computing Teacher*, 1981, *9*(2), 55-56.
Suggests using computer name instead of subject headings (among other things) and a seven digit classification system.

894. Skow, J. Those beeping, thinking toys. *Time*, 1979, *114*(24), 86-88.
Describes computer games marketed for Christmas sales in 1979. Silicon chip industry will have to increase production because of the insatiable demands of the toy industry. Many toys combine fantasy with education. "Civilization as we know it will have disappeared beneath a pile of spent alkaline cells" (p. 88).

895. Software. *Educational Computer*, 1982, *2*(4), 44.
Any program written in BASIC for the TRS-80 Model I can be transferred to the IBM personal computer for $15 (includes disk and shipping). This service is also available at the same price per program for transfers from the IBM personal computer to the TRS-80 Model I, and between the Apple II Plus and either the TRS-80 Model I or the IBM. Send $15 for each BASIC program to be transferred along with the program to: Solartek, RD#1, Box 255A, West Hurley, NY 12491.

896. Souviney, R. There's a microcomputer in your future. *Teacher*, 1980, *97*(5), 52-58.
Broadbased help for teachers preparing to use microcomputers. The article contains a short essay by Geraldine Carlstrom entitled "Operating a Microcomputer Convinced Me—and My Second Graders—to Use it Again. . .and Again. . . ."

897. *Space waste race.* San Francisco: Storybooks of the future, 1981.
Version 1.2 is a tape or diskette program in BASIC for the TRS-80, Model I or III, consisting of three parts: 1) Poem-story with each line animated; 2) Funtime (includes number and letter recognition games, position concept games, direction concept games, and alphabetical order); 3) Look, Nod, and Shake—moons nod, shake, and look in different directions on command by children-users.

898. Staples, B. Potato chips to panty hose: The future of personal computing. *Creative Computing*, 1982, *8*(2), 78, 80, 82.
Report of Boston Computer Society's forum on The Future of Personal Computers. One company VP (Apple) wanted to do away with software protection. The others were strongly for it. All agreed that programing was best investment for the eighties.

899. Steffin, S.A. A challenge to Seymour Papert. *Educational Computer*, 1982, *2*(4), 34, 36.
Challenges several of Papert's assertations: 1) that a *medium* can be a *mode* of instruction; 2) that electronics can reverse developmental processes, and 3) that the medium can *design and implement* instructional strategies.

900. Stein, S. *Read about me and the bee.* Hicksville, New York: Me-Books, 1973.
One of the several computer personalized and computer printed books for young children. These books are about the children who own them and contain references to their home addresses, brothers and sisters, and pets.

901. Suppes, P. Third annual dean lecture: The future of computers in education. *Journal of Computer Based Instruction*, 1979, *6*(1), 5-10.
Describes Computer Curriculum Corporation's courses, their fre-

quency of use, and the correlation of their test placements with standardized test scores. Also describes research on computer generated speech using the MISS machine, a microprogramed, intoned, 48-channel machine generating as many as 16 simultaneous conversations with either single-phoneme or whole-word synthesis and with some intonational variations. Predicts CAI in homes, uniformly audio-delivering computers with speech input.

902. Talk and type. *Technology Illustrated*, August/September 1982, 16.
Describes a computer program developed for the U.S. Air Force by Threshold Technologies of Debran, New Jersey. Users type the first letter of each word as they speak and the machine types the rest. An experienced typer-speaker can top 160 wpm with 99 percent accuracy. However, to start, users must orally enter every word in the vocabulary of the system.

903. University of Virginia plants apple orchards. *Apple Education News*, 1982, *3*(2), 3.
Faculty at the University of Virginia firmly believe that in the not too distant future, students will be required to bring their own computers.

904. White, R.M. Disk-storage technology. *Scientific American*, 1980, *243*(2), 138-148.
Relates the history of magnetic storage devices and predicts that optical (laser beam) recordings will provide low cost memory in great quantities on any one disk.

905. World Book will test on-line, full text version with compuserve. *Educational Marketer*, November 23, 1981, *7*.
World Book and Compuserve announced an agreement to make available all of World Book's contents to on-line customers of the Compuserve network.

906. World Book Encyclopedia, Compuserve sign pact. *Today*, January 1982, *5*.
Compuserve is available in more than 190 North American cities and has more than 19,000 subscribers. The contract for an on-line version of the encyclopedia was announced by Robert King, chair of the board of directors of World Book.

Additional References

907. Gallese, L.R. Electronic switch. *Wall Street Journal*, May 25, 1979, 1, 72.

908. Kleinman, J.H. *The ABC-NEA school disc project*. Paper presented at the 27th Annual Convention of the International Reading Association, Chicago, April 1982.

909. Lesgold, A. Computer games for the teaching of reading. *Behavior Research Methods and Instrumentation*, 1982, *14*, 224-226.

910. Sanders, W.R.; Benbassat, G.V.; & Smith, R.L. Speech synthesis for computer assisted instruction: The MISS system and its applications. *SIGCUE Bulletin*, 1976, *8*(1), 200-211.

INDEX

C

302
345
482-483
516
558
560
607
618
622
634
715 ✓ +4
727 ✓
758
803
804

DATE DUE

DEC 13 1991
MAY 11 1992
APR 13 1992

GAYLORD PRINTED IN U.S.A.